KU-014-804

# Contents

**PART ONE Introduction**     **5**

**PART TWO Changing Needs**     **7**
Demographic changes     8
Changing treatments and demands for care     12
'Equal health for all?'     15

**PART THREE The Record of Achievement:**
**The NHS — A growing service?**     **36**
Impressive statistics?     36
More money?     37
More staff?     50
More beds?     56
More patients treated?     59
Shorter waiting lists?     64
Whose priorities?     68

**PART FOUR The Record of Achievement:**
**More Community Care?**     **72**
What is community care?     73
More money?     74
More facilities?     78
More staff?     84
Informal care     87
The gap between services and needs     88
What happened to targets and guidelines?     92
Who cares?     •     95

**PART FIVE Current Issues**     **99**
The NHS service — some international comparisons     99
Health services in the USA     103
Commercial medicine     108
The contracting out of ancillary services in the NHS     122
Increased charges to patients     130
Equal opportunities for NHS staff?     136
Prescribing and the pharmaceutical industry     143
Dentistry and dental health     151
Health education — blaming the victim?     155
Food, health and welfare     164

**PART SIX Monitoring the System**     **172**

**PART SEVEN Has the Health Service Achieved its Original Aims?**     **185**

Appendix One: Some questions to ask when looking at
official health statistics     187
Appendix Two: Conducting a local health canvass.     191

R/A
74/1
.FAC

# Facing The Figures

## What Really Is Happening to the National Health Service?

# Acknowledgements

THIS BOOK was written by Radical Statistics Health Group which includes statisticians and others working in health services and medical research and in the National Health Service. We are not affiliated to any other group or organisation except the British Society for Social Responsibility in Science (BSSRS). Contributors to this book include:

Mel Bartley, Steve Bennett, Ashok Bhat, Eric Brunner, Mary Corcoran, Christine Cousins, George Davey Smith, Alastair Gray, Christine Hay, Jenny Head, Jacky Holloway, Kevork Hopayian, Alison Macfarlane, Luise Parsons, Aubrey Sheiham, Jerry Shulman.

We should like to thank the following for the permission to use material from their forthcoming books:

Mike Grimsley and Ashok Bhat (Health, Chapter 7 of *Britain's black population, a new perspective* to be published by Gower Press, 1988).

Christine Cousins (*Controlling social welfare: a sociology of state welfare work and organisations* by Christine Cousins, to be published by Wheatsheaf Press, 1987).

Ben Griffith (Appendix to *Banking on sickness: commercial medicine in Britain and the USA*, by Ben Griffith, Geof Rayner and Steve Iliffe, to be published by Lawrence and Wishart, 1987).

We should also like to thank everyone else who helped or commented on earlier versions, including:

NUPE Research Department, London Food Commission, Colin Thunhurst, David Jones, Robin Frampton, Martin Bland, Lee Bennett, Gavin Ross, Derek Cook, Russell Ecob, David Fruin, Bob Harrison, David Southgate, Charlie Brooker, Alan Walker, Matthew Hall and Martin Brown.

Cover photograph: Mike Abrahams / Network. Cover design: Sophie Gibson.

**Facing the Figures:**
**What's Really Happening to the Health Service**
First published 1987
ISBN 0 906081 07 6
© Copyright Radical Statistics
Published by Radical Statistics, c/o BSSRS, 25 Horsell Road, London N5 1XL.
Designed and typeset by Gwasg Rydd (TU), 25 Cathedral Road, Cardiff, CF1 9HA. Tel: (0222) 42403.
Printed by Pensord Press (TU), Pontllanfraith, Blackwood, Gwent.
Trade distribution by Turnaround Distribution, 27 Horsell Road, London N5 1XL.

# 1
# Introduction

'1. Objects in view
(1) To ensure that everyone in the country — irrespective of means, age, sex or occupation — shall have equal opportunity to benefit from the best and most up-to-date medical and allied services available.
(2) To provide, therefore, for all who want it, a comprehensive service covering every branch of medical and allied activity from the care of minor ailments to major medicine and surgery; to include the care of mental as well as physical health and all specialist services, e.g. for tuberculosis, cancer and infectious diseases, maternity, fracture and orthopaedic treatment, and others; to include all normal general services, e.g. the family doctor, the midwife and nurse, the care of the teeth and of the eyes, the day-to-day care of the child; and to include all necessary drugs and medicines and a wide range of appliances.
(3) To divorce the care of health from questions of personal means or other factors irrelevant to it; to provide the service free of charge (apart from certain possible charges in respect of appliances) and to encourage a new attitude to health — the easier obtaining of advice early, the promotion of good health rather than the treatment of bad.'
*A national health service,* **1944**[1]

THESE OBJECTIVES set out over forty years ago in the White Paper on the National Health Service have a very different flavour from the news of cuts, closures and falling standards in the 1980s. Alongside these reports, the Conservative government quotes statistics which claim that it has poured unprecedented sums of money into health services, and that record numbers of people have been treated.

Many people find these statistics so at odds with their experience that they do not know how to respond to them. Are they merely 'cooked' while the 'true' figures are hidden, for example? Although there is an element of truth in this view, the position is not that simple. Dismissing the misleading statistics as 'damned lies' is no help either in defending the National Health Service or in campaigning to improve it.

The aim of this book is to look at the present state of our National Health Service and ask how it relates to its original aims and to the needs of the population today. In doing so, we look at the statistics commonly quoted on the subject and the way they are selected and interpreted, while pointing to the many questions they fail to answer.

To set the scene, we start by looking at the changing needs of the population and at some of the factors outside the health service which have affected people's health and created additional demands on the services. We also look at the pressures arising from the development of new types of treatment, and conclude by discussing inequalities in health and health care.

Against this background of growing need and demand, the next part looks at the claims, often quoted by politicians, that the health service is beating all records in terms of resources, facilities, staff and patients treated. This updates and expands the arguments made in 1985 in our report 'Unsafe in their hands'[2].

It is important not to equate the health service with hospital care and many people have conditions which are not curable or do not require the type of care given in hospitals. In the light of this, the next part of this book, examines government claims that the contraction of the hospital service has been offset by the additional care provided elsewhere in homes and hostels, day centres and people's own homes. ·

This is followed by a look at current issues in health and health care. Many of them show some inter-relationship between commercialism in health care and the widening inequalities in health. The issues examined include comparisons with other countries, the growth of commerical medicine, privatisation of services, increasing charges for NHS treatment, the pharmaceutical industry, dental health, food and health education.

The concluding part returns to the question of what is happening to our health service and how it should be monitored by statistical and other means. It suggests some ways in which user groups, unions and local campaigns can set about doing this from their own perspectives.

This raises the question of who should control the health services. A democratically run health service would need to ask different questions and collect different information than one which is, increasingly, being run simply as a business. Is this the health service we want? Our book concludes by pointing out the link between the nature of a health service and the types of information needed to run it effectively, and asking whether the National Health Service is moving towards the objectives for which it was set up.

### References

1. Ministry of Health, Department of Health for Scotland. A national health service. Cmd 6502. London: HMSO, 1944.
2. Radical Statistics Health Group. Unsafe in their hands. London: Radical Statistics, 1985.

# 2
# Changing needs

THE IMPACT of changing needs and demands for health care has to be understood in the context of the wider social policies of which the health service was intended to be part. The idea underlying the package of reforms introduced after the Second World War was that they should improve people's lives by acting in combination. Full employment was seen as the keystone, because it would allow people the stability to plan their own lives and, in cooperation with their employers and the state, insure themselves against illness, incapacity and old age.

In a manner of speaking, full employment and better housing and schooling were seen as 'preventive' measures. The concept of health embodied in the idea of a welfare state was one which placed the individual in her or his social environment. National Assistance, or Social Security, as we now call it, was only intended as a safety net for those few people who were not covered by comprehensive national insurance. In a similar sort of way, the curative hospital service was seen as somewhat of a last resort, the need for which would 'wither away' as the population became healthier under the influence of the other policies.

What actually happened was quite different. The reforms did not go far enough in the first place. Levels of benefit were set too low, so that insured people had to fall back on National Assistance / Social Security when they became unemployed or retired. 'Full employment' was never a reality for women, or for people with disabilities, for example. We need to look at changing patterns of demand on the health services in the light of these failures of the wider social policies.

Health problems such as TB and rheumatic heart disease, which were previously caused by preventable conditions, have disappeared. In their place, the health service is now called upon to deal with the health consequences of, for example the alienation of unemployed young people, the isolation and poor housing of many people with young families, and material and social deprivation in old age. These are also, of course, preventable, but the measures required to do so are less politically acceptable.

The health service responds to these demands in two ways. One is by providing hospital beds for many people whose problems are a product of their material and social circumstances. The other medical response is 'high technology' forms of treatment. Increasingly, these are seen as being inappropriate responses which impose an 'expensive burden' on society.

It is not the inappropriateness of these measures which causes their expense, however. The health service is caught in the dilemma that, in many instances, better preventive strategies would be more expensive. As we show later, there is more ill health among disadvantaged people in society and this leads to greater demands on the health service. To prevent this 'excess demand' would require political action to ensure improved access to better food, housing and working conditions and income. All of this would cause expense.

The 'problem' of the growing numbers of elderly people in the population, and of the increasing demand for hospital treatment, especially of the high technology kind, have to be looked at in this light. It is by no means inevitable that a person of 75 or 85 will need enormous amounts of hospital care or will have lost their intellectual faculties even if they are physically unwell. The 'problem' of the health care needs of elderly people is caused by the the inability of the welfare and health care systems to meet the needs of older citizens. This is, perhaps, the most striking example of the way in which the health service is called upon to make up for the failure to develop broader policies which could ensure material and social support for groups in the population with a wider variety of different needs.

# Demographic changes

Demographic changes mean changes in the size and age structure of the population. In 1901, 4.2 per cent of men and 5.1 per cent of women were aged 65 or over, while in 1981, the corresponding figures were 12.2 and 17.6 per cent.[1] This is a result of changing patterns of life expectancy.

Life expectancy is the average number of further years which people of a given age can expect to live. Life expectancy at birth is the average total lifetime, including those who die in infancy as well as people who die in old age. Table 2.1 shows the life expectancy of men and women of different ages in 1901 and 1981, eighty years apart.[2] Over this period, life expectancy at birth increased

**Table 2.1**
Expectation of life, United Kingdom

| Expectation of life, years | Males | | Females | |
|---|---|---|---|---|
| | 1901 | 1981 | 1901 | 1981 |
| From birth | 48 | 70 | 52 | 76 |
| From age | | | | |
|   15 years | 47 | 56 | 50 | 63 |
|   45 years | 23 | 28 | 25 | 34 |
|   65 years | 11 | 12 | 12 | 17 |

Source: Government Actuary's Department, quoted in Social Trends, 1987[2]

dramatically, but the increase in later life was much less. Thus we can see that the change is not an extension of every man's life by 22 years and every woman's by 24, which would be seen at every age. Instead it follows from the fall in mortality in childhood and early adulthood. Mortality in later life has changed very little.

Now a big reduction in mortality in childhood would result in an increase in the numbers of young people, as more children survived, unless there was a corresponding fall in the numbers of babies being born. In the nineteenth century, women had many children. Despite the high mortality in childhood, the number who survived into adulthood to have children of their own exceeded that of their own parents. Thus the population expanded as each generation more than replaced itself. In the twentieth century, infant mortality fell and people responded to this by having fewer children. As the younger members of the 1901 population grew older, the numbers of old people in the population increased. Had the birth rate not fallen, the population would have continued to expand and we would have as great or greater a proportion of young people in 1981 as we did in 1901, and a vastly larger population. Thus the increase in the proportion of elderly people is not because adult lives have been extended, but because the birth rate has declined.

The major drop in fertility occurred in the early 1920s. There was a sharp decline in the number of babies born during the First World War, followed by the usual post-war 'baby boom'. This was, however, very short lived and by the late 1920s, the birth rate was lower than it had been during the war. It stayed low until after the Second World War, dropped during the early 1950s, and rose again in the 1960s,[3] as Figure 2.1 shows.

**Figure 2.1 Mid-1981 age distribution compared with past births, England and Wales.**

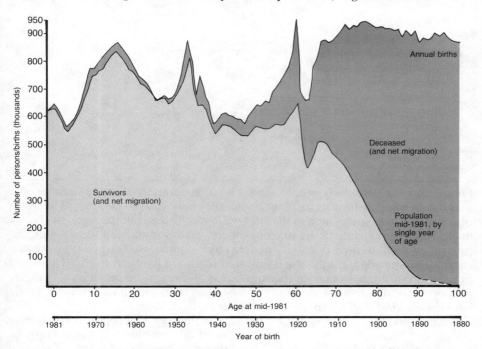

These marked fluctuations in the birth rate affected not only the numbers of elderly people in each age group, but also their family structure. This, in its turn, influenced the size of their potential pool of carers in the community. There are increasing numbers of 'very elderly' people, aged 75 or over and born before the First World War. As Table 2.2 shows, this age group will form up to 40 per cent of the total population of pensionable age by 2001, as the number of pensioners aged under 75, who were born during and just after the First World War, decline.[4,5] From then on, the total number of elderly people will increase as the children of the post-war 'baby boom' reach retiring age.

**Table 2.2**
Mid-1985 based population projections for Great Britain

| | | | | | Thousands |
|---|---|---|---|---|---|
| Age group | 1985 | 1991 | 2001 | 2011 | 2021 |
| All Ages | | | | | |
| Males | 26,810 | 27,282 | 28,156 | 28,471 | 28,723 |
| Females | 28,250 | 28,564 | 29,120 | 29,227 | 29,412 |
| Persons | 55,060 | 55,846 | 57,275 | 57,698 | 58,135 |
| 15 to pensionable age† | | | | | |
| Males | 18,129 | 18,270 | 18,459 | 18,931 | 18,671 |
| Females | 16,449 | 16,651 | 16,842 | 16,816 | 16,478 |
| Persons | 34,577 | 34,921 | 35,301 | 35,747 | 35,148 |
| Pensionable age† to 74 | | | | | |
| Males | 2,117 | 2,209 | 2,163 | 2,358 | 2,749 |
| Females | 4,323 | 4,164 | 3,914 | 4,515 | 4,975 |
| Persons | 6,440 | 6,373 | 6,077 | 6,873 | 7,724 |
| 75 and over | | | | | |
| Males | 1,176 | 1,341 | 1,572 | 1,670 | 1,852 |
| Females | 2,367 | 2,584 | 2,748 | 2,704 | 2,826 |
| Persons | 3,543 | 3,925 | 4,320 | 4,374 | 4,678 |

† 65 for men, 60 for women
Totals may not agree, because of the way figures have been rounded
Source: OPCS Monitor PP2 86/1[4]

**Family support for elderly people.** The present generation of very elderly people may have had many brothers and sisters but they had very few children. The death of several million young men in the 1914-1918 war also meant that these include a much higher proportion than usual of women who never married. As a result, the present generation of very elderly people have a much smaller pool of potential carers than the generations which followed them are likely to have.[6] The lower proportion of single women in the future may, however, be offset by the higher proportion of divorced women in the 45-64 age group shown in Table 2.3 Those who do not find new partners may be freer to help their parents.

Because so many are single or no longer married, a high proportion of elderly people live alone. By 1981, nearly a quarter of all households consisted only of pensioners, and 14.2 per cent consisted of one pensioner living alone.[7] Table 2.4 shows that in 1985, 36 per cent of people aged 65 or more and living in private households lived alone and 45 per cent lived with their spouse only.[2] They were more likely to be in unsatisfactory housing, with a higher than average proportion occupying privately rented accommodation or accommodation without proper facilities,[8] as Table 2.5 shows. Very elderly people living alone fare worst in this regard.

**Table 2.3**
Marital status by age group, Great Britain, 1981

| Marital status | Percentage of people in age group | | | | | |
| | 45-64 | | 65+ | | 85+ | |
| | M | F | M | F | M | F |
|---|---|---|---|---|---|---|
| Married | 84.4 | 77.3 | 72.9 | 37.2 | 38.6 | 7.3 |
| Widowed | 2.8 | 11.2 | 17.4 | 48.9 | 53.7 | 76.3 |
| Divorced | 3.7 | 4.5 | 1.6 | 1.8 | 0.6 | 0.6 |
| Single | 9.0 | 7.0 | 8.0 | 12.2 | 7.1 | 15.9 |

Source: 1981 Census, National report[7]

---

**Table 2.4**
Who elderly people lived with, Great Britain, 1985

| Household Composition | Percentage of people aged 65+ living in private households |
|---|---|
| Spouse only | 45 |
| Spouse and others | 7 |
| Brother/sister/children children-in-law | 10 |
| Others | 2 |
| Living alone | 36 |

Source: General Household Survey 1985, quoted in Social Trends 1987[2]

---

**Table 2.5**
The housing conditions of elderly people in Great Britain, 1981

| | Percentage of all households | Percentage of households with elderly persons | Percentage of elderly people aged 75+ living alone |
|---|---|---|---|
| Housing | | | |
| Owner occupied | 58.7 | 50.7 | 41.7 |
| LA owned | 29.0 | 35.5 | 39.4 |
| Privately rented/ unfurnished | 4.0 | 9.5 | 12.9 |
| Amenities | | | |
| No bath or inside WC | 0.64 | 2.5 | 4.5 |
| No inside WC | 1.6 | 4.4 | 6.8 |

Source: OPCS, 1981 census (persons of pensionable age)[8]

Transport can also be a problem. Table 2.6 shows that elderly people are less likely than younger people living in the same sort of area to have their own cars.

Inner city areas also have above average proportions of elderly people who tend to be more disadvantaged than those able to move house when they retire. They are the people left behind when the younger generations move out to the suburbs.

**Table 2.6**
Car ownership in some Metropolitan and non-Metropolitan counties in England, 1981

| County | Percentage of households with car | |
| --- | --- | --- |
| | all households | pensioners only households |
| Greater London | 55 | 22 |
| Metropolitan Counties | | |
| Merseyside | 50 | 20 |
| South Yorks | 50 | 16 |
| Tyne and Wear | 44 | 13 |
| W. Yorks | 53 | 19 |
| Non-Metropolitan Counties | | |
| Devon | 66 | 38 |
| Dorset | 70 | 43 |
| E. Sussex | 59 | 33 |
| Isle of Wight | 63 | 36 |
| W. Sussex | 70 | 40 |

Source: OPCS, 1981 census[9]

An additional factor affecting the availability of carers for elderly people in the community is the rising proportion of women, especially married women, who are in paid employment. In 1951, 25 per cent of married women aged 16-59 did paid work. By 1981, this had reached 55 per cent, although the increase was smaller between 1971 and 1981 than it had been between 1961 and 1971.[6]

In 1981, the proportion of married women in paid employment was higher in the more industrial areas than in the rural areas of Britain, although there were pockets which did not fit the general pattern.[9] This is especially true of the south coast of England, North Wales and the Borders of Scotland These are all areas with very high proportions of elderly people. Services for these people provide large numbers of part time jobs, which are usually taken by married women.

To sum up, over the next 20 years, there will be a large increase in the numbers of very elderly people. They are likely to make more use of the statutory services, as there are now fewer family members and other informal carers available to them. The situation is likely to ease early in the next century, but may recur as people born in the 1960s reach retirement age from the year 2020 onwards.

# Changing treatments and demands for care

Partly, but only partly because of the increased risk of illness in old age, and partly because of the failure of social policies to prevent poverty and isolation in their homes, elderly people make greater use of hospital in-patient treatment. On average, the length of hospital stays increases with age.

Continuing developments in medical care have increased the range of treatments that can be offered both to elderly people and to people of all ages. An example of this is total hip replacement operations, the estimated numbers of which increased from 20,280 in 1979 to 25,300 in 1984.[10] The success of this operation has had a major impact on orthopaedic waiting lists throughout the country. Other 'high technology' solutions to chronic disorders which have become more common and more successful over the last ten years include dialysis and transplantation for chronic kidney disease and coronary artery bypass grafts for coronary heart disease.

The Kings Fund report 'Back to back planning'[11] summarised the policies which DHSS urged Regional Health Authorities to implement, in circulars it issued between 1983 and 1986. Among other things these included:

'... develop services for kidney failure, coronary artery surgery, joint replacement and bone marrow transplant; (Health Circular HC(84)2)'

'... achieve a target of 40 new kidney dialysis patients per one million population; (Health Circular HC(85)5)'

'... plan new services for people with AIDS; (Health Circular HC(86)2)'

Major changes in non-surgical treatments include the development of day hospitals and a more active attitude towards rehabilitation for elderly people. Although, as we show in Part 3, there are problems in interpreting these statistics, Figure 2.2 gives some idea of the impact of these changes on geriatric departments.[12] The average length of stay dropped by over half, from 98.8 days in

**Figure 2.2 Activity of geriatric departments, England, 1974-85.**

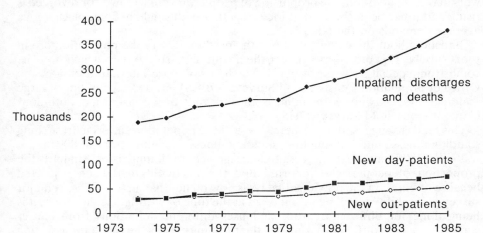

Source: Data from DHSS statistical bulletin 2/86.[12]

1974 to 47.8 in 1985, while the numbers of new day patients nearly trebled and the numbers of in-patient stays doubled. As elderly people are increasingly seen to be entitled to the same range of treatments as younger people, geriatric medicine more and more resembles general medicine.

Changes in the pattern of diseases and especially the emergence of new diseases also affects the needs of the population. The Acquired Immune Deficiency Syndrome (AIDS) was first recognised in the United States in 1981. People with the syndrome were reported in the United Kingdom in the same year. It was estimated in the latter half of 1986 that there were 30,000 people in the United Kingdom who were carriers of the human immunodeficiency virus (HIV) which causes AIDS and that 3,000 of them may develop the disease by 1988.[13] Such estimates and projections have to be treated with caution, however, because of the lack of reliable estimates of the numbers of carriers of the virus or the way it has spread in the population.

The treatment of people with AIDS, which is currently concentrated in a few centres, will soon have to be more evenly spread throughout the country. At the moment hospital care is very labour intensive due to barrier nursing requirements to limit the spread of infection. The treatments available at the time of writing are expensive and only temporarily effective. The government campaign to publicise the facts about the disease and how to avoid catching the disease in the first place may help to curb the epidemic, but effective prevention is unlikely until a vaccine is available. The indications are that this is some years away.

As well as the ageing of the population. there are other changes which are likely to create increasing demands for health care. Although the government has not estimated the costs to the NHS of the health consequences of the growth in unemployment since 1979,[14] there is evidence that it can increase the NHS workload.[15] In addition, the proportion of people who are widowed or divorced is rising and it has been shown that they, together with single people, place above average demands on the NHS.[16]

Statistics about the extent of ill health and disability in the population are in short supply. It is difficult to collect them routinely, so the data which do exist come from special surveys, of which we shall say more later. In addition, the Office of Population Censuses and Surveys (OPCS) has done a number of large scale surveys, as well as including some relevant questions in its continuous General Household Survey (GHS).

This tends to suggest that the percentage of the population suffering from 'long standing illness' and 'limiting long standing illness' is higher in the 1980s than it was in the 1970s, although there is no clear sign of a continuing rise.[17] Similarly the proportion of people who reported that their activities had been restricted because of illness in the previous 14 days is now higher than in the 1970s. A major survey of disability is still being analysed at the time of writing. As, however, it is being done for different reasons and uses different definitions from earlier surveys, it will be difficult to compare their findings. Thus the scope for assessing trends in the prevalence of chronic illness and other disabling conditions is severely limited.

# 'Equal Health for All?'

As recently as 1979, the Report of the Royal Commission on the National Health Service reaffirmed these stated aims of the NHS:

'We believe that the NHS should: encourage and assist individuals to remain healthy; provide equality of entitlement to health services; provide a broad range of services of a high standard; provide equality of access to these services; provide a service free at the time of use; satisfy the reasonable expectations of its users; remain a national service responsive to local needs'.[18]

Is there any evidence that the NHS is moving towards these aims or that, in combination with wider policies, has it succeeded in removing inequalities in health? This section focuses on three particular aspects of inequality by looking at class, race and gender differences. Although we consider them separately, they are, of course, strongly interrelated.

**Class.** A review of the inequalities in the nation's health was commissioned by the last Labour government, but by the time it was completed, the Conservatives were in power. After some delay, the report[19] was 'made available for discussion' as a photocopied typescript 'without any commitment by the government to its proposals'. Only a small number of copies was run off but when a revised paperback version[20] was published commercially, it was widely read. This section summarises the main findings of that report, commonly known as 'the Black report', and takes a brief look at some more recent information. Some of this was brought together in 'The health divide',[21] which was commissioned by the Health Education Council to follow up the findings of the Black report.

Many of the report's findings are expressed in terms of the occupational classes used by the Registrar General. These are:

I Professional
II Intermediate professional or managerial
IIIN Skilled non-manual
IIIM Skilled manual
IV Semi-skilled manual
V Unskilled manual

**Equal Health?** Because there are so few statistics about ill health and disability, extensive use is made of information about death rates. To overcome differences between populations with different age structures, this is most frequently expressed in terms of the Standardised Mortality Ratio (SMR), which compares the death rate for any given group of people with the national rate.

The national rate is set at 100, so that a group with an SMR of 70 would be quite a lot better off, according to this measure of health, than the country as a whole, and a group with an SMR or 130 would be considerably worse off. The way in which the measure is calculated makes allowance for differences in the distribution of ages of people in different groups. For example, a high 'crude', or unstandardised, death rate in a town like Bournemouth would probably be due to the large numbers of elderly people in the town rather than to any particular disease or health hazard. After being standardised, the death rate (expressed now as an SMR) would be around 100, or perhaps even lower. So that by looking at SMRs, we can be sure that the measure of health for a social group is not the result of the age of that group, but must be due to other factors.

The report quoted from the Registrar General's Decennial Supplement on Occupational Mortality.[22] This compared occupations recorded on death certificates during the years 1970-72 with occupations recorded in 1971 census returns. As at earlier censuses, this Decennial Supplement showed that death rates for unskilled workers and members of their families were consistently much higher than those for professional workers, as Figure 2.3 shows. This difference

**Figure 2.3 Mortality by social class and age, England and Wales, 1970-72.**

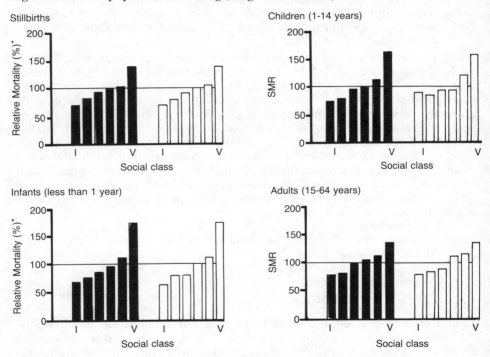

* Relative mortality (%) is the ratio of rates for the occupational class to the rate for all males or females

existed at all ages, and was particularly marked in infancy and childhood. These class differences were greatest for deaths from accidents and respiratory disease, causes which are both closely related to social and economic conditions. Accidents were by far the biggest cause of childhood deaths, and boys from Class V had a ten times greater chance of dying from fire, falls or drowning than those in Class I. The ratio for adults was greatest for respiratory diseases (4 adults in class V die of these conditions for every 1 in class I). Some examples are given in Table 2.7.

**Table 2.7**
Mortality by class and cause of death. Some selected SMRs for men of working age.

| | Men aged 15-64 England and Wales 1970-72 Social class | | Men aged 20-64 Great Britain 1979-80, 1982-83 Social class | |
|---|---|---|---|---|
| | I | V | I | V |
| Lung cancer | 53 | 143 | 43 | 178 |
| Stomach cancer | 50 | 147 | 50 | 158 |
| Duodenal ulcer | 45 | 201 | 45 | 253 |
| Respiratory diseases | 37 | 187 | 36 | 210 |
| Hypertensive disease | 71 | 141 | 56 | 190 |
| Cerebrovascular disease | 80 | 136 | 62 | 179 |
| Motor vehicle accidents | 77 | 174 | 65 | 181 |

Source: Occupational mortality 1970-72[22] (page 60-61).
Occupational mortality 1979-80, 1982-83[26] (Table GD 28)

As well as gender and racial differences, which we discuss later, the Black report pointed to geographical differences. Death rates were found to be lower in the south of England and the West Midlands than in the rest of England and Wales, even when allowance was made for age and social class. These regional differences, shown in Table 2.8 had been with us for many years, and still have not disappeared.[21] As, however, there are also differences between the more

**Table 2.8**
Regional variations in mortality of men aged 15-64, England and Wales, 1970-72

| Standard region | S.M.R. standardized for: | |
|---|---|---|
| | Age | Age and class |
| Northern | 113 | 113 |
| Yorkshire and Humberside | 106 | 105 |
| North West | 116 | 116 |
| East Midlands | 96 | 94 |
| West Midlands | 105 | 104 |
| East Anglia | 84 | 83 |
| South-East | 90 | 90 |
| South-West | 93 | 93 |
| Wales I (South) | 114 | 117 |
| Wales II (North and West) | 110 | 113 |
| England and Wales | 100 | 100 |

Source: Occupational Mortality 1070-72[22], p.180

deprived and more affluent areas within regions,[21,23] and even within a given city such as Sheffield,[24] it is an oversimplification to talk only of a north-south divide, without considering more localised inequalities.

Statistics from the OPCS Longitudinal Study, which follows a one per cent sample of the population, showed that people living in owner occupied households at the time of the 1971 census had lower death rates in the five following years than people in other types of housing.[25] As Table 2.9 shows, these differences could be seen within each social class group.

**Table 2.9**
Mortality of men and married women by household tenure and social class, England and Wales, 1971-75

Social class

Standardised mortality ratios†

| | Owner occupied | Privately rented | Local authority tenancy |
|---|---|---|---|
| Men aged 15-64 at death | | | |
| I | 79 | 93 | 99 |
| II | 74 | 104 | 99 |
| IIIN | 79 | 112 | 121 |
| IIIM | 83 | 99 | 104 |
| IV | 83 | 100 | 106 |
| V | 98 | 126 | 123 |
| Other | 186 | 270 | 250 |
| Women aged 15-64 at death (husbands' social class) | | | |
| I | 65 | 81 | 57 |
| II | 84 | 96 | 142 |
| IIIN | 69 | 94 | 99 |
| IIIM | 88 | 106 | 115 |
| IV | 93 | 105 | 111 |
| V | 108 | 161 | 131 |
| Other | 97 | 120 | 173 |

† In this table expected deaths are calculated separately for each sex using death rates for 1971-75 (in five-year age-groups) for all men/married women in the LS 1971 Census sample who were enumerated in private households.
Source: OPCS Longitudinal Study [25]

Information on chronic sickness from the General Household Survey showed considerable class differences in 'long standing illness' and 'limiting long standing illness' in the early 1970s. Table 2.10 shows that there were still differences in 1984.[17] This table uses the slightly different classification of occupations into 'socio-economic groups'.

**More recent trends.** Among the information to become available since the Black Report was published, is a new Decennial Supplement.[26] This related deaths in the years 1979-80 and 1982-83 to data from the 1981 census. As Table 2.11 shows, social class differences had not disappeared.

Indeed, they appeared to have widened, but it was no simple task to check whether this was so. Because of changes in the way occupations are coded into different social classes, comparisons between the two Decennial Supplements can

**Table 2.10**
Chronic sickness, acute sickness and doctor consultations by socio-economic group, Great Britain, 1984

| Socio-economic group | Percentage with limiting long-standing illness | | Average number of days of restricted activity per year | | Percentage who had consulted a doctor in previous 14 days | |
|---|---|---|---|---|---|---|
| | M | F | M | F | M | F |
| Professional | 9 | 9 | 16 | 18 | 9 | 12 |
| Employers & managers | 14 | 15 | 16 | 19 | 10 | 13 |
| Intermediate and junior non-manual | 14 | 17 | 18 | 26 | 10 | 14 |
| Skilled manual | 18 | 17 | 23 | 24 | 12 | 15 |
| Semi-skilled manual | 20 | 25 | 23 | 36 | 13 | 17 |
| Unskilled manual | 24 | 34 | 27 | 43 | 13 | 19 |
| All | 17 | 19 | 20 | 27 | 11 | 15 |

Source: General Household Survey, 1984[17]

---

**Table 2.11**
Social class differences in mortality, early 1980s. Standardised mortality ratios

Men of working ages, England and Wales

| Class | Men aged 20-64 1979-80, 1982-83 | Men aged 15-64 1981-1983 |
|---|---|---|
| I Professional occupations | 66 | 63 |
| II Intermediate occupations | 74 | 84 |
| IIIN Skilled non-manual | 93 | 89 |
| IIIM Skilled manual | 103 | 94 |
| IV Partly skilled | 114 | 103 |
| V Unskilled | 159 | 131 |

The figures in the first column come from the Decennial Supplement for 1981[26]. They were described as being subject to bias and do not give reliable estimates of mortality by social class, particularly for Class V.[27] The second column comes from the OPCS longitudinal study which does not have this bias, but is based on only 1 per cent of the population[27].

Women aged 20-59, Great Britain 1979-80, 1982-83

| Class | Married | Single | All women |
|---|---|---|---|
| I Professional | 75 | 75 | 69 |
| II Intermediate | 83 | 68 | 78 |
| IIIN Skilled non-manual | 93 | 80 | 87 |
| IIIM Skilled manual | 111 | 111 | 100 |
| IV Partly skilled | 125 | 107 | 110 |
| V Unskilled | 160 | 117 | 134 |

Married women were classified by their husbands' occupations in the tables from which these figures were taken.
Source: Registrar General's Decennial Supplement for 1981[26]
(Tables GD31, GD34, GD35)

---

**Figure 2.4 Standardised mortality ratios for select causes of death in Great Britain 1970-72 and 1979-83 for manual and non-manual groups.**

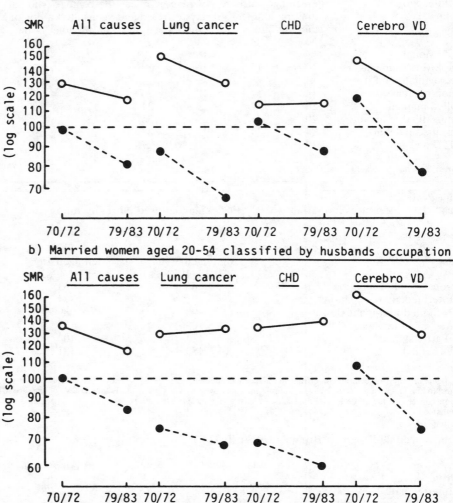

a) Men aged 20 - 64

b) Married women aged 20-54 classified by husbands occupation

**Standardised mortality ratios\* for select causes of death in Great Britain 1970–72 and 1979–83 for manual (○—○) and non-manual (●—●) groups.**

\*For each cause the SMR in 1979–83 is 100 for each sex.

Source: Mortality decline and widening inequalities.[28]  Reproduced by permission of the Lancet.

---

only be made in terms of the wider groupings into non-manual workers (classes I, II and IIIN) and manual workers (classes IIIM, IV and V).

When this is done, as in Figure 2.4, it can be seen that for adults, the class inequalities have widened.[28] Mortality from all causes has fallen in both groups for both men and women, but more so for non-manual workers. If we look at specific diseases, we see that the same is true for lung cancer in men and cerebrovascular disease (strokes) in both men and women. Death rates from lung cancer in women and from coronary heart disease in both sexes have increased for manual workers, while decreasing for non-manual workers.

It is likely that there is some connection between these widening social inequalities in health and the widening gap in income between rich and poor over this period, not to mention the enormous increase in unemployment which has hit manual workers much harder than non-manual workers.

The 1987 edition of the Central Statistical Office's publication Social Trends drew attention to the increasing differences between the economic circumstances of rich and poor.[2] These had also been discussed in a British Medical Journal editorial.[29] In 1976, the poorest 20 per cent of the British population received 7.4 per cent of the national income, while the richest 20 per cent received 37.9 per cent. In 1983, the equivalent figures were 6.9 per cent to the poorest and 39.3 per cent to the richest. In 1974, 2.7 million people were living on supplementary benefit. By 1983, the number had risen to 4.6 million.

The same British Medical Journal editorial[29] speculated that the Registrar General's Decennial Supplement on Occupational Mortality for 1979-83,[24] which was about to be published, would show a corresponding widening of mortality differences. Apart from the analysis described above, however, and very cautious comments on one table, publication of the Supplement has not shed much light on this question. Breaking with a tradition which dates back to the 1850s,[30] there is no detailed commentary on the data. In addition, more detailed figures which might allow people to check more carefully are not in the printed report at all, but in a separate folder containing 22,000 tables on microfiche which costs £40 and can only be read with the aid of viewing equipment costing some £200. The press reacted to this with headlines such as 'How the government buried its dead reckoning' (The Guardian), 'What death penalty do the poor pay?' (New Society) and even ' Lies, damned lies, and suppressed statistics' (the British Medical Journal itself).

In a rather quieter tone, an editorial in the Lancet made these comments on what should be learned from the latest official government figures on inequalities in the risk of death:

'A whole conglomerate of undesirable exposures is concentrated among those who, being socially less privileged, tend to have worse education, less money, worse housing, less access to medical care — in many kinds of ways less personal and material resources for health. Society's inequitable distribution of those resources, and their effects on health and survival, seem to be remarkably well measured by social class differentials in mortality ... To understand what is happening calls for a detailed and critical scrutiny of the time-trends, such as the Occupational Mortality Supplement might have provided, but did not.'[31]

**Figure 2.5 Perinatal and postneonatal mortality by father's social class, England and Wales.**

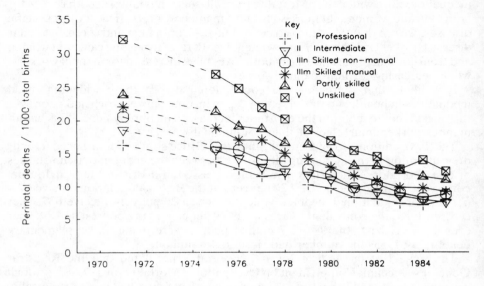

Perinatal mortality by father's social class, England and Wales

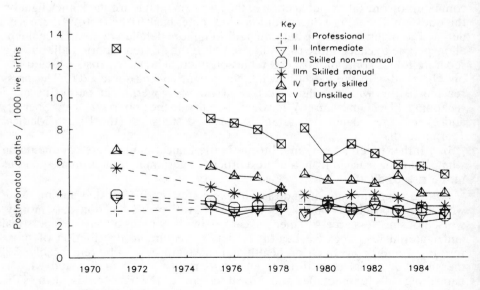

Postneonatal mortality by father's social class, England and Wales

Source: OPCS mortality statistics, series DH3.

Instead, the report was largely confined to technical criticisms of the deficiencies of the methods used to derive the data. These were said to be less reliable than those used in the OPCS Longitudinal Study. This may well be true, but as Table 2.11 shows, mortality rates for men from this source also show marked class differences.[27]

It has to be acknowledged that there are numerous technical problems with using social class classifications based on occupations.[19,21] These inadequacies apply even more acutely to analyses of women's health.[32,33] Despite this, these analyses do point to marked inequalities in health.

Furthermore, there is evidence that a number of these differences have widened over the past ten to fifteen years,[21,28] although there are gaps in the information. Information about the mortality of children is being published in a separate Decennial Supplement, but it has yet to appear as we go to press. For babies, the differentials in perinatal mortality (stillbirths and deaths in the first week after live birth) have remained undiminished since the early 1970s, as Figure 2.5 shows. For postneonatal deaths (at ages 1 to 11 months), there was some narrowing of the differential in the 1970s, but the picture is a complex one.[34]

Turning to chronic illness, there is some evidence that the gap between manual and non-manual classes is wider in the 1980s than it was in the 1970s.[17]

It cannot therefore be concluded that equal health has been provided for people of all classes. What, then, of the aim of making health care equally available to all?

**The inverse care law?** 'The inverse care' law was the title of an article written in 1971 by Julian Tudor Hart, a GP in South Wales. He postulated that 'The availability of good medical care tends to vary inversely with the need for it in the population served'.[35] In support of this, he cited 'massive but mostly non statistical evidence' in favour of the generalisation made by Richard Titmuss in 1968 that:

We have learnt from 15 years experience of the health service that the higher income groups know how to make better use of the service; they tend to receive more specialist attention; occupy more beds in better equipped and staffed hospitals; receive more elective surgery; have better maternal care, and are more likely to get psychiatric help and psychotherapy than low income groups — particularly the unskilled.'[36]

Julian Tudor Hart admitted that 'these generalisations are not easily proved statistically because most of the statistics are either not available or else they are essentially use rates.'[35]

This was, by and large, still true 16 years later in 1987. The new system of hospital statistics, like its predecessor, does not record patients' social class or any alternative socio-economic information.

There is rather more information about consultations with GPs. Table 2.10 shows that manual workers tend to consult GPs more often than do non-manual workers. The most important question, though, is whether these difference are wide enough to allow for the class differences in ill health.

A different survey, which looked at specific medical conditions separately, found that social class differences in consultation rates were much less marked than corresponding differences in mortality.[37] It is also clear that non-manual workers are likely to make much fuller use of preventive services, particularly those for children, such as vaccination. The Black report quoted surveys which found that middle class patients are likely to be given more time by doctors and more information about their illnesses. Taken as a whole, however, the answer to the question is much less clear cut. Different research projects have tended to produce contradictory findings, partly because they define need in different ways.[17,19,21]

In 'The inverse care law', Julian Tudor Hart opposed the growth of private practice and moves to an insurance based system of health care on the grounds that market forces would be unlikely to direct care towards the people and places in greatest need. This is one of the aspects of commercial medicine which we discuss in Part 5.

The only aspect of inequality on which there has been any action in the past 15 years is the geographical distribution of NHS resources. Attempts have been made through 'RAWP' in England and 'SHARE' in Scotland to redistribute NHS spending more equitably to NHS regions and districts. It is not known what effect this has had on class differences in access to care by individual people within the regions and districts.

**Race.** The Black report also mentioned race, though very briefly, in its discussion on 'race, ethnicity and health':

'Another important dimension of inequality in contemporary Britain is race. Immigrants to this country from the so-called New Commonwealth, whose ethnicity is clearly visible in the colour of their skins, are known to experience greater difficulty in finding work and adequate housing .... Given these disabilities [in finding work and adequate housing] it is to be expected that they might also record higher than average rates of mortality and morbidity. This hypothesis is difficult to assess from official statistics since race has rarely been assessed in official censuses and surveys.'[20]

The previous section showed that people in the lowest socio-economic groups suffer the worst health. It is clear that black people in this country are over-represented at the disadvantaged end of the socio-economic spectrum. By black we mean people who were either born in, or who would state their ethnic group as originating from what official sources euphemistically labels as the New Commonwealth and Pakistan.

This section looks at some some of the few data that there are on the subject of race and health. Most of the data are classified by place of birth rather than ethnic group. Thus we have little knowledge, at present, of the health of black people born in this country, although the evidence that does exist confirms the suspicion that they too are disadvantaged with respect to their health.

**Mortality.** It was only in 1984 that what was described as 'the first comprehensive study of mortality of immigrants to England and Wales'[38] was published. The opportunity for such an analysis came about when place of birth was added to information collected at death registration in 1969.

Standardised mortality ratios were calculated by country of birth and sex for all causes and for selected individual cases. Table 2.12 shows the SMRs for people born in the New Commonwealth and Pakistan (NCWP), for all causes and three major cause groups. These are circulatory diseases, which include heart disease and strokes, cancers and respiratory diseases. The most strikingly high SMRs are for men and women born in the African Commonwealth for all causes and for those born in the African and Caribbean Commonwealth for strokes.

**Table 2.12**
Standardised mortality ratios for immigrants aged 20-69 year by sex and country of birth, 1970-72

| Cause of death | Indian sub-continent | Country of birth Caribbean commonwealth | African commonwealth |
|---|---|---|---|
| **Men** | | | |
| All causes | 99 | 95 | 133 |
| All circulatory diseases | 116 | 90 | 137 |
| Heart attacks | 119 | 45 | 105 |
| Strokes | 117 | 207 | 203 |
| Cancer | 64 | 77 | 101 |
| Respiratory disease | 83 | 66 | 115 |
| **Women** | | | |
| All causes | 111 | 131 | 144 |
| All circulatory diseases | 114 | 166 | 142 |
| Heart attacks | 128 | 88 | 78 |
| Strokes | 121 | 227 | 190 |
| Cancer | 84 | 88 | 88 |
| Respiratory disease | 112 | 99 | 122 |

Source: Immigrant mortality in England and Wales[38]

**Health and health care.** As with class, it is clear that black people are not equal with respect either to their state of health or to the care which they receive. Four specific areas of concern are discussed below. These are maternity care, sickle-cell anaemia and rickets, both of which are more prevalent among ethnic minority communities than among white Britons, and mental health, which is a topic on which the black communities have recently expressed a great deal of concern.

**Maternity care.** In the analysis of immigrant mortality, above average death rates due to conditions of pregnancy and childbirth were found among women born in the New Commonwealth and Pakistan.[38] The highest death rates were among women from Africa and the Caribbean. The Confidential Enquiry into Maternal Deaths in the years 1976-1978[39] found a maternal death rate of 0.32 per 1,000 total births for women from the New Commonwealth and Pakistan compared with 0.11 for all other women.

These figures were not updated in the most recent report, covering the years 1979-1981,[40] as according to the reply to a parliamentary question 'information about the birth place of the mothers concerned was not collected as part of the enquiry'.[41] Data about direct maternal deaths released in response to subsequent parliamentary questions[42] made it possible to estimate death rates. While the gap appeared to have narrowed by 1982-4, it had by no means disappeared. The combined direct maternal death rate for these years was 0.108 per 1000 live births

**Figure 2.6 Perinatal and postneonatal mortality by mother's country of birth, England and Wales.**

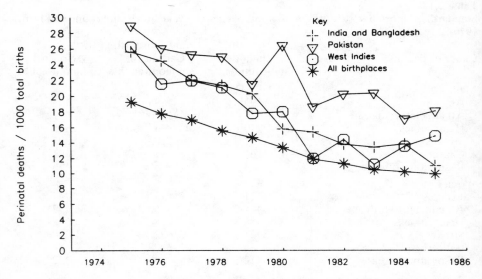

Perinatal mortality by mother's country of birth, England and Wales

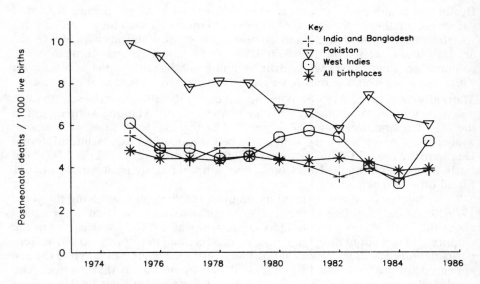

Postneonatal mortality by mother's country of birth, England and Wales

Source: OPCS mortality statistics, series DH3.

for women born in the New Commonwealth and Pakistan compared with 0.064 for all other women.

Black women also run additional risks, if they have a general anaesthetic for delivery or abortion. As the Maternal Deaths Enquiry report for 1979-81 explained:

'Dark-skinned patients have even greater risks of death and morbidity from anaesthetic causes than white-skinned ones because cyanosis from hypoxia [the woman's face becoming first very pale and then blue in colour, which happens when she is not getting enough oxygen] is so easily missed.'[40]

The report recommended that all women be monitored with especially great care throughout the administration of any anaesthetic. Pulse rate, breathing rate and blood pressure then provide the necessary signs of any problem, before it becomes serious. Despite the fact that similar points had been made in earlier reports, this lesson had still not been learned.

Figure 2.6 shows perinatal and postneonatal mortality rates in England and Wales for the years 1975-1985, tabulated according to the mother's country of birth. Perinatal mortality includes still births and deaths in the first week after live birth and postneonatal mortality is the proportion of live born babies who die at ages of at least a month but under a year.

In the mid 1970s, perinatal mortality rates for babies with mothers from the Caribbean and the Indian subcontinent were well above the England and Wales average. After this, there were some signs that perinatal mortality rates for babies with mothers from India and Bangladesh were falling nearer the national average, and until 1983 this seemed to be true of babies with Caribbean mothers. For these mothers, postneonatal mortality rates were similar to the rates for all births. In both the perinatal and postneonatal period, however, death rates among babies of mothers from Pakistan remained persistently high. This group has a high rate of congenital malformations.[43,44] There is also some evidence of an above average prevalence of severe mental handicap among Asian children.[43] Although both official statistics and research studies have a tendency to group together either Indians and Bangladeshis or all Asian women, it is important to remember that there is considerable diversity in social class, levels of deprivation and in obstetric characteristics.[45]

Although there are exceptions, there is generally a very low take-up of antenatal care by black women. Conventional wisdom would have us believe that this is the reason for the raised perinatal mortality rates amongst their babies. Similar statements are often made about the reasons for the high perinatal mortality rates among babies with fathers in manual occupations.

In fact, there is little substance in the claims[46-48] and antenatal care in its present form has been criticised even by the middle class white women who make the most use of it.[46,49] It is far more inappropriate to the needs of black women, and those who do not speak English are at a particular disadvantage. Although recent developments such as link workers, patients' advocacy schemes and the pilot projects set up under the Asian Mother and Baby Campaign are welcome they are on a very small scale indeed compared with what is needed. In addition, the workers in these schemes are not in a strong position to tackle the underlying problems, many of which stem from institutionalised racism.

**Sickle-cell disease and rickets.** Two specific conditions again highlight the lack of effective action by the NHS in areas of concern to ethnic minorities. Sickle-cell disease, or sickle-cell anaemia, describes a group of genetically transmitted disorders of haemoglobin which affects mainly people of Afro-Caribbean origin. The sickle-cell disease sufferer has a less efficient form of haemoglobin and because of this, the body's tissues may be deprived of oxygen, particularly in times of stress, and give pain. The pain of this 'sickling crisis' may be very severe. There may also be subsequent jaundice and skin ulcers. Children with the condition may be particularly susceptible to infection, and, because the disease reduces the life of red blood cells, anaemic fatigue is not uncommon.

There is very little information in this country about the numbers of people suffering from sickle-cell disease and information on mortality is sparse and indirect. It is estimated that around 1 in 400 black persons in Britain are affected by sickle-cell anaemia[50] but there are reports that this could well be a conservative estimate.[51] The research that has been done has concluded that there are probably many undiagnosed individuals with the disease in the community, and that the main risk to such individuals would be an unexpected and potentially fatal sickling episode during pregnancy or after surgery.[52]

In addition, there is evidence that sickle-cell disease is asssociated with increases in rates of miscarriage, spontaneous premature delivery, lower birthweights and a large increase in perinatal mortality rates. Associated ante-natal complications include anaemia, urinary tract infections, sickling crisis and pre-eclampsia. One study states that the 'maternal death rates in this country associated with sickle-cell disease remains a matter of educated guesswork.'[53] Although deaths associated with sickle cell disease are reported in each of the DHSS' reports on Confidential Enquiries into maternal deaths, it is impossible to calculate death rates without knowing how many of the women who gave birth each year have the condition.

Because there is no screening to detect the disease at an early stage, it is likely that childhood deaths from sickle cell disease are under-reported. If a child is not known to have the disease, then 'the pneumococcal infection with which a child presents and for which treatment is given is seen as the cause of death, without associating it with sickle-cell disease.'[51]

It is possible to identify babies with the condition at birth by a test using blood from the cord, and to take measures to prevent them from dying from illnesses associated with sickle cell disease. The NHS does not, however, have a screening programme to detect this conditions. There is, however, screening for phenylketonuria, which is less common than sickle-cell disease. So why not screen? As Protasia Torkington has tersely stated, 'Phenylketonuria virtually affects only white children.'[51]

Another condition particularly prevalent among ethnic minorities, this time mainly Asians, is rickets and its adult equivalent, osteomalacia. Both conditions are thought to be caused by vitamin D deficiencies. Rickets affects the growing skeleton and its main features are pain in the bone and bone swelling which may produce obvious skeletal deformities. In the Committee on Medical Aspects of

Food Policy (COMA) report,[54] rickets is reported to be declining and osteomalacia slightly on the increase. But individual surveys of Asian communities have found alarmingly high proportions of affected individuals. For example, one study in Glasgow found that about 5 per cent of Asian children had rickets,[55] while another investigation among Asians in Bradford[56] found that around 40 per cent of the study population had some evidence of bone changes related to rickets. It has also been found that average vitamin D blood levels are lower in Asians than for the rest of the population and it seems that the commonest cause of this deficiency is the combination of inadequate exposure to sunlight and insufficient vitamin D in the diet.[57,58]

Vitamin D levels can be raised by increased exposure to sunlight and by raising the amount of the vitamin in the diet, for example by fortifying foodstuffs with vitamin D. Margarine has been fortified in this way since the war, and rickets virtually disappeared from the 'indigenous' population. Some have argued, therefore, that Asian foodstuffs for example, chappati flour, should be fortified in the same way. Indeed, a low dose vitamin supplement campaign was successful in Glasgow.[59] COMA, however, came out strongly against the idea of fortification. Though there are arguments against fortification of foodstuffs it does seem strange that they do not apply equally to margarine and chappati flour.

A final example of another area of concern is mental health. There is not a great deal of information on the mental health of members of ethnic minorities. Although differences in admission rates to hospital do not provide a consistent picture of any differences between ethnic groups,[60,61] we can see that members of different group tend to receive different diagnoses.

There is widespread evidence that people from ethnic minorities with mental illnesses are more likely to be diagnosed as psychotic than 'natives'. It has been found that Afro-Caribbeans are between 3 and 5 times more likely to be diagnosed as schizophrenic than UK born admissions. In addition, Asians tend to have higher rates of diagnosis of schizophrenia. Schizophrenia and psychotic disorders represent the 'harder' end of the diagnostic spectrum while psychoneuroses and non-psychotic disorders are the 'softer' end. There seems to be little 'medical' evidence for this imbalance, though some studies have shown that there is evidence of misdiagnosis.[62]

A matter which is perhaps of even greater concern has been the way in which black people come to psychiatric services. This has led some black people to state that psychiatry is now a form of social control.[63] Under the Mental Health Act people can come to hospital either voluntarily or, in extreme cases, under a section of the Act where the referral agencies referring them have the legal power to enforce admission to hospital.

The few studies that have looked at routes of admission have shown that black people are over-represented among compulsory admissions. In addition, police or social workers seem to be involved in a greater proportion of black admissions than white. One study, although only looking at a single hospital, found that black patients were twice as likely as whites to have been detained under Section 136 of the Mental Health Act. This is the clause which empowers the police to take people to a psychiatric hospital.[64] There is also some evidence that black patients tend to be on harsher forms of medication than white patients with equivalent types of diagnosis, and seem to be viewed differently once in hospital.[65]

**Gender.** Women are often presented as being iller than men and, as a result, placing more demands on the health services. To what extent is this true?

As Table 2.1 shows, women have a much longer expectation of life than men and have a lower death rate in every age group. In fact, as Figure 2.7 shows, these differences have widened since the 1930s.[66,67] The differences become even wider if the causes of death peculiar to men and women are excluded.[32]

**Figure 2.7 Percentage excess of male over female death rates by age, 1841-1980.**

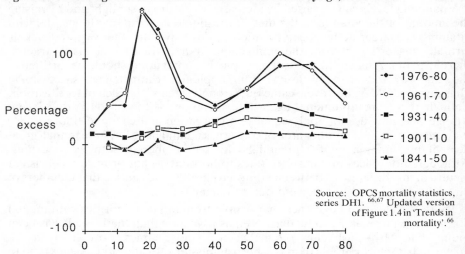

Source: OPCS mortality statistics, series DH1. [66,67] Updated version of Figure 1.4 in 'Trends in mortality'.[66]

The differences in death rates and expectation of life have important implications for health services. Although there are slightly more women than men in the population as a whole, there are many more women in the older age groups, when people make greater use of health services. More boys than girls are born and among children under 15 there were 105 boys to every 100 girls in England and Wales at the time of the 1981 census.[40] The excess of men then decreased with age and from the 50-54 age group on there were more women than men, with for example, 59 men for every 100 women aged 75-79.

Despite the differences in death rates and age at death, taking all age groups together, the percentages of men and women dying from the main causes of death are roughly similar, as Table 2.13 shows, but they are not the same for each age group. For example, mortality between the ages of 35 and 54 from diseases of the circulatory system (heart disease and strokes) is about three times higher for men than women.[69]

Despite the fact that the the percentages of deaths from circulatory disease in men and women are similar and the fact that a study in East London found that the mortality rates of Asian men less than 65 years old was three times that of their UK-born contemporaries,[70] the major research on heart disease has been on

**Table 2.13**
Most common causes of death, by sex, England and Wales, 1985

| | Percentage of deaths attributed to each cause | |
| --- | --- | --- |
| | Male | Female |
| Cancer | 25 | 23 |
| Diseases of the circulatory system | 48 | 49 |
| Respiratory diseases | 12 | 10 |
| Accidents, poisoning and violence | 4 | 3 |
| All other causes | 11 | 15 |
| Number of deaths All causes | 292,327 | 298,407 |

Source: OPCS Mortality statistics 1985, Series DH1[69]

middle aged white men.[71-74] This may tell us more about the values of the people doing the research than about the disease itself.

How about the quality and appropriateness of the care offered by the NHS to men and to women? Rather than answering these questions, the available statistics tell us more about the use made of services.

Given that women live longer than men, it is not surprising that, particularly in the older age groups, they account for a considerable proportion of hospital bed use,[75] as Figure 2.8 shows. When the numbers of hospital stays and the use of beds

**Figure 2.8 Percentage of average daily bed use by age and gender, England, 1984.**

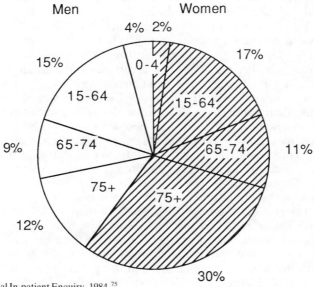

Source: Data from Hospital In-patient Enquiry, 1984.[75]

is related to the number of women in each age group, however, a different picture appears. In Table 2.14 it can be seen that, on average, women in the 45-74 age group make less use of hospital beds than men, and among children girls use them less than boys. Men aged 75 or over have more in-patient stays than women, but

**Table 2.14**
Comparison between hospital in-patient stays and bed use by men and women, England, 1984

| Age | Hospital in-patient stays per 10,000 population | | Average beds used daily per million population | |
|---|---|---|---|---|
| | M | F | M | F |
| All ages | 1,015 | 1,091 | 2,634 | 3,766 |
| 0- 4 | 1,668 | 1,174 | 2,158 | 1,688 |
| 5-14 | 712 | 517 | 907 | 568 |
| 15-44 | 561 | 909 | 911 | 1,110 |
| 45-64 | 1,081 | 994 | 2,628 | 2,564 |
| 65-74 | 2,106 | 1,481 | 7,661 | 7,019 |
| 75-84 | 3,216 | 2,326 | 15,477 | 17,794 |
| 85+ | 4,594 | 3,661 | 33,225 | 41,550 |

Source: Derived from Hospital In-patient Enquiry, Summary Tables, 1984[75]

they tend to be shorter. As we show in Part 3, statistics about in-patient stays are difficult to interpret as people are counted each time they are discharged from hospital, without making links between successive stays by the same person. This makes it difficult to relate gender differences in numbers of hospital stays to the availability of carers outside hospital.

Table 2.14 excludes not only mental illness and mental handicap hospitals but also admissions to maternity departments. It does, however, include some stays in gynaecology departments such as those for miscarriages, abortions and infertility investigations, which are related to pregnancy rather than illness.

As we have already suggested when discussing class differences, use of services may not necessarily relate to need. As Table 2.15 shows, adult women report more acute illness, but no more chronic illness than men, except at ages 75 and over.[17,76] As, however, this excludes people in long stay hospitals, homes and old people's homes, there may be some biases in this. Women do tend to consult GPs more often than men.[17] This may result from their higher rates of acute sickness, or possibly because, when taking children to see a doctor, they also ask about a problem of their own.

Because of these and other problems, it is not easy to see to what extent the health services meet the respective needs of men and women.[3]

We have shown here that there are clear class, race and gender differences in health and the provision of health services within the United Kingdom. The health service has not eliminated them, and removing inequalities in the future does not feature on the political agenda. Instead the government quotes statistics about overall levels of resources provided, to try to convince the public that the service is

**Table 2.15**
Chronic and acute sickness by age and sex, Great Britain, 1985

| Age | Percentage of each age group who reported: | | | | | |
| | Long standing illness | | Limiting long standing illness | | Restricted activity in previous 14 days | |
| | M | F | M | F | M | F |
|---|---|---|---|---|---|---|
| All ages | 29 | 31 | 16 | 18 | 11 | 14 |
| 0- 4 | 11 | 9 | 4 | 3 | 13 | 13 |
| 5-15 | 18 | 13 | 8 | 6 | 11 | 12 |
| 16-44 | 21 | 22 | 10 | 11 | 9 | 13 |
| 45-64 | 42 | 43 | 27 | 26 | 11 | 14 |
| 65-74 | 55 | 56 | 38 | 38 | 13 | 18 |
| 75+ | 58 | 65 | 43 | 51 | 17 | 23 |

Source: General Household Survey, 1985[76]

making record achievements. The next two parts of this book examine these claims.

# References.

1. OPCS. Census 1981. Historical tables 1901-1981, England and Wales. CEN 81 HT. London: HMSO, 1982.
2. Central Statistical Office. Social Trends 17, 1987 edition. London: HMSO,1987.
3. Craig J. The growth of the elderly population. Population Trends 1983; 32: 28-33.
4. OPCS. Population projections, mid-1985 based. OPCS Monitor PP2 86/1. London: OPCS,1986.
5. Family Policy Studies Centre. An ageing population. Fact sheet 2. London: FPSC, 1986.
6. Beacham R. Economic activity, Britain's workforce 1971-81. Population Trends 1984; 37: 6-14.
7. OPCS and Registrar General Scotland. Census 1981. National report, Great Britain, Part I. CEN 81 NR(1). London: HMSO, 1983.
8. OPCS and Registrar General Scotland. Census 1981. Persons of pensionable age, Great Britain. CEN 81 PEN. London: HMSO, 1983.
9. OPCS and Registrar General Scotland. Census 1981. Key statistics for local authorities, Great Britain. CEN 81 KSLA. London: HMSO, 1984.
10. OPCS. Hospital In-patient Enquiry (England) Trends 1979-84. OPCS Monitor MB4 86/1. London: OPCS,1986.
11. Kings Fund. Planned health services for London. Back to back planning. London: Kings Fund, 1987.
12. DHSS. NHS hospital activity statistics for England 1974-85. Statistical bulletin 2/86. London: DHSS,1986.
13. Tillett H E, McEvoy M. Reassessment of predicted numbers of AIDS cases in the UK. Lancet 1986; ii: 1104.
14. Written reply. Hansard, July 25 1986, col 715.
15. Beale N, Nethercott S. Job loss and family morbidity: a study of factory closure. Journal of the Royal College of General Practitioners 1985; 35: 510-514.
16. Real resources and unreal assumptions: the case of the NHS. Public money; December 1984: 58-62.
17. OPCS Social Survey Division. General Household Survey 1984. Series GHS No 14. London: HMSO, 1986.
18. Royal Commission on the National Health Service. Report. Cmnd 7615. London: HMSO, 1979.
19. DHSS. Inequalities in Health. Report of a working party. London: DHSS, 1980.
20. Townsend P, Davidson N. Inequalities in health: the Black report. Harmondsworth: Penguin, 1982.
21. Whitehead M. The health divide. Inequalities in health in the 1980s. London: Health Education Council, 1987.

22. Office of Population Censuses and Surveys. Occupational mortality 1970-72. Series DS No 1. London: HMSO, 1978.

23. Townsend P, Phillimore P, Beattie A. Inequalities in health in the Northern Region. Northern Regional Health Authority and University of Bristol, 1986.

24. Thunhurst C. Poverty and health in the city of Sheffield. Sheffield: Sheffield City Council, 1985.

25. Fox A J, Goldblatt P O. Longitudinal Study. Socio-demographic mortality differentials 1971-1975. Series LS No 1. London: HMSO, 1982.

26. Office of Population Censuses and Surveys. Occupational mortality. The Registrar General's decennial supplement for Great Britain, 1979-80, 1982-83. Series DS No 6. Part I Commentary and Part II Tables. London: HMSO, 1986.

27. OPCS. Longitudinal study data quoted in Population Trends 1986; 45: 2-4.

28. Marmot M G, McDowall M E. Mortality decline and widening social inequalities. Lancet 1986; ii: 274-276.

29. Smith R. Whatever happened to the Black report? British Medical Journal 1986; 293: 91-92.

30. McDowall M. William Farr and the study of occupational mortality. Population Trends 1983; 31: 12-14.

31. Editorial. The occupational mortality supplement: why the fuss? Lancet 1986; ii: 610-612.

32. Macfarlane A J. Official statistics and women's health and illness. Equal Opportunities Review 1980; 4: 43-77.

33. McDowall M. Measuring women's occupational mortality. Population Trends 1983; 34: 25-29.

34. Macfarlane A J. Letter. British Medical Journal 1986; 293: 503-504.

35. Tudor Hart J. The inverse care law. Lancet 1971; i: 405-412.

36. Titmuss R. Commitment to welfare. London: Allen and Unwin, 1968.

37. Royal College of General Practitioners, OPCS, DHSS. Morbidity statistics from general practice 1970-71. Socio-economic analyses. Studies on Medical and Population Subjects No 46. London: HMSO, 1982.

38. Marmot MG, Adelstein AM, Bulusu L. Immigrant mortality in England and Wales 1970-1978. Studies on Medical and Population Subjects No 47. London: HMSO, 1984.

39. DHSS. Report on confidential enquiries into maternal deaths in England and Wales 1976-1978. Report on Health and Social Subjects No 26. London: HMSO, 1982.

40. DHSS. Report on confidential enquiries into maternal deaths in England and Wales 1979-1981. Report on Health and Social Subjects No 29. London: HMSO, 1986.

41. Written reply. Hansard May 23, 1986, col 375.

42. Written reply. Hansard Nov 27 1986, col 353.

43. Barnes R. Perinatal mortality and morbidity rates in Bradford. In: McFadyen I, MacVicar J. Obstetric problems of the Asian community in Britain. London: Royal College of Obstetricians and Gynaecologists, 1982.

44. Dhariwal HS. Leicestershire — decline in perinatal mortality. In: McFadyen I, MacVicar J. Obstetric problems of the Asian community in Britain. London: Royal College of Obstetricians and Gynaecologists, 1982.

45. Terry PB, Condie RG, Settatree RS. Analysis of ethnic differences in perinatal statistics. British Medical Journal 1980; 281: 1307-1308.

46. Enkin M, Chalmers I. Effectiveness and satisfaction in antenatal care. Clinics in Developmental Medicine Nos 81/82. London: Spastics International Medical Publications/ William Heinemann Medical Books, 1982

47. Pearson J. Is early antenatal attendance so important? British Medical Journal 1982; 284: 1064.

48. Simpson H, Walker G. When do pregnant women attend for antenatal care? British Medical Journal 1980; 2: 104-107.

49. Oakley A. The Captured Womb. Oxford: Blackwell Scientific Publications, 1984.

50. Clarke P, Clare N. Sickle cell anaemia: a challenge to health education. Health Education Council Journal 1981; 40: 50-53.

51. Torkington P. The racial politics of health — A Liverpool profile. Merseyside Area Profile Group. University of Liverpool, 1983.

52. Anionwu E, Walford D, Brozovic M, Kirkwood B. Sickle cell disease in a British urban community. British Medical Journal 1981; 282: 283-286.

53. Tuck S. Sickle cell disease and pregnancy. British Journal of Hospital Medicine 1983; 28: 125-127.

54. DHSS. Rickets and osteomalacia. Report of the Working Party on Fortification of Food with Vitamin D. Committee on Medical Aspects of Food Policy (COMA) London, HMSO, 1980

---

55. Goel K, Sweet EM, Logan RW, Warren JM. Arneil GC, Shanks RM. Florid and sub-clinical rickets among immigrant children in Glasgow. Lancet 1976; i: 1141-1145.

56. Ford J. Clinical and sub-clinical vitamin D deficiency in Bradford children. Archives of Disease in Childhood 1976; 51: 39-40.

57. Preece MA, Tomlinson S, Ribot CA et al. Studies in vitamin D deficiency in man. Quarterly Journal of Medicine 1975; 44: 575-577.

58. Stamp T. Sources of vitamin D nutrition. Letter. Lancet 1980; i: 316.

59. Dunnigan MG, Glelan BM, Henderson JB, et al. Prevention of rickets in Asian children: an assessment of the Glasgow comparison. Br Med J 1985; 291: 239-242.

60. Cochrane R. Mental illness in immigrant in England and Wales: an analysis of mental hospital admissions in 1971. Social Psychiatry 1977; 12: 2-35.

61. Dean G, Walsh D, Downing H, Shelley E. First admissions of native born and immigrants to psychiatric hospitals in SE England 1976. Br J Psychiat 1981; 139: 506-512.

62. Ineichen B. Mental illness among New Commonwealth migrants to Britain. In Boyce A (ed.) Mobility and Migration. London: Taylor and Francis, 1980.

63. Black Health Workers and Patients Group. Psychiatry and the corporate state. Race and Class 1983; XXV: 49-54.

64. Lipsedge M, Littlewood RK. Compulsory hospitalisation and minority status. 11th Biennial Conference of the Caribbean Federation for Mental Health. Gosier, Guadaloupe, 1977.

65. Littlewood RK, Cross S. Ethnic minorities and psychiatric services. Sociology of Health and Illness 1980; 2: 194-201.

66. OPCS. Trends in mortality, England and Wales 1951-1975. Series DH1 No 3. London: HMSO, 1978.

67. OPCS. Mortality statistics, England and Wales, Serial tables, 1841-1980. Series DH1 No 15. London: HMSO, 1985.

68. Britton M, Edison N. The changing balance of the sexes in England and Wales, 1851-2001. Population Trends 1986; 46: 22-25.

69. OPCS. Mortality statistics 1985, England and Wales. Series DH1 No 17. London: HMSO, 1987.

70. Tunstall Pedoe H, Clayton D, Morris JN, Brigden W, McDonald L. Coronary heart attacks in East London. Lancet 1975; ii: 833.

71. Committee of Principal Investigators. A co-operative trial in the primary prevention of ischaemic heart disease using clofibrate. British Heart Journal 1978; 40: 1069-1118.

72. Dayton S, Peace ML, Hashimoto S, Dixon WJ, Tumiyasu U. A controlled trial of diet in unsaturated fat. Circulation 1969; 39-40; Suppl III; 1-63.

73. Rose G, Shipley MJ. Plasma lipids and mortality: a source of error. Lancet 1980; 1: 523-527.

74. Stamber J, Wentworth D, Neaton JD. Is relationship between serum cholesterol and premature risk of death from coronary heart disease continuous and graded? Journal of the American Medical Association 1986; 282: 2823-2828.

75. DHSS, OPCS. Hospital In-patient Enquiry 1984, summary tables. Series MB4 No 24. London: HMSO, 1986.

76. OPCS. General Household Survey. Preliminary results for 1985. OPCS Monitor GHS 86/1. London: OPCS, 1986.

# 3
# The Record of Achievement:
# The NHS — A Growing Service?

*'May I point out, in regard to the National Health Service, that the only cuts we have made are cuts in waiting lists.'*
Margaret Thatcher.[1]

THE GOVERNMENT repeatedly quotes statistics which claim that it is spending more on the health service and treating more patients than ever before. Yet this comes at a time when it is unusual to find a local or national paper which does not contain a report of cuts in the National Health Service. In this section, we look at the statistics most commonly mentioned, and the way they are selected and used to support the government's claims.

Because the statistics which are most often quoted are, by and large, those for England, we have tended to focus our comments on them. The very same points can, however, be made about the similar statistics collected in Wales, Scotland and Northern Ireland. Many of these are published annually in 'Health and Personal Social Services Statistics for Wales', 'Scottish Health Statistics', 'Health and Personal Social Services Statistics for Northern Ireland', and the Central Statistical Office's 'Annual Abstract of Statistics'.

## Impressive statistics?

Before looking in detail at the government's specific claim about the NHS, it is worth outlining some common features in the way it uses statistics.

Firstly, many statistics relate to two years only. The annual reports of the Health Service in England and the DHSS leaflets issued in January 1985 and July 1986 compared statistics for the most recent year with those for 1978. No explicit explanation is given for choosing 1978, the year before which the Conservatives returned to power.

Quoting statistics for just two years can give a very misleading picture. It is important to seek out statistics for the years before 1978, as doing so reveals that many of the changes referred to are the continuation of longer term trends which were already established before 1978 and are not direct consequences of the present government's policies. For example, the government often gives itself credit for the fall in the perinatal mortality rate, which is the proportion of babies who are stillborn or who die in the first week after live birth. Yet the rate has been falling for many years under both Labour and Conservative governments.

In other instances, the changes which have occurred since 1978 have been spread equally over the time period. For example, increases in NHS spending were concentrated in the years up to 1981, while the numbers of people on waiting lists for in-patient treatment have gone up and down twice since 1978.

In addition to this, there have been changes since 1978 in the way some of the statistics were defined. This happened both with waiting list statistics and with statistics about the numbers of nurses and midwives. In both examples, the changes are usually ignored or mentioned in very small footnotes.

Very often health service statistics are quoted as raw numbers without trying to relate them to the population for which they are intended by expressing them as rates. Thus, little attempt is made to relate changes in the levels of services to changes in the size or age structure of the population or to assess unmet need.

Finally, quoting statistics for England as a whole can mask very large local differences both in the population using the services and in the way health service spending is changing. Some parts of the country are experiencing much larger cuts than others in the name of reallocation of resources. This is aimed at diverting funds away from the Thames and Oxford regions in the south-east of England to the rest of the country.[2] Within the Thames regions, funds are being diverted away from Inner London, which has lost population, to the surrounding counties, whose population has grown[3]. We published a detailed critique of the way this is done in 'RAW(P) deals'[4], and mention some of its effects in what follows.

While cuts in prestigious London teaching hospitals get wide coverage in the press, they may not fare as badly as neighbouring less powerful non-teaching hospitals. Perhaps the most telling way to measure the impact of government spending policies would be to look at what is really happening in the 'gaining' districts in the regions which are said to be 'gaining' resources. As we have not had time to do this ourselves, we leave this as a suggestion to readers and take a look at the government's most commonly repeated claims about the state of the NHS.

# More money?

'The government have already increased spending from £7¾ billion in 1978-79 to £18¾ billion this year.[5] This is just one of many versions of the claim that NHS spending has more than doubled under Conservative rule. In the example above, the figures apply to health service spending in England plus combined spending on health and personal social services in Scotland, Wales and Northern Ireland. On the other hand, combined health and social services spending in England is shown in Figure 3.1 which is taken from the government's annual public expenditure white papers.[6,7]

**The effects of inflation.** It is readily admitted that these comparisons do not allow for inflation. In the statement quoted above, Norman Fowler went on to say, 'That is a real terms increase of 24 per cent after general inflation'.[5] After adjustment in this way, expenditure on the NHS in England rose by 21.0 per cent between 1978-79 and 1984-85[8] and decreased by 0.2 per cent in 1985-86.[9]

These so-called 'real terms' measure the 'economic cost' of the National Health Service, that is, its cost to the Exchequer. They are arrived at by adjusting annual spending figures using a statistic called the Gross Domestic Product (GDP) deflator. This allows for the way inflation affects the internal economy of the country as a whole. The effect of making this adjustment to the public expenditure figures adjusted in shown in Figure 3.1 can be seen in Figure 3.2. The series does not go back before 1978-79, making comparisons with earlier years difficult.

**Figure 3.1 Public expenditure by selected departments in cash terms.**

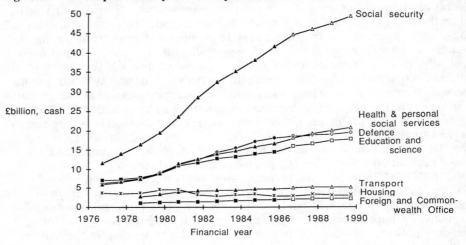

Source: 1982[6] and 1987[7] Public expenditure white papers.

**Figure 3.2 Public spending by department in 'real terms' as presented in the 1987 public expenditure white paper.**

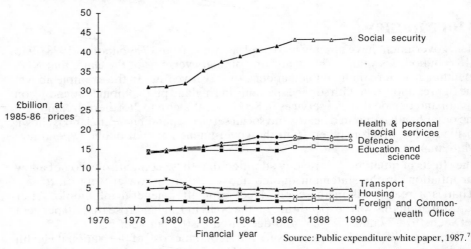

Source: Public expenditure white paper, 1987.[7]

The way the National Health Service spends its money is not, of course, typical of the economy as a whole, and the costs of the goods and services it buys have increased faster than general inflation since 1979. Thus, allowing for this, between 1978-79 and 1984-85, 'input volume', that is, what money can actually buy for the

NHS in England, increased by only 8.4 per cent,[8] with a further increase of 0.6 per cent in 1985-86.

Up to 1981, the government's annual public expenditure White Papers presented figures in these 'volume' terms adjusting spending figures on each programme of public spending for changes in the relevant pay and prices. This allowed year to year comparisons to be made of the volume of goods and services used. Figure 3.3 comes from the 1981 White Paper[10] and shows expenditure up to 1980-81 in volume terms at 1980 survey prices, together with planned spending for the following three years.

**Figure 3.3 Actual and planned public expenditure at '1980 survey prices' as presented in the 1981 white paper.**

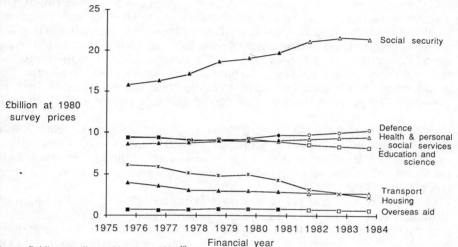

Source: Public expenditure white paper, 1981.[10]

Since 1982, the White Paper spending figures have been presented in the cash terms shown in Figure 3.1 without any adjustment for inflation. This followed the announcement by the Chancellor of the Exchequer in his March 1981 budget statement that public expenditure was now being planned in cash terms. The rationale for this is clearly part of the government's policy of cutting public spending. As the 1982 White Paper put it, 'The cash plans embody the principle, already well established in the system of cash limits, that levels of service must be determined in the light of finance available'.[6]

Since 1985 the White Papers have also included a table of figures giving spending in the 'real terms' shown in Figure 3.2. As these spending figures were both adjusted for inflation on a different basis and cover a different time period from those in Figure 3.3, it is almost impossible to compare what happened in the late 1970s and the early 1980s across different areas of public spending. Spending totals for the NHS and the social services have, however, been produced on both 'economic cost' and 'input volume' bases. Figures for England are published annually in the reports of the House of Commons Social Services Committee, and information for all four countries of the UK has been given in reply to parliamentary questions.

**Changes in accounting methods.** As well as this major change in the way figures are presented, there are a number of smaller differences to look out for. Usually, gross spending, which includes money collected from charges to patients, is quoted, but sometimes figures are presented in net terms, without the income from charges. As we show later, the relative contribution of charges has increased since 1978. Similarly, figures for capital spending now often include the proceeds from land sales as well as funds from central government.

In April 1985, the costs of administering Family Practitioner Committees were transferred from the Hospital and Community Health Services to the Family Practitioner Committees themselves. At the same time, a change was made in the accounting methods used for current spending in the Hospital and Community Health Services in England. Instead of being based on 'accruals', that is total spending incurred and income arising during the year, they are now based on cash flow.[9] Revised spending figures for 1978-79 onwards, adjusted to this basis, have been published.[9,11] It is interesting to note that on the new 'cash' basis the increase in input volume for total expenditure on the NHS in England from 1978-9 to 1984-5 was 9.2 per cent,[11] whereas on the old 'accruals' basis it was 8.4 per cent.[8]

**Uneven patterns of growth.** The data for England[11] shown in Figure 3.4 and corresponding information for Scotland,[12] Wales[13] and Northern Ireland[14] tell similar stories. Increases in both the 'economic cost' of the health service and in the 'input volume' were not evenly spread over the years, nor between different types of spending.

Over half of the 21.0 per cent growth between 1978-79 and 1984-85 in the 'economic cost' of the NHS in England had already taken place by 1981, and 40 per cent of it happened in the single year 1980-81.[8] Revised figures suggest that 47 per cent of the 21.3 growth occurred in this year.[11] It was largely confined to the Hospital and Community Health Services and resulted from the Clegg awards agreed by the Labour government and the shortening of the working week to comply with an EEC directive.

This aside, the 'economic cost' of the Hospital and Community Health Services, which are subject to cash limits, has grown less since 1978-79 than that on the Family Practitioner Services, which are not.

There were also differences between growth in current spending (salaries and supplies) and capital spending (mainly buildings) within the Hospital and Community Health Services. Table 3.1 shows there has been a much greater percentage growth in capital than in current spending since 1979. This accounts for the heavy emphasis on new buildings and facilities in the government's claims of record growth in the NHS and the comparisons it makes with the record of its Labour predecessors. Yet, as Table 3.2 and Figure 3.5 show, capital spending accounted for under 6 per cent of all NHS spending in England in 1985-86,[7] and was lower in earlier years.[15] It made up a similar proportion of spending in the other three countries of the United Kingdom.

In contrast to capital expenditure, current spending on hospital and community

# Figure 3.4 Cost of the NHS in terms of percentage growth since 1974-5, England.

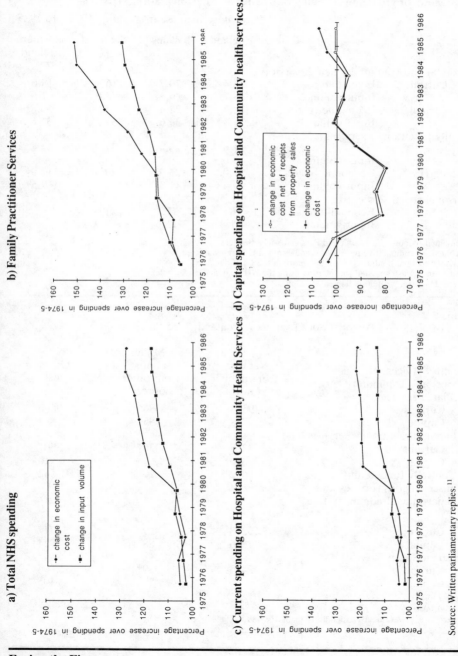

a) Total NHS spending

b) Family Practitioner Services

c) Current spending on Hospital and Community Health Services

d) Capital spending on Hospital and Community health services.

Source: Written parliamentary replies.[11]

**Table 3.1**
Two views of growth in spending on Health and Personal Social Services

Percentage increase in spending 1978-9 to 1985-6

| | | England | Wales | Scotland | Northern Ireland |
|---|---|---|---|---|---|
| **Hospital and community health services** | | | | | |
| Current | Economic cost | 16.4 | 20.7 | 16.9 | 18.6 |
| | Input volume | 5.7 | 9.5 | 6.0 | 7.6 |
| Capital | Economic cost | 28.7 | 22.4 | 25.0 | − 35.8 |
| | Input volume* | 34.8* | 30.6* | 33.3* | − 31.6* |
| **Family practitioner services** | | | | | |
| | Economic cost | 31.6 | 28.4 | 27.9 | 24.4 |
| | Input volume | 13.0 | 9.0 | 8.2 | 5.7 |
| **Total NHS** | Economic cost | 21.0 | 23.3 | 20.0 | 17.9† |
| | Input volume | 9.4 | 11.4 | 8.4 | 7.5† |
| **Personal social services** | | | | | |
| | Economic cost | 16.9 | 17.1 | 21.4 | |
| | Input volume | 11.4 | 11.6 | 9.9 | |

†Combined spending on Health and Personal Social Services
*Included for comparative purposes although not strictly relevant (see text)
Economic cost: cash adjusted for inflation using the GDP deflator
Input volume: cash adjusted for inflation using the NHS pay and prices index
Source: Hansard, written parliamentary replies[11-14].

---

**Table 3.2**
Cost of NHS and Personal Social services, England, 1985-86

| | Net cost from public funds | £ Million Funds from other sources | Gross cost |
|---|---|---|---|
| **Health Services** | | | |
| Hospital, community and related services | | | |
| Current | 9574 | 86† | 9660 |
| Capital | 798 | 85* | 884 |
| **Family Practitioner Services** | | | |
| Current | 3265 | 336† | 3601 |
| Capital | 10 | | 10 |
| Centrally funded and miscellaneous services and departmental administration | 532 | 10 | 542 |
| **Total** | | | |
| Current | 13288 | 429 | 13717 |
| Capital | 836 | 88 | 924 |
| **Personal Social Services** | | | |
| Current | 2415 | 389† | 2804 |
| Capital | 76 | 29 | 105 |

† Charges
* Land sales
Source: The government's expenditure plans 1987-88 to 1989-90[7]

**Figure 3.5 How the NHS in England spent its money, 1985-86.**

a) Total NHS budget

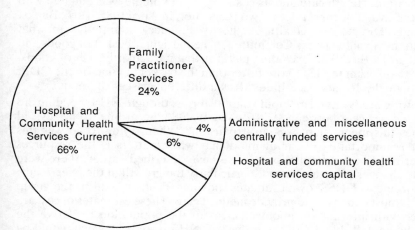

b) Family practitioner services

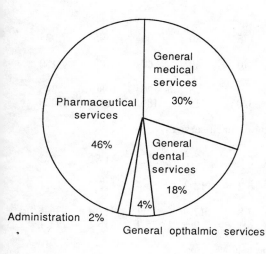

Source: Public expenditure white paper, 1987.[7]

health services, which accounts for about two-thirds of NHS expenditure, grew very slowly in 'input volume' terms and fell by 0.1 per cent in 1984-85.[9] Perhaps this is the reason why government ministers now refuse to accept that 'input volume' is 'a sensible measure of "expenditure in real terms" '.[8] Yet in 1983, in a DHSS publication 'Health care and its costs,'[16] 'input volume' was equated with 'real resources' available for services. Two years later, in April 1985, Terry Banks, who was then Director of Health Authority Finance, admitted somewhat cryptically to the Social Services Committee, 'The particular basket of goods and services bought by the NHS, excluding pay, for that particular basket of goods, the prices in that basket tended to rise faster than the basket of goods in the GDP, the economy or the Retail Price Index. It is a different basket of goods'.[17]

**Meeting growing needs?** Even in 'input volume' terms, though, NHS spending did increase by 9.4 per cent between 1978-79 and 1985-86, according to the revised figures. Does this mean there was an expansion? When trying to answer this question, it is important to bear in mind that what matters is the resources available per head of the population. As we have described earlier, there were considerable changes over this period, particularly the growth in the over 75 age group. According to DHSS' own estimates shown in Table 3.3, this is the group for whom it is most expensive to provide medical care. These estimates of cost are put together with information about changes in the population to derive the estimates, shown in Table 3.4 of the growth in NHS resources which would be

**Table 3.3**
Estimated gross current spending per person by age and type of service, England, 1984-85

| | All ages | All births | Age 0-4 | 5-15 | 16-64 | 65-74 | 75+ |
|---|---|---|---|---|---|---|---|
| a) £ per head | | | | | | | |
| Hospital and community health services | 195 | 1075 | 175 | 80 | 100 | 395 | 925 |
| Family practitioner services | 70 | 80 | 70 | 60 | 60 | 100 | 150 |
| Personal social services | 60 | 25 | 75 | 75 | 20 | 80 | 345 |
| Total | 325 | 1180 | 320 | 215 | 180 | 575 | 1420 |
| b) Estimated percentage of total spending on each service† | | | | | | | |
| Hospital and community health services | 100.0 | 7.0 | 5.6 | 5.9 | 32.5 | 17.2 | 29.8 |
| Family practitioner services | 100.0 | 1.4 | 6.2 | 12.3 | 54.4 | 12.2 | 13.4 |
| Personal social services | 100.0 | 0.5 | 7.8 | 17.9 | 21.1 | 11.4 | 36.1 |
| Total | 100.0 | 4.6 | 6.1 | 9.5 | 35.1 | 15.1 | 27.4 |

†Estimated using 1984 births and mid-1984 population estimates
Source: Hansard, written reply[18]

**Facing the Figures**

required to maintain the same level of service.[19] Published statements give figures which have less appearance of precision.

In 1976, the report of the Resource Allocation Working Party said, 'It is generally accepted that the resources available to the NHS need to grow at a rate of 1 per cent per annum in order to accommodate the increasing cost effects of demographic change' (para 2.41).[2] A few years later, a growth rate of 0.7 per cent was being quoted,[16,20] whereas in 1985, it was stated that, 'In the period since the late 1970s, it has usually been estimated that on average the Hospital and Community Health Services require each year nearly one per cent more of real resources to deal with demographic pressures'.[8] In fact, as Table 3.4 shows, the estimated requirement fluctuated considerably over the years.

**Table 3.4**
DHSS estimates of growth in expenditure. Hospital and Community Health services required to meet demand from demographic change.

| Year | Percentage growth | Year | Percentage growth |
|------|------|------|------|
| 1975-76 | 0.0 | 1986-87 | 1.0 |
| 1976-77 | 0.2 | 1987-88 | 0.9 |
| 1977-78 | 0.3 | 1988-89 | 0.8 |
| 1978-79 | 0.9 | 1989-90 | 0.7 |
| 1979-80 | 1.2 | 1990-91 | 0.6 |
| 1980-81 | 0.9 | 1991-92 | 0.5 |
| 1981-82 | 0.3 | 1992-93 | 0.2 |
| 1982-83 | 0.5 | 1993-94 | 0.0 |
| 1983-84 | 0.5 | 1994-95 | 0.1 |
| 1984-85 | 0.6 | 1995-96 | 0.6 |
| 1985-86 | 1.1 | | |

Source: Written reply, Hansard, June 23 1986, col 67.[19]

The DHSS also tries to allow for the cost of technological innovation which is increasing the NHS' ability to purchase goods and carry out procedures which were not available in 1978. The DHSS usually estimates that a growth rate of 0.5 per cent per year in spending on the Hospital and Community Health Services is needed to cover the cost of technological innovation.

The way these growth rates are arrived at is discussed in detail in a series of reports from York University.[20,22] In the first two of these, Nick Bosanquet pointed out that the increase in spending on services for elderly people was less than the amount thought to be necessary and the estimate of 0.5 per cent per year for technology was somewhat haphazard.[20,21] He estimated that an overall rate of growth of 2 per cent would be necessary to cover these increases plus new investments needed to develop community care and provide new forms of acute care. The third of these reports, 'Public expenditure on the NHS — recent trends and future problems', by Alan Maynard and Nick Bosanquet, spelled out pressures for increased spending in more detail.[22]

Some pressures are likely to follow from changes in policy. The move from institutional to community care will create demands for increased spending in the community before savings are made on institutions. If screening programmes for cervical and breast cancer are to be extended, more funds will be needed. Changing nursing education along the lines proposed in Project 2000 would decrease the extent to which student nurses are used as cheap labour on the wards. If family practitioner services were developed along the lines set out in the 1986 Green Paper, more funds would be required especially if attempts were also made to reduce geographical inequalities by levelling services upwards.

Alan Maynard and Nick Bosanquet also mentioned the increasing need for care resulting from the AIDS epidemic and the difficulty in predicting the number of people likely to be affected.[22] They are likely to be concentrated in the Thames regions in the inner city districts which are losing money under RAWP.

There are other changes which they, like the government, did not take into account, but which are likely to create increasing demands for health care. As we mentioned earlier, these include the growth in unemployment[24,25] and the rising proportion of people who are divorced or widowed.[26]

The second[22] and third[23] reports from York University were commissioned jointly by the Royal College of Nursing, the British Medical Association and the Institute of Health Service Administration, who used them in their campaigns for increases in NHS funding. The DHSS responded in February 1986 to Nick Bosanquet's report 'Public expenditure on the NHS: recent trends and the outlook'.[22] Mentioning demographic pressure, technological change and its own specific priorities, the DHSS admitted, 'HCHS services therefore need to grow by about 2 per cent a year in order to meet both the inexorable and policy pressures. This tallies with the report's own estimate'.[27]

**More efficient use of resources?** The DHSS followed this by what seems to have become its stock response to accusations of inadequate funding, 'But it is important to recognise, as the Report's sponsors do, the contribution to developing services from cost improvement programmes as well as from higher cash spending'.[27]

This was reiterated in June 1986 when Health Minister Barney Hayhoe was questioned by the House of Commons Social Services Committee: 'I said yes when you mentioned 2 per cent, but I was saying yes then to 2 per cent increases in the level of services. However, that is not resources, it is services; because if, for example, we are able, through cost improvements, to get some services such as cleaning services done more cheaply, then there is more money for dealing with patients'.[9]

The extent and growth of cost improvements, or efficiency savings as they used to be known is set out in Table 3.5.[28] Further increases are planned for future years. No-one would deny that increasing efficiency in the NHS is a worthwhile objective, but there are no data to show that all the savings are in fact the result of better use of resources. Savings could have been made in other ways, for example, by cutting services, delaying the introduction of new services, or postponing repairs.

The DHSS view given in evidence to the Social Services Committtee is set out in Table 3.6.[9] Nearly a third of planned savings in 1986-87 were attributed to competitive tendering. As we show later, there may well be hidden costs in this

**Table 3.5**
Efficiency savings and cash releasing cost improvement programmes, England

| Year | £ million |
|---|---|
| 1981-82 | 15.2 |
| 1982-83 | 25.5 |
| 1983-84 | 42.0 |
| 1984-85 | 105.2 |
| 1985-86 | 138.4 |

In 1983-4 health authorities were expected to achieve the efficiency savings shown equivalent per cent of their cash allocations. Figures for other years are based on cash savings reported by regions.
Source: Written parliamentary reply, Hansard February 4, 1987[28]

**Table 3.6**
Planned cost improvement programmes, England 1986-87

| | £ million | Per cent |
|---|---|---|
| Rationalisation of patient services | 37 | 24 |
| Competitive tendering | 48 | 31 |
| Other reductions in labour costs | 23 | 15 |
| 'Rayner scrutiny' savings | 7 | 4.5 |
| Supply cost savings | 7 | 4.5 |
| Fuel cost savings | 9 | 6 |
| Other savings† | 24 | 15 |
| Total | 155 | 100 |

†Includes items such as the introduction of cook/chill catering, centralisation of laundry services, savings in Blood Transfusion Service, rationalisation of telephone services etc.
Source: Social Services Committee. Public expenditure on the social services, 1985-86,[9]. Table 1.2

method of reducing the pay and increasing the workload of the lowest paid NHS workers.

A report early in 1986 from the Comptroller and Auditor General warned that some health authorities were saving costs 'without necessarily any matching improvements in efficiency'.[29] This was based on a survey of 11 authorities at the end of 1984, five of whom were found to be cutting services. Eighteen months later these five authorities still faced considerable problems which they could only solve by cutting services.[30]

**The impact of pay awards.** The government used arguments about efficiency savings to defend its decision not to meet the full cost of the pay settlements awarded in 1985 and 1986 by the review bodies for doctors and dentists, nurses and midwives, and professions supplementary to medicine. Nurses', health visitors' and midwives' pay is a critical item of spending. They are not well paid, but because there are so many of them, their pay accounts for a third of current spending on Hospital and Community Health Services. Figure 3.6 shows information for England, and the position is similar in Wales, Scotland and Northern Ireland.

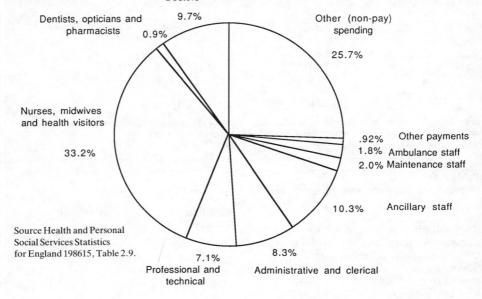

**Figure 3.6 Current spending on the Hospital and Community Health Services, England, 1984-85.**

Doctors 9.7%

Dentists, opticians and pharmacists 0.9%

Other (non-pay) spending 25.7%

Nurses, midwives and health visitors 33.2%

.92% Other payments
1.8% Ambulance staff
2.0% Maintenance staff

10.3% Ancillary staff

Source Health and Personal Social Services Statistics for England 198615, Table 2.9.

7.1% Professional and technical

8.3% Administrative and clerical

The review body pay awards announced in June 1985 were well ahead of the 3 per cent allowed for in the budget. Rises for doctors and dentists led to an increase of 5.25 per cent in their pay bill. Had the nurses', health visitors' and midwives' pay award been paid in full, it would have led to an increase of 8.6 per cent, their bill rose by only 5.9 per cent in 1985-86.

Initially the government refused to meet the additional cost of these pay awards but later, in the Chancellor's autumn statement, funds due to be allocated to the NHS were increased by £250 million for 1986-87 and £300 million for 1987-88.'[31] In 1986 further pay rises for these groups of staff increased their pay bill by 6 per cent, and the government 'decided exceptionally to provide an extra £60 million for health authorities' cash limits' to help meet this.[32] This applied to the UK as a whole, and £50 million of this increase was allocated to England.

Although some health authorities were saved by the fall in oil prices and the fact that inflation was less than forecast, many have had major problems meeting these pay rises plus those for other NHS staff. To add to the confusion, some districts may have anticipated the pay rises and already made cuts to fund them, while others may have blamed cuts made for other reasons on them. The impact of the pay rises is also likely to have depended on each district's staffing structure.[21]

**Regional differences.** Districts and regions which were losing funds under NHS resource allocation were probably particularly vulnerable to the effects of the pay rise. Table 3.7 shows the considerable variation in changes in input volume in each English region. As their population structures differ, the same assumptions made

**Table 3.7**
National and regional differences in changes in current spending on Hospital and Community Health Services.
Percentage change in input volume

| Region or country | Three year periods | | Six years | |
|---|---|---|---|---|
| | 1978-79 1981-82 | 1981-82 1984-85 | 1978-79 1984-85 | 1984-85 1985-86 |
| Northern | 4.2 | 2.6 | 6.8 | |
| Yorkshire | 4.7 | 1.3 | 6.0 | |
| Trent | 4.9 | 4.0 | 9.0 | |
| East Anglian | 4.2 | 5.4 | 9.7 | |
| Thames† | 1.4 | -1.6 | -0.3 | |
| Wessex | 4.0 | 5.0 | 9.1 | |
| Oxford | 1.7 | 3.0 | 4.7 | |
| South Western | 4.2 | 1.6 | 6.0 | |
| West Midlands | 3.9 | 3.3 | 7.4 | |
| Mersey | 2.4 | 0.2 | 2.6 | |
| North Western | 6.4 | 1.3 | 7.7 | |
| England | 4.4 | 0.7 | 5.2 | 0.4 |
| Percentage increase which would allow for a) 'demography' and 'innovation' | 4.0 | 3.1 | 7.2 | 1.1 |
| b) 2 per cent increase each year | 6.1 | 6.1 | 12.6 | 2.0 |
| Wales | 4.6 | 3.2 | 7.9 | 1.5 |
| Scotland | 3.4 | 2.0 | 5.5 | 0.4 |
| Northern Ireland | 6.0 | 1.7 | 7.8 | -0.2 |

†Including Special Health Authorities
Source: Written Parliamentary replies[12, 13, 14, 33]

nationally about the need for resources for demographic change do not apply locally. What can be seen is much smaller growth over the period 1981-82 to 1984-85 in most of the poorer regions compared with the preceding three-year period. Most striking is the net decrease over the second three-year period in the Thames regions. This contrasts with the ostensible purpose of RAWP which is to distribute growth money,[2] and is likely to affect not only losing districts in the Thames regions but also losing districts in regions with very little growth.

A report by the Kings Fund on the consequences of the Thames regions' strategic plans on 12 inner London health districts illustrated the combined effects of RAWP and government spending policies. One result was that while 74 per cent of the cuts in local acute beds which were planned to have taken place by 1993 had already been made in the first two years of the ten year period, this yielded only 34.5 per cent of the planned reduction in spending on local acute services.[34]
**Getting ready for a general election?** Though the picture is a complex one, it is

apparent that while there has been some growth in the resources available to the NHS, some of this has come from property sales and increased charges to patients. Relatively little growth occurred in the past three or four financial years. Over this period it has been insufficient to meet the DHSS' stated requirements for demographic change and technological change and technological innovation, let alone other consequences of changes both in need and policy.

Increases in funding in 1987-88 and the two succeeding years, announced in the 1986 autumn statement,[35] were claimed by the DHSS to be 'substantial increases on our published plans and show the importance the government attach to the health service'.[36] In Hospital and Community Health Services current spending it promised 'an increase of £626 million over the total funds this year — 6 per cent more in cash and 2.2 per cent more in real terms. The plans provide for real terms increases of about 1 per cent in each of the succeeding.'[36] The public expenditure White Paper issued in January 1987[7] put these increases as 2.5 per cent in 1987-88 and 0.9 per cent in each of 1988-89 and 1989-90.[37]

Closer inspection showed that £25 million of this was earmarked for half the cost of the two-year initiative to reduce waiting lists, as was £15 million for half the cost of the special fund to deal with transitional problems of resource allocation. After deducting this and the remaining cost of the 1986-87 pay rise, the rise in the economic cost was just under 1 per cent.[38] This would not be enough to meet the rising demands to which we have referred.

The position will be even more severe in 1988-89 and 1989-90 with the much smaller planned rises of 0.9 per cent in current spending on the Hospital and Community Health Services. The 1987 White Paper also shows that land sales will continue to account for 15 per cent of capital spending in England. This cannot go on forever as, like North Sea oil, the supply of saleable NHS assets will eventually run out. Figures given for the Family Practitioner Services point to a sharp increase in charges to patients in 1988-1989. In other words, even the somewhat illusory increases in spending in the run up to the general election will disappear afterwards.

The government's repeated response to evidence that the growth in resources has been adequate over the past few years and the signs of continued inadequacies in the future is that it has 'responded to demand by providing a record level of service to patients'.œ3œ9 In the sections which follow, we look at the government's claims about the growth of NHS resources and activity.

# More staff?

'The fact is that more doctors and nurses are working for patients than at any stage in the history of the health service — over 70,000 more than when we came to office.'[40] Government claims that there have been large increases in NHS staff under Conservative rule are usually based on comparing 1978 with a recent year. It is not difficult to see why. Numbers of staff had been rising throughout the 1970s.

**Changes in definition.** This rise, which continued up to 1982, was artificially inflated by a major change in definition in 1980. Apart from general practitioners and dentists, who are independent contractors, statistics about NHS staff usually expressed as 'whole time equivalents', to allow for the fact that so many work part-time. In 1984, 34.1 per cent of nurses and midwives in England did so.[15] Each part-time employee is counted according to the fraction of the full-time week that she or he works.

In 1980, following the Clegg Committee's recommendations and to comply with Common Market legislation, the full working week of nurses and midwives, who make up nearly half the whole time equivalent NHS staff, were reduced from 40 to 37.5 hours per week. Then, additional staff had to be employed to make up for the shorter hours worked by full-time staff. As a result, the whole time equivalent numbers of nurses and midwives increased by 7 per cent without a single extra hour being worked.

This is not always taken into account in published statistics which show, for example, a 14.3 per cent increase between 1978 and 1985 in whole time equivalent numbers of all nursing and midwifery staff in England. When the change in the working week is accounted for, however, the rise was only 7.0 per cent.[39] In evidence to the House of Commons Social Services Committee, the DHSS said that the apparent increase of 50,000 nurses and midwives between 1978 and 1985 would amount to some 26,000 or so after allowing for the reduction in their hours.[9]

**Cuts in ancillary staff.** Whole time equivalent ancillary staff (including operating department assistants who were redesignated professional and technical on April 1, 1984) decreased by 17.5 per cent over the same period. Even though some may have been replaced by staff working for private contractors, this might mean that some nurses and midwives had extra work to do to compensate for them. There is no shortage of individual accounts of instances where this is happening, but it is difficult to quantify, partly because of the problem of agreeing what exactly are 'non-nursing' duties, and partly because there is a shortage of systematically collected information.

A study of two wards at St Mary Abbots Hospital, Kensington, showed that nurses spent much of their time on jobs other than direct nursing, particularly duties normally thought of as the work of ancillary staff.[41] Evidence given to the Auditor and Comptroller General[42] supported this, and suggested that it was particularly likely to occur at night and at weekends when nurses also did some of the work of medical and paramedical staff.

**Changing demands.** Amongst the changes in the population over the period 1978 to 1984 were fluctuations in the numbers of births. As a result, there were 6.4 per cent more births in England in 1984 than in 1978. Yet, after adjustment for the change in the working week, the whole time equivalent numbers of all midwives, including community midwives and pupil midwives, rose by only 3.2 per cent.

Looking over a slightly earlier period, Nick Bosanquet showed that there were marked changes over the period 1976 to 1982 in the relative numbers of different grades of nursing staff.[21] While the position varied between NHS regions and between the acute, geriatric, psychiatric and mental handicap sectors, the general picture was a decrease in the contribution from student nurses, pupil nurses and nursing sisters, and increases in the contribution of other registered nurses, enrolled nurses and unqualified nurses.

It is not easy to assess the impact on the workload of hospital nursing staff of the increases in the numbers of people aged 75 or over, particularly as the shortening of hospital stays is likely to mean that a higher proportion of the people in hospital will require a more intensive level of nursing.

In addition, it is unclear whether the community health services have been able to keep pace with both demographic changes and the consequences of earlier discharge from hospital. Between 1978 and 1984, the adjusted increase in whole time equivalent numbers of district nurses was 8 per cent,[43] but they treated 12 per cent more people and 26 per cent more people aged 65 and over in 1984 compared with 1978.[15] The corresponding rise in numbers of health visitors was 4.9 per cent but they visited 10.8 per cent more people. Does this mean shorter or less frequent visits? There is no easy answer, but we shall return to this question later.

The increase in the number of general practitioners from 21,040 in 1978 to 24,035 in 1985, and the decrease over the same period in their average list size from 2,312 in 1978 to 2,089 in 1984, also has to be offset against demographic changes. Older people consult GPs more often than the population as a whole, and are more likely to do so through a home visit. The General Household Survey estimated that in 1984 22 per cent of consultations by people aged 65-74 and 45 per cent of those by people aged over 75 took place at home, compared with only 10 per cent of those by people aged under 65.[44]

The numbers of dentists in the General Dental Service increased from 11,919 in 1978 to 14,334 in 1985, so it is hardly surprising that the number of courses of dental treatment increased from 27.1 million in 1978 to 31.4 million in 1985. The statistics are not collected in a way which would enable us to see whether more people are receiving treatment or the same people are receiving more treatment, nor do they relate the increases to changes in the population. As dental caries has been declining, the question of whether the increased amount of dental activity is appropriate or necessary needs to be raised. These questions are discussed in more detail later.

**'Front line' and 'support' staff.** Stress is often laid on the increase in the numbers of so-called 'front line' staff including doctors, dentists, nurses, midwives, and professional and technical staff who are seen to be giving direct services to patients. The government contrasts this approvingly with the decrease in the proportion of 'support' staff including administrative, clerical, ancillary, works and ambulance staff who are not categorised as serving patients. This ignores the interdependence between staff doing different types of work, the possibility mentioned earlier that nurses may have to take on an increasing proportion of clerical and cleaning work in addition to their own duties, and the extent to which 'support' staff give patient care in ways which may not be formally recognised.[45]

The distinction between 'front line' and 'support' staff has been reflected in the pay settlements made since the Clegg awards which gave average pay increases ranging from 20 to 26 per cent to all categories of staff. Between 1980-81 and 1984-85, the average pay of directly employed NHS medical and dental staff rose by 73.6 per cent in cash terms. The corresponding increases were 60.5 per cent for

# Table 3.8a
NHS whole-time equivalent directly employed staff

Whole time equivalent staff on September 30

| Category | 1976 | 1977 | 1978 | 1979 | 1980 | 1981 | 1982 | 1983 | 1984 | 1985 | March 1986 |
|---|---|---|---|---|---|---|---|---|---|---|---|
| **England only** | | | | | | | | | | | |
| Medical and Dental | 34,100 | 35,000 | 35,900 | 37,100 | 38,200 | 39,000 | 39,400 | 40,200 | 40,200 | 40,800 | 41,800 |
| Hospital and Community Nursing and Midwifery | 341,700 | 343,200 | 351,000 | 358,400 | 370,100† | 391,800† | 397,100† | 397,100† | 397,500† | 401,200† | 403,000 |
| Professional and Technical (excl. Works) | 52,500 | 54,800 | 57,200 | 60,100 | 61,900 | 65,200 | 67,200 | 68,700 | 72,700* | 74,300* | 74,000 |
| Works Professional | 5,300 | 5,500 | 5,600 | 5,600 | 5,900 | 6,200 | 6,100 | 6,000 | 6,000 | 6,100 | 6,000 |
| Maintenance | 19,700 | 19,900 | 19,900 | 20,100 | 20,600 | 27,000 | 21,000 | 20,800 | 20,200 | 19,800 | 19,000 |
| Administrative and Clerical | 98,500 | 99,000 | 100,300 | 103,000 | 105,400 | 108,800 | 108,800 | 110,000 | 110,300 | 111,000 | 110,000 |
| Ambulance | 17,200 | 17,400 | 17,500 | 17,100 | 17,800 | 18,200 | 18,300 | 18,400 | 18,100 | 18,200 | 18,000 |
| Ancillary | 173,600 | 172,800 | 172,200 | 171,900 | 172,000 | 172,200 | 170,500 | 166,200 | 152,200* | 139,400* | 132,000 |
| **Total Employed Staff** | | | | | | | | | | | |
| England | 742,500 | 747,700 | 759,700 | 773,300 | 791,900† | 822,400† | 828,500† | 827,400† | 817,200† | 810,700† | 805,000† |
| Wales | 47,438 | 47,912 | 49,088 | 50,320 | 52,025† | 53,272† | 54,062† | 54,131† | 54,528† | 55,321† | |
| Scotland | 111,325 | 111,439 | 113,800 | 115,737 | 118,896† | 122,208† | 124,011† | 124,491† | 123,497† | 123,894† | |
| Northern Ireland | 31,622 | 32,865 | 33,992 | 34,869 | 36,027† | 37,325† | 38,670† | 38,192† | 37,730† | 37,631† | |

† Not adjusted for the reduction of nurses' and midwives' working week from 40 to 37½ hours in 1980.
* Not adjusted for the transfer on April 1 1984 of 2,700 Operating Department Assistants from the ancillary to the technical and professional staff group.

Source: Data derived from Scottish Health Statistics
DHSS Census of Medical and Non-medical 'manpower', Health and Personal Social Services Statistics for Wales
Trends in Health and Personal Social Services Statistics in Northern Ireland.

nurses and midwives, and 60.9 per cent for professions allied to medicine. In contrast, technicians and works staff received average increases of 39.1 per cent, administrative and clerical staff 39.9 per cent, ancillaries 41.0 per cent, and maintenance staff 44.3 per cent.[46] In the 1985 pay settlements the 'support' staff received lower percentage rises than the 'front line' staff covered by review bodies. Similarly, in 1986, doctors and dentists received 7.6 per cent, nurses and midwives 7.8 per cent, and all other staff 6.0 per cent.[18] Thus, the gap between the lowest and the highest paid NHS staff has widened since 1981.

**'Manpower' cuts after the 1983 general election.** While government statements usually compare just two years, we have shown a longer series in Table 3.8 and

---

**Table 3.8b**

Effect of adjusting NHS staff statistics for England for change in nurses' working hours and reclassification of operating department assistants

| | Percentage change in whole time equivalent staff, 1978-85 | |
| --- | --- | --- |
| | Published | Adjusted |
| Nurses and Midwives | 14.3 | 7.0* |
| Professional and Technical | 29.8 | 24.1† |
| All 'front line' staff | 16.2 | 9.7* |
| Ancillary | − 19.0 | − 17.8 |
| Total directly employed staff | 6.7 | 3.5* |

* Adjusted for the reduction in nurses' and midwives' working week in 1980
† On April 1 1984, 2,600 Operating Department Assistants were reclassified as Professional and Technical staff.
Source: Derived from Annual report of the health service in England, 1985-86[39]

---

Figure 3.7. These reveal that the increase in overall numbers of staff slowed down in 1982 and all but stopped in 1983, then turned into decreases in 1984 and 1985. Then came the 'manpower' cuts imposed in September 1983 when the government ordered health authorities to make reductions of staff totalling 4,800 between September 1983 and March 1984.

According to the 1984-85 report of the Social Services Committee, the target was overshot by 7,000.[17] As a result, it estimated, there was a decrease of about 11,000 staff, including 3,100 nurses by March 1984, compared with March 1983. Most published statistics, like those in Table 3.8 and Figure 3.7, compare September with September, and these show a decrease of 10,200 whole time equivalent directly employed NHS staff between September 1983 and September 1984, and a further decrease of 6,500 by September 1985.

Although the DHSS set targets for March 1985 which provided for an increase of 6,800 staff, some health authorities could not afford to take back staff to achieve this. It is likely that with the financial problems which followed the 1985 pay settlements, some authorities were obliged to freeze posts and a few may have made staff redundant. On the other hand, it appears that some health authorities, especially in the south of England, have been unable to fill vacancies for nurses and lower paid staff.

In the event, all regions fell below their March 1985 'manpower' ceilings, and the national total was 10,000 whole time equivalent below the national ceiling.

**Figure 3.7 Numbers of directly employed NHS staff, England, 1976-86.**

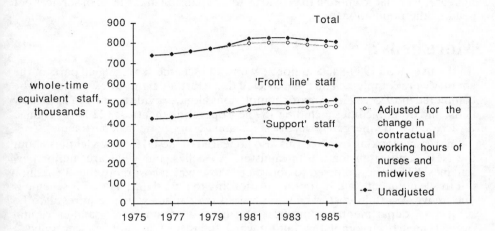

Source: Derived from data from DHSS annual censuses of medical and non-medical 'manpower'.

**Table 3.9**
Doctors and dentists in the Family Practitioner Services

|  | England* | Wales* | Scotland† | Northern† Ireland |
|---|---|---|---|---|
| **Doctors** | | | | |
| 1974 | 21,531 | 1,354 | 2,959 | 745 |
| 1979 | 23,062 | 1,448 | 3,190 | 788 |
| 1984 | 25,788 | 1,661 | 3,529 | 909 |
| 1985 | 26,197 | 1,699 | 3,575 | 943 |
| **Dentists** | | | | |
| 1974 | 11,023 | 505 | 1,176 | 315 |
| 1979 | 12,146 | 604 | 1,234 | 358 |
| 1984 | 14,066 | 714 | 1,405 | 444 |
| 1985 | 14,334 | 742 | 1,407 | 466 |

† As at September 30
* As at October 1
Source: Data from Health and Personal Social Services statistics for England. Health and Personal Social Services statistics for Wales. Scottish Health Statistics.
DHSS, Northern Ireland

The position was similar in March 1986.[9]

In conclusion, it is likely that instead of increasing, numbers of NHS staff are still decreasing. There is also no evidence to support the claim that the earlier increases were large enough to provide a real expansion in the level of services per head of the population.

## More beds?

'In the five years 1980-84 35 major new hospital schemes covering all parts of the country were completed and it is expected that a further eight such schemes will be completed in 1985… These major completions alone provide a total of 11,500 new beds, and other facilities including 189 new operating theatres, 122 X-ray rooms, 27 accident and emergency departments and 25 out-patient departments'.[43]

Impressive looking lists like this also appeared in the DHSS' two leaflets about the NHS, and often feature in ministers' speeches, but what are 'major new schemes'? The ones referred to above are those which cost more than £5 million but this is not a constant definition. According to the DHSS, 'A major scheme is one above a certain cost, which has varied over time, which requires it to be subject to departmental approvals. During the period many smaller capital projects have been completed, but for which full records are not held centrally'.[49]

**Widening the goal posts.** Statistics given in reply to a parliamentary question in July 1985 gave numbers of beds provided in new schemes costing over £2 million from 1974-78 and over £5 million from 1979 onwards.[50] Since mid 1985 the threshold appears to have been lowered again. For example, the leaflet 'The Health Service Today', issued in July 1986, mentions schemes costing more than £2 million , while the 1985-86 annual report issued in December 1986 featured schemes costing more than £1 million.[39]

In October 1986, Norman Fowler's speech to the Conservative Party Conference and the computer printout he used as a visual aid referred to schemes costing more than £1 million.[40] Many of these referred to successive phases of building schemes within the same hospitals, so many hospitals were mentioned more than once and one was mentioned as many as 11 times.

Changes in definition, together with inflation, make it difficult to interpret changes over time. Available data for England are summarised in Table 3.10. This is based on schemes actually completed. In fact, it is difficult for the present government to claim full credit for them. According to the DHSS, of the 45 hospital schemes each costing over £5 million completed between May 1979 and June 1986, 39 were approved before May 1979.[51]

More recent statements refer to building schemes approved since May 1979 and further schemes planned for the future. Thus, the 1986 leaflet states that 'over 150 more hospital schemes — together worth over £1,000 million — are being planned, designed and built'. Norman Fowler's 1986 conference speech mentioned 88 schemes costing more than £1 million under construction on 1st October 1986, 113 due for completion in the next three years, 84 with budget cost approval, 45 schemes with approval in principle, and 163 programmed with their approximate cost known. Closer inspection of his list reveals a number of

**Table 3.10**
Beds provided in new hospital schemes opened in England

| Year Opened | Over £1 million | | Over £2 million | Over £5 million | |
|---|---|---|---|---|---|
| | Schemes | Beds | Beds | Schemes | Beds |
| 1974 | | | 793 | | |
| 1975 | | | 1109 | | |
| 1976 | | | 1335 | | |
| 1977 | | | 3993 | | |
| 1978 | | | 2522 | | |
| 1979 | 3 | 1,521 | | 4 | 1,519 |
| 1980 | 8 | 2,198 | | 4 | 2,058 |
| 1981 | 10 | 2,146 | | 5 | 1,776 |
| 1982 | 16 | 2,553 | | 7 | 2,067 |
| 1983 | 47 | 4,334 | | 12 | 3,235 |
| 1984 | 45 | 2,712 | | 8 | 1,380 |
| 1985 | 49 | 1,696 | | 7 or 8 | |
| 1986 | 39 | 3,310 | | | |
| | | | | | |
| 1980-85 | | 15,639 | | | 'over 11,500' |

Source: Hansard, written parliamentary replies [50, 52]
Annual report of the NHS, 1985[43]

instances where the same phase of the same scheme in the same hospital appears again under more than one heading, adding up to 493 items. In contrast, his speech referred to 380 schemes, 267 of which are not due to be completed until after October 1989.

**Table 3.11**
Complete and partial permanent closures of hospitals, England

| Year approved | Complete closures | | Permanent partial closures | Total |
|---|---|---|---|---|
| | Hospitals | Beds | Beds | Beds lost |
| 1980 | 41 | 2,500 | 17 | 2,517 |
| 1981 | 32 | 2,017 | 705 | 2,722 |
| 1982 | 17 | 895 | 262 | 1,157 |
| 1983 | 52 | 3,738 | 598 | 4,336 |
| 1984 | 57 | 4,037 | 785 | 4,822 |
| 1985 | | 2,434 | 813 | 2,947 |
| 1986 (to end Sept.) | n.a. | 1,930 | 108 | 2,038 |
| | | | | |
| 1980-85 | n.a. | 15,621 | 2,880 | 18,501 |

Source: Hansard, written parliamentary replies [50, 53]

**Gains and losses.** The 1985 Annual Report stated that 'new facilities often replace old, outdated and inefficient hospitals, thereby providing better health care environment for patients and a more productive and efficient working environment for staff'.[43] This may well be true, but it is certainly not the whole story. Statistics about closures are never quoted, making it difficult to compare them with new schemes in terms of capacity or geographical position.

According to DHSS, in England over the years 1980-85, 15,639 beds were provided in new schemes costing more than £1 million.[52] Over the same period, 15,621 beds were approved for closure by closing complete hospitals, and a further 2,880 by closing parts of hospitals.[50,53]

This does not tell us when the closures eventually took place. What is more, the statistics are incomplete on their own terms. As former DHSS minister Kenneth Clarke claimed, in reply to a parliamentary question, 'I see no sensible purpose in keeping centrally a full inventory of furniture in each of our hospitals. We only acquire information centrally on permanent partial closures when they are sufficiently significant to require formal consultation. In every case bed closures are only approved by Ministers when they are no longer necessary for patient care and the resources can be put to better use elsewhere'.[54]

The mismatch between these various sets of statistics means that it is more helpful to look at others. A much better picture is provided by the statistics on the average numbers of beds available daily, shown in Figure 3.8 and Tables 3.12 and 3.13. In England these showed a decline of 12,900 between 1980 and 1983, and further falls of 8,600 in 1984 and 9,000 in 1985, making an overall decrease of 30,500. The numbers of beds have been falling in all NHS regions and most districts over the past ten years, and this has affected all sectors of hospital in-patient care except geriatrics.[50,55,56]

**Figure 3.8 Average number of beds available daily, England, 1974-85.**

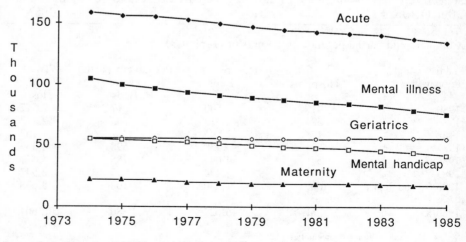

Source: Derived from data in DHSS statistical bulletin 2/86.[55]

**Table 3.12**
Average number of beds available daily, NHS hospitals, England

|      | Total* | Acute | Geriatric | Mental illness | Mental handicap | Maternity |
|------|--------|-------|-----------|----------------|-----------------|-----------|
| 1974 | 396,200 | 158,400 | 55,400 | 104,400 | 55,200 | 21,700 |
| 1979 | 361,700 | 147,000 | 55,100 | 89,000 | 50,100 | 18,600 |
| 1984 | 334,500 | 137,200 | 55,600 | 78,900 | 44,000 | 17,200 |
| 1985 | 325,500 | 134,500 | 55,300 | 75,900 | 41,600 | 16,600 |

* Includes units for younger disabled people, which are not counted in any of the other columns shown
Source: DHSS Statistical Bulletin 2/86[55]

**Table 3.13**
Average number of beds available daily, all countries of the United Kingdom

|      | England | Wales | Scotland | Northern Ireland |
|------|---------|-------|----------|------------------|
| 1974 | 396,200 | 24,700 | 61,514 | 17,504 |
| 1979 | 361,700 | 23,500 | 58,501 | 17,126 |
| 1984 | 334,500 | 22,300 | 57,216 | 16,715 |
| 1985 | 325,500 | 22,100 | 56,334 | 16,595 |

Source: Data from DHSS Statistical Bulletin 2/86[55], Health and Personal Social Services Statistics for Wales, Scottish Health Statistics, CSO Annual Abstract of Statistics

These all show a clear decline in resources available for in-patient care. The government responds to this by pointing to the rising numbers of 'in-patient cases'.

# More patients treated?

'... When confronted with the facts our critics say that they are just *statistics*.'

'When they hear that in England last year we treated nearly 1 million more in-patient cases than in 1978, they dismiss that as *statistics*. When they hear that we treated 40,000 more day cases, they dismiss it as *statistics*. When they hear that we provided for over 3¼ million more out-patient attendances, they dismiss it as *statistics*.

'What they forget is that each and every one of those 4½ million *statistics* is a personal story — a story of care. Of dedicated staff working night and day. Of patients' pain relieved and hope renewed'.[40]

When confronted with evidence that NHS resources are no longer growing in 'real terms' and that the numbers of available hospital beds are falling, government spokespeople dismiss it as irrelevant. Instead, they quote statistics which, they claim, show that record numbers of patients are being treated. They usually quote increases in numbers of 'in-patient cases', 'day cases' and out-patient attendances, adding comments such as, 'These are the real figures of health care in this country. They show how health care has developed. Above all they show that the National Health Service today — under this government — is bringing more help to more people than ever before'.[40] On closer examination, however, it is unclear what the statistics do show.

**More patients or more readmissions?** The number of 'in-patient cases' is defined as the total number of discharges from and deaths in NHS hospitals in the given time period. As there is no linkage between successive stays in hospital by the same person, people who have been in hospital more than once will have been counted each time they were discharged.

There is no secret about this. The DHSS and the Office of Population Censuses and Surveys warns us in every volume of statistics from the Hospital In-Patient Enquiry (HIPE) that 'patients discharged more than once during a calendar year may be included in the sample on each discharge'.[57] Thus, while HIPE shows increases between 1979 and 1984 in hospital discharge rates per head of the population in all age groups,[58] it is not clear whether more people were being admitted to hospital or some of the same people were being admitted increasingly often.

This was confirmed in the response to a parliamentary question asking how many of the discharges from NHS hospitals in the years 1973 to 1983 were of patients who had been readmitted after having previously been discharged in the same year. It received the all too common reply that, 'We do not have sufficient information centrally to answer this question'.[59]

There are a number of reasons for this. One is that the Hospital In-Patient Enquiry which, until the end of 1985, was used to collect information about hospital in-patient stays in England, was based on a 10 per cent sample of information collected in each region through Hospital Activity Analysis (HAA).

The Hospital Episode System which will replace HIPE from 1987 onwards will analyse all records nationally and will at least link each person's hospital stays in the same episode of in-patient care within the same health district. Some districts are installing systems which will enable them to do much more than this locally. At present, it is sometimes possible to distinguish locally between first admissions and readmissions to a given hospital and transfers from other hospitals using information in computerised patient information systems or from Hospital Activity Analysis.

Meanwhile, as both the average length of stay and the average number of beds occupied daily are decreasing steadily,[55] it is tempting to jump to the conclusion that the increase in numbers of 'in-patient cases' has come about simply because people are being discharged too soon and have to be readmitted as a result.

It is not difficult to find anecdotal accounts of instances where this has occurred,[60] but it is unlikely to be the whole story. Some people may receive treatment in a specialist centre and then be transferred back to a local hospital before being discharged home. Others may have a planned series of short admissions instead of a single long stay. In both cases, they will be counted each time they are discharged.

A comparison of hospital in-patient stays in Leicestershire in 1977 and 1983 in the specialties of medicine, surgery and geriatric medicine found that readmissions to the same hospitals increased and transfers between hospitals decreased as a proportion of the increasing numbers of discharges.[61] At the same time, the rates of admission of new patients also increased and their average length of stay fell. An analysis of a sample of 338 records of people who had been readmitted showed that 49 per cent had been readmitted within 30 days of discharge with the same main diagnosis, 28 per cent were readmitted with the same diagnosis, and 23 per cent with a different diagnosis more than 30 days after discharge.

There is, of course, no guarantee that similar results would be obtained elsewhere, and indeed different patterns might well be expected in districts with more than one acute hospital and in large conurbations. Also, specialties analysed excluded the 'supradistrict' specialties of maternity, psychiatry and mental handicap, in which there is some evidence that the proportions of readmissions are increasing.

The only area of in-patient care where any sort of direct crosscheck is possible is maternity. There, the average length of stay and average daily bed use fell over the years 1974-85, but the ratio of 'in-patient cases' to births in NHS hospitals rose from 1.28 in 1974 to 1.33 in 1978 and 1.40 in 1985.[5] Data from the Hospital In-Patient Enquiry maternity tables show that this is the consequence of a rise in the proportion of antenatal admissions which goes back at least to the mid 1960s.[60]

There is also some limited information from the Mental Health Enquiry, through which information is collected about stays in mental illness and mental handicap hospitals and units. The Enquiry distinguishes between first admissions and readmissions.

First admissions to both types of institution fell from 1975 to 1979, both in terms of numbers and rates per 100,000 population.[62,63] Between 1979 and 1984 first admission rates rose again, with a sharp rise in 1984, followed by a slight fall in 1985, in the number of people admitted for the first time to a mental illness hospital or unit.

Readmission rates rose very sharply over the whole period, particularly in mental handicap institutions. In both types of hospital there was a significant increase in stays lasting under one month and, as in other types of hospital, it is not possible to identify how many people were readmitted more than once in a given year.[64]

As a result, although there were small increases in first admission rates, some of which arose from changes in the age structure of the population, most of the increase in 'in-patient cases' in mental handicap and mental illness hospitals arose from changes in patterns of care which led to shorter lengths of stay and easier readmission, or out-patient treatment if necessary.[55,62,63]

**The growth in new types of care.** 'Day cases' are hospital admissions which do not involve an overnight stay. Because these are a relatively recent development, the numbers appear to have increased dramatically when they are expressed as a percentage of the numbers in 1973 or 1978, as has been done in the annual reports of the health service.[39] Despite this, they accounted for only 13.2 per cent of hospital stays in England in 1985.[55] Figure 3.9 puts them into a more realistic perspective.

The same principle is applied in claims about 'advances in care'. The operations most often mentioned include new forms of treatment such as heart and bone

**Figure 3.9 Two ways of looking at hospital activity statistics.**

**a) as presented in the annual report of the Health Service in England 1985-86.**

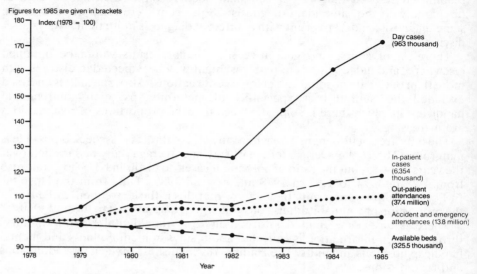

Source: Reproduced from the annual report of the health service in England 1985-86.[39]

**b) an alternative view**

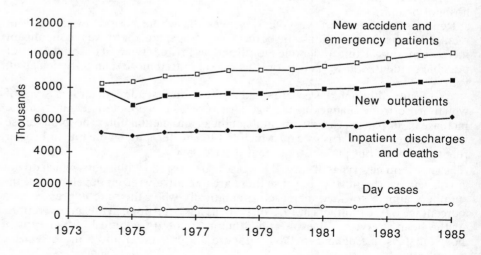

Source Drawn using data in DHSS statistical bulletin 2/86.[55]

**Facing the Figures**

marrow transplants which show similarly impressive rises when expressed in percentage terms, although they form a minute proportion of all NHS operations. Indeed, these, taken together with the larger numbers of hip replacement, coronary bypass and cataract operations which also often feature in ministers' statements, accounted for under 5 per cent of all operations under the NHS in England in 1984.[58] Yet it is these which have been selected for special targets to be achieved before 1990.[36]

**More outpatients?** When talking about out-patient care government spokespeople show a tendency to quote the total numbers of attendances rather than the much smaller numbers of new out-patients. The latter is, of course, nearer to being a measure of the numbers of people involved. Even so, people who attend more than one type of out-patient clinic are counted separately at each one. In addition, with shorter in-patient stays and a rising proportion of day case admissions, it is hardly surprising that numbers of out-patient attendances have risen.

Statistics about out-patient attendances are not at present subdivided by age, so it is not clear to what extent they reflect changes in the age structure of the population. Data from the General Household Survey show that, while the percentage of people who reported having attended an out-patient clinic in a three-month reference period is higher than in the mid 1970s in most age groups, there is little evidence of an increase in the percentage attending over the years 1979 to 1984 except in men aged 75 and over.[44]

The only conclusion to be drawn is that it is unclear what the frequently quoted statistics about 'cases treated' mean, let alone whether they are 'the real figures of health care in this country'. It would be tempting, for example, to respond with the claim that 'they show we are getting iller under the Tories', but this is too crude. Although there is evidence that government policies, for example on housing and unemployment, may have adverse effects on the most vulnerable people in the population, there is no simple relationship with the demands they make on the NHS. While OPCS' HIPE Trends Monitor gives a useful picture of changes in patterns of diagnosis and treatment among people of different ages discharged from hospitals in England over the years 1979 to 1984,[58] it is not possible to assess the extent to which changes observed reflect changes in supply and demand or changes in morbidity.

**What about the outcome of treatment?** Hospital activity statistics also tell us nothing about the outcome of the care given. Was it, for example, appropriate and effective? Were the patients satisfied with the care they received, and the staff satisfied with the work they did? Is unmet need increasing or decreasing? Have the changes made led to better care? For example, as there is little evidence about the relative effectiveness of different lengths of hospital stay,[65] there is no way of knowing whether the shortening of hospital stays is leading to greater or lesser efficiency in the use of hospital beds and resources, let alone its impact on the work of general practitioners and community nurses.

The statistics answer none of these questions. They do not even tell us whether or not more people were being treated, let alone whether this kept pace with the increasing numbers of very elderly people. All we do know is that the average numbers of hospital beds occupied daily decreased.[55]. Of course, this is not necessarily a bad thing as most people would rather be at home than in hospital, provided they are able to have the help they need to do so when, say, recovering from an operation. The article describing the analysis of hospital admissions in Leicestershire mentioned above added pressure on community services. The question of whether the contraction of hospital care has been offset by increasing resources in the community is discussed later.

# Shorter waiting lists?

'Waiting lists have also come down. In England at 31 March 1979 they stood at 752,422. By September 1985 they had fallen to 661,249. This was in spite of industrial action in 1982 following which waiting lists rose by about 100,000 cases'.[66]

At a time when private health insurance companies and some doctors point to the length of NHS waiting lists as a reason for 'going private', the government continually claims to have reduced them. What is actually happening?

Industrial action taken in 1975, 1979 and 1982 was followed by peaks in the numbers of people on waiting lists for in-patient treatment, as Figure 3.10 shows. In order to show a decrease in the size of waiting lists, government statements usually compare the most recent figures with the peak value reached in March 1979, instead of following their usual practice of comparing current statistics with those for 1978.

The figure for September 1985 quoted above was still 10 per cent higher than the 603,240 reported for March 1978. After falling between March 1983 and September 1985 the numbers on waiting lists rose to 673,107[67] in March 1986 and 681,901 in September 1986.[68]

When asked in a parliamentary question, 'What criteria were used to determine that the 1984 treatment figures should be compared with 1978?', John Patten replied, 'These were the figures which best reflected activity in the National Health Service at the end of the last Labour Government's tenure of office'.[69]

In England, statistics about waiting lists on December 31 are collected annually as part of the SH3 Hospital Return. More detailed data about the position on March 31 and September 30 are collected half-yearly via the SBH 203 Waiting List Return. These are shown in Figure 3.10, together with June figures from the SBH1 return discontinued in 1980.

**Changes in definition.** Since March 1979, there have been two changes in the way waiting list statistics are collected. One of these will have had the effect of reducing numbers. As health authorities were unclear whether or not to include people waiting for day surgery, the DHSS instructed them not to in a 'note of clarification' issued in September 1979.[70]. This is an important omission, given the rise in day case surgery. Data about people waiting for day surgery will, however, be collected when the recommendations of the Steering Group on Health Services Information are implemented.

A second change relates to the description of the degree of urgency of treatment. The Waiting List Return asks for a breakdown by specialty in which

**Figure 3.10 Numbers of people on waiting lists for in-patient treatment, England 1956-85.**

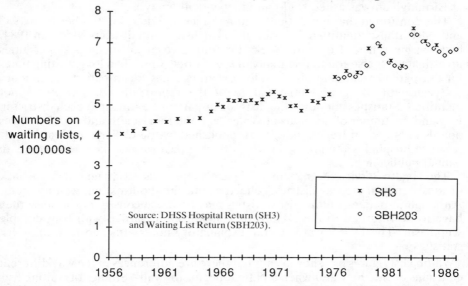

Numbers on waiting lists, 100,000s

Source: DHSS Hospital Return (SH3) and Waiting List Return (SBH203).

| | |
|---|---|
| x | SH3 |
| o | SBH203 |

patients are categorised as 'urgent' or 'non-urgent'. 'Urgent cases' who have been on the waiting list for more than a month, and 'non-urgent cases' who have been on the waiting list for more than a year, are tabulated separately.

Some health authorities keep more detailed information. In March 1980, Statistical Memorandum SM(80)2/1[71] instructed authorities who used intermediate degrees of urgency between 'urgent' and 'non-urgent' to classify the patients in the intermediate categories as 'non-urgent'. The DHSS issues no guidance as to how urgency is defined. Instead, this is left to 'clinical judgment'.

Statistics for Scotland show that waiting lists there rose during the periods of industrial action in 1979 and 1982, particularly during the latter period. Although the numbers fell in 1984 and 1985, the figure of 77,677 for September 1985 was still 9 per cent higher than the corresponding total of 70,970 for September 1979.[72] Provisional figures for March 1986 showed a rise to 81,250.[73]

In Wales, numbers on waiting lists rose during the periods of industrial action and remained high after 1982, the figure being 43,000 in December 1985 compared with 36,000 in December 1978 and 38,400 in December 1979.[74]

**Out-patient waiting lists.** Before being put on a waiting list for in-patient treatment, most people have to go to an out-patient clinic and there is often a waiting list for this. As out-patient waiting list statistics are not collected centrally by the DHSS, the British Medical Association (BMA) sent a questionnaire to all health districts in England and Wales asking about waiting times for a first out-patient appointment. It asked for the position on March 31 in 1983 and 1984 in six specialties — general medicine, general surgery, gynaecology, ear nose and throat (ENT) and orthopaedics. The BMA's preliminary analysis suggested that there had been a 20 per cent increase in waiting times between 1983 and 1984. In

---

**Facing the Figures**

agreement with the Minister of Health, the Health Services Management Centre at Birmingham was asked to do an independent analysis.[75]

This confirmed that out-patient waiting times had deteriorated between 1983 and 1984. It also identified a cluster of 36 English health districts which, in 1984, had waiting times of over 10 weeks for four, five or all of the six specialties investigated. It also found that many of the districts which had long waiting times for out-patient treatment also had long waiting times for in-patient treatment.

Because of the confidential nature of the report, the districts were not identified. Statistics about waiting lists for in-patient treatment in each district in England, a number of hospitals in Wales, and the four health and social services boards in Northern Ireland have been published by the College of Health.[76] Its guide to hospital waiting lists, in which they appear, looks likely to become an annual publication.

The Health Services Management Centre's report also commented on the lack of consistency in the way districts collected data about out-patient waiting times. Although in-patient waiting list statistics may be less inconsistent, because they have to be returned to the DHSS, they should be regarded with considerable scepticism. The DHSS warns in the explanatory notes attached to waiting list statistics:

"Waiting list figures can show trends but there are differences in the way different clinicians decide how and when a patient begins to 'wait'. Studies of waiting lists have shown that a proportion of those on lists have died, moved to another area, do not want or need the intended operation, or appear on more than one list. The amount of overstatement cannot be readily estimated but it is thought to exceed 10 per cent nationally and could be considerably more." The figures cannot therefore be relied upon as absolute indicators of the demand for elective admission to hospital.[77]

**The drive to reduce waiting lists.** Having noticed this scope for improving waiting list statistics in a downward direction, the government wrote to health authorities in December 1984, asking them to review in-patient waiting lists and remove patients who no longer required treatment. The numbers fell from 682,599 in September 1984 to 674,453 in March 1985 and 661,249 in September 1985. The DHSS commented, 'It is not possible, however, to separate changes in waiting list numbers resulting from the validation exercise from other changes which would have taken place in any case'.[77]

This was followed in July 1986 by a further drive to reduce waiting lists and waiting times,[66] and £50 million was earmarked for this purpose in the Autumn Budget statement.[35] Could it be that these developments were inspired by an early inspection of the returns for March 1986? When these statistics were published in November 1986 they showed the rise in numbers mentioned earlier although the DHSS was at pains to point out that the total was 'slightly lower than a year earlier'.[67] The further increase revealed in the September 1986 figures was dismissed by comparing the total with the peak value for March 1979.[68]

**How important are waiting lists statistics?** Despite the prominence given to waiting list statistics only about a quarter of non-maternity admissions to

**Table 3.14**
NHS hospital patients and activity, England

| | In-patient discharges and deaths thousands | Day cases thousands | Out-patients New new | Out-patients Attendances per new patient | Accident and Emergency patients new patients thousands | Accident and Emergency Attendances per new patient |
|---|---|---|---|---|---|---|
| 1974 | 5171·7 | 449·6 | 7824·8 | 4·26 | 8258·1 | 1·56 |
| 1979 | 5400·1 | 592·1 | 7713·5 | 4·42 | 9197·4 | 1·44 |
| 1984 | 6177·5 | 902·9 | 8508·1 | 4·35 | 10212·5 | 1·35 |
| 1985 | 6353·8 | 962·8 | 8682·1 | 4·31 | 10402·7 | 1·33 |

Source: DHSS Statistical Bulletin 2/86[55]

non-psychiatric hospitals are from waiting lists. About half the admissions for surgical operations and procedures are from waiting lists. In both cases the proportions vary widely according to diagnosis and operation.[78]

The notes also explain that the waiting list statistics include people who are booked for admission, possibly some months ahead. As was pointed out in the British Medical Journal, however, people who have been given a firm date for admission are in a different position from those who may have to wait just as long but have very little notice about their date of admission.[79]

This suggests that comparisons between districts or specialties may often fail to compare like with like. Thus, statements based on them need to be regarded with equal scepticism as those about changes over time. Clearly, waiting list statistics have little value as measures of unmet need. Given this, the government's claim that the only cuts in the NHS are in the length of waiting lists is a contradiction in terms.

**Table 3.15**
Hospital and Community Health Services spending by client group

| | Percentage of current spending in year | |
|---|---|---|
| England | 1976-77 | 1984-85 |
| Geriatric services | 8·7 | 9·5 |
| Community services | 8·4 | 9·4 |
| Mental handicap | 5·3 | 5·1 |
| Mental illness | 11·5 | 5·0 |
| Obstetric services | 5·4 | 5·0 |
| Acute hospital services | 47·2 | 45·9 |
| Other services | 13·4 | 13·6 |
| Scotland | 1977-78 | 1984-85 |
| Geriatric Services | 11·7 | 12·4 |
| Community Services | 7·3 | 8·2 |
| Mental handicap | 5·1 | 5·2 |
| Mental illness | 15·1 | 15·0 |
| Obstetric services | 6·3 | 5·6 |
| Acute hospital services | 54·4 | 53·5 |

Source: Hansard, written parliamentary reply[78] Scottish Office [79]

# Whose priorities?

In 1976, DHSS produced a consultation document, 'Priorities for health and personal social services in England', in an attempt 'to establish rational and systematic priorities'.[80] This set out a strategy for a shift of emphasis away from acute hospital and maternity services and towards services for elderly, mentally ill and mentally handicapped people, community services and prevention.

Our response 'Whose priorities?' supported these aims but concluded, sceptically that 'detailed examination suggests that the proposed changes in emphasis will leave the service very much in the same shape as at present'.[81] Table 3.15 reveals that since then, there has been very little shift in the way money has been spent in England[82] and none at all in Scotland.[83] There are no corresponding figures for Wales or Northern Ireland.

'Whose priorities?' also suggested that the change of emphasis 'will have little effect on the people who are at present in receipt of the poorest services'.[81] It is more difficult to assess whether this is so, but there is little evidence to contradict it.

We have shown here that a closer look at the statistics calls into serious doubt the picture the government has painted of a growing health service. Although there has been some increase in resources, it is unlikely that this has been enough to achieve the government's own objectives. These leave aside questions about the extent of unmet need and whether the government's policies in other areas have affected the national health or created additional demands on the NHS.

It is tempting, faced with this, to fall into the trap of assuming that more treatment necessarily means better care. As we pointed out in 1977 in 'In Defence of the NHS', many treatments and procedures are of unproven effectiveness.[84] While some of those in use at that time have since been appraised in terms of their clinical effectiveness and acceptability to patients, others have not. The same can be said of the 'technological innovations' which have appeared on the scene since then. Meanwhile, the DHSS has reduced, in cash terms, the funding of health service research, much of which is geared to answering these very questions.

Although considerable sums are being spent on new information systems for NHS managers, these will yield very little information about the outcome of the care provided. Instead, the government's approach to information strategies is one which 'turns the key objectives of the authority's strategic plan into a 'business plan' which adds time scales, workload and priority considerations to the plan objectives'.[85]

Another item which will not appear in the new statistical systems is information about the socio-economic circumstances of users of the NHS. Thus, it will continue to be impossible to identify which sections of the population are losing and gaining in the geographical redistribution of NHS resources.

While the shift in NHS spending towards the so called 'priority groups' has been small, there has been a marked contraction in the extent of in-patient care both in services for these groups of people and in the acute hospital services. This is not necessarily a bad thing if it has been offset by providing more appropriate care elsewhere. The next part of this book takes a look at government claims that this has, in fact, happened.

## References

1. Hansard, May 23 1985, col 1151, amongst many other occasions.
2. DHSS. Sharing resources for health in England. Report of the Resource Allocation Working Party. London: HMSO, 1976.
3. Wiles R. A critical guide to resource allocation in London. London : GLC, 1984.
4. Radical Statistics Health Group. RAWP deals. London: Radical Statistics, 1977.
5. Fowler N. Clear demonstration of growth in health services. DHSS press release 86/280. September 1 1986.
6. The government's expenditure plans 1982-83 to 1984-85. Cmnd 8494-I. London: HMSO, 1982.
7. The government's expenditure plans 1987-88 to 1989-90. Vol. II. Cm 56-II. London: HMSO, 1987.
8. Written parliamentary reply. Hansard, May 14 1985, col 119- 120.
9. House of Commons. Fourth Report from the Social Services Committee, Session 1985-86. Public expenditure on the social services. Vol.II. London: HMSO, 1986.
10. The government's expenditure plans 1981-82 to 1983-84. Cmnd 8175. London: HMSO, 1981.
11. Written parliamentary replies. Hansard, July 1 1985, col 47-48, July 25 1986, col 732-734, November 6 1986, col 623-624, July 23 1986, col 311-314, February 16 1987, col 501-502.
12. Written parliamentary replies. Hansard, July 25 1986, col 637-641, November 4 1986, col 397-398, January 19 1987, col 395-396.
13. Written parliamentary replies. Hansard, July 25 1986, col 693-696, January 19 1987, col 419-422.
14. Written parliamentary replies. Hansard, January 20 1987, col 492-494.
15. DHSS. Health and personal social services statistics for England 1986. London: HMSO, 1986.
16. DHSS. Health care and its costs. The development of the National Health Service in England. London: HMSO, 1983.
17. House of Commons. Sixth report from the Social Services Committee, Session 1984-85. Public expenditure on the social services. London: HMSO, 1985.
18. Written reply. Hansard, February 25 1987, col 331-334.
19. Written reply. Hansard, June 23 1986, col 66-67.
20. Bosanquet N. Public expenditure rules and the NHS. Discussion Paper 3, Centre for Health Economics. York: University of York, 1985.
21. Bosanquet N. Public expenditure on the NHS: recent trends and the outlook. London: Institute of Health Services Management, 1985.
22. Maynard A, Bosanquet N. Public expenditure on the NHS — recent trends and future problems. London: Institute of Health Services Management, 1986.
23. DHSS, Welsh Office, Northern Ireland Office, Scottish Office. Primary health care: an agenda for discussion. Cmnd 9771. London: HMSO, 1986.
24. Written reply. Hansard, July 25 1986, col 715.
25. Beale N, Nethercott S. Job loss and family morbidity: a study of a factory closure. Journal of the Royal College of General Practitioners 1985;35:510-514.
26. Real resources and unreal assumptions: the case of the NHS. Public Money 1984; :58-62.
27. DHSS. Response to 'Public expenditure on the NHS'. London: DHSS, 1986.
28. Written reply. Hansard, February 4 1987, col 701-702.
29. Comptroller and Auditor General. Value for money developments in the NHS. HC212. London: HMSO, 1986.
30. Davies P. Counting the cost of cuts. Health Service Journal 1986; :850-851.
31. HM Treasury. Autumn statement. London: HMSO, 1985.
32. Written reply. Hansard, May 22 1986, col 240.
33. Written reply. Hansard, July 11 1986, col 219-222.
34. Kings Fund. Planned health services for London. Back to back planning. London: Kings Fund, 1987.
35. HM Treasury. Autumn statement 1986. CM 14. London: HMSO, 1986.
36. DHSS. Health and personal social services spending plans. Press release 86/348. London: DHSS, 1986.

37. DHSS. Public expenditure White Paper — Norman Fowler's statement. DHSS press release 87/21. London: DHSS, 1987.
38. Day S. An autumn windfall? Health Service Journal 1986; :1480.
39. DHSS. The health service in England. Annual report 1985-86. London: DHSS, 1986.
40. Fowler N. Speech to Conservative Party Conference, October 8 1986. Conservative Party Press Release 550/86.
41. MacLeod M. The professional ancillary. Nursing Times 1985; Nov.27:24-27.
42. National Audit Office. National Health Service control of nursing manpower. Report by the Comptroller and Auditor General. London: HMSO, 1985.
43. DHSS. The health service in England. Annual report 1985. London: HMSO, 1985.
44. Office of Population Censuses and Surveys, Social Survey Division. General Household Survey 1984, Series GHS No.14 (SS457M). London: HMSO, 1986.
45. Davies JA. An exceptional cleaner. Lancet 1986;ii:585.
46. Written reply. Hansard, July 1 1985, col 60.
47. DHSS. Annual censuses of medical and non-medical manpower.
48. DHSS. Press Release 86/323. October 20 1986.
49. Written reply. Hansard, January 14 1986, col 554.
50. Written replies. Hansard, July 1 1985, col 49-55.
51. Written reply. Hansard, June 27 1986, col 355.
52. Written reply. Hansard, February 6 1987, col 864.
53. Written replies. Hansard, May 20 1985, col 189-192, November 24 1986, col 369-370.
54. Written reply. Hansard, June 5 1985, col 189.
55. DHSS. NHS hospital activity statistics for England 1974-85. Statistical Bulletin 2/86. London: DHSS, 1986.
56. Written reply. Hansard, November 24 1986, col 98-106.
57. DHSS, OPCS, Welsh Office, Hospital In-Patient Enquiry Maternity Tables 1977-81. Series MB4, No.19. London: HMSO, 1986.
58. Office of Population Censuses and Surveys. Hospital In- Patient Enquiry (England) Trends 1979-84.
59. Written reply. Hansard, May 13 1985, col 34.
60. Holdstock DJ, Parsons S. Letters. Guardian, July 13 1985.
61. Jones J. The price of early discharge. Health Service Journal 1986; :825.
62. DHSS. Mental illness hospitals and units in England: results from the Mental Health Enquiry 1985. Statistical Bulletin 4/86. London: DHSS, 1986.
63. DHSS. Mental handicap hospitals and units in England: results from the Mental Health Enquiry 1985. Statistical Bulletin 6/86. London: DHSS, 1986.
64. Written reply. Hansard, May 15 1985, col 156.
65. McPherson K. Length of stay and health outcome. Editorial. British Medical Journal 1984;288:1854-1855.
66. DHSS Press Release 86/237, July 21 1986.
67. DHSS Press Release 86/368, November 21 1986.
68. DHSS Press Release 87/114. March 13 1987.
69. Written reply. Hansard, July 26 1985, col 959.
70. DHSS. Health Notice HN(79)103, September 1979.
71. DHSS. Statistical Memorandum SM(80)2/1, March 1980.
72. Information Services Division. Scottish Health Statistics. Edinburgh: HMSO, various years.
73. Written reply. Hansard, February 17 1987, col 539.
74. Welsh Office. Health and Personal Social Services Statistics for Wales. Cardiff: Welsh Office, various years.
75. Yates JH, Wood K. Inter-Authority comparisons and consultancy. Out-patient waiting time. Birmingham: Health Services Management Centre, 1985.
76. College of Health. Guide to hospital waiting lists. London: College of Health, 1985.
77. DHSS. Hospital in-patient waiting lists at 30 September 1985. London: DHSS, 1986.
78. OPCS. Hospital In-Patient Enquiry. Trends 1979-84, England. Additional tables. Titchfield: OPCS, 1986.
79. Morris D. Surgical waiting lists. British Medical Journal 1984;289:271-272.
80. DHSS. Priorities for health and personal social services in England. London: DHSS, 1976.

81. Radical Statistics Health Group. Whose priorities? London: Radical Statistics,1976.
82. Written reply. Hansard, July 25 1986, col 729-732.
83. MacKay J. Letter to Frank Dobson MP. August 29 1986.
84. Radical Statistics Health Group. In defence of the NHS. London: Radical Statistics, 1977.
85. DHSS. A national strategic framework for information planning in the Hospital and Community Health Services. London: DHSS, 1986.

# 4
# The Record Of Achievement: More Community Care?

'Patients have also benefited from the trend in recent years to care for a greater proportion of the elderly, the mentally ill and mentally handicapped in the Community'.

Primary health care, an agenda for discussion,1986.[1]

'..we shall continue the move towards community care for the mentally handicapped and other groups of patients. This means, for example, that in Northern Region by July 1986 only four children will still be in mental handicap hospitals and in South East Thames region no children will be remaining in such hospitals by March 1987. In Oxford the outdated Bradwell Grove mental handicap hospital will be closed, allowing the staff to be deployed to care for people in community units...'

Norman Fowler, March 14 1986.[2]

GOVERNMENT STATEMENTS about community care tend not to quote statistics. Instead, they either make vague claims, like the first one quoted above, or they list sums of money allocated to specific projects. Another approach, illustrated in the second quotation above, is to focus on the closure of institutions rather than the care being provided elsewhere.

Although the statistics in Table 4.1 do not distinguish between hospitals and residential homes, they show that the numbers of people living permanently in these institutions decreased by over 63 thousand between 1971 and 1981, while the numbers in homes for disabled and elderly people increased by nearly 40

**Table 4.1**
Residents in communal establishments present on census night, Great Britain 1971 and 1981

| Type of Establishment | 1971 | Thousands | 1981 |
|---|---|---|---|
| Hotels and boarding houses | 160.3 | | 101.3 |
| Hospitals and homes | 314.2 | | 250.7 |
| Homes for the old and disabled | 172.9 | | 212.8 |
| Children's homes | 42.9 | | 26.7 |
| Educational establishments | 41.7 | | 29.6 |
| Other | 177.8 | | 175.5 |
| | | | |
| Total in communal establishments | 909.9 | | 796.6 |
| | | | |
| Total resident population | 53,978.4 | | 54,285.4 |

Source: 1981 census[3]

thousand.[3] What they do not tell us is the extent to which the contraction of hospital services has been offset by providing more appropriate services elsewhere. Nor do they tell us about the extent to which services meet the needs of the majority of people who, as Table 4.2 shows, live in private households. It is likely that the position has changed further since 1981, when the last census was taken.

**Table 4.2**

Residents (including staff) in communal establishments, Great Britain 1981

| Age | Number, thousands | Percentage of resident population in age group |
|---|---|---|
| Under 16 | 47.5 | 0.4 |
| 16-24 | 180.4 | 2.4 |
| 25-44 | 141.3 | 1.0 |
| 45-64 | 114.8 | 1.0 |
| 65-74 | 74.3 | 1.5 |
| 75-84 | 132.1 | 5.3 |
| 85 and over | 106.3 | 19.2 |
| Total in communal establishments | 796.6 | 1.5 |

Source: 1981 census [3]

Statistics about community care tend to give a patchy picture of the activities of a variety of services and agencies and focus even less than hospital statistics on the people receiving help. In what follows we look at the information which is available about money, staff and facilities for community care and about the circumstances of people who provide informal care. Before looking at them, however, it is necessary to ask what community care actually is.

# What is community care?

'That over used word community' is the title of an article by none other than the Chief Medical Officer of DHSS. In it he said 'The word community is now widely used but unfortunately in so many different senses that this is leading to confusion'.[4] It would be tempting to suggest that this is the very reason why the government uses it so often.

According to Philip Abrams, community care is the 'provision of help, support and protection to others by lay members of societies acting in everyday domestic and occupational settings'.[5]

There was a shift in meaning in the 1950s and 1960s, when community care was redefined in terms of services provided to individuals outside institutions by professional staff of local authority health and welfare services. A report published in 1963 summarising local authorities' community care plans said:

'Most of the needs which the health and welfare services are designed to meet arise among four broad groups of people: the mothers and young children; the elderly; the mentally disordered and the physically handicapped.'[6] These overlap considerably with the so-called 'priority groups' defined fourteen years later in 'Priorities for Health and Personal Social Services in England',[7] following the reorganisation of local authority social services in 1971 and the reorganisation of both local government and the NHS in 1974.

Perhaps because residential care continued to take up the major part of the budget, in the mid 1970s DHSS extended its official definition of community care to include hospitals, hostels, residential homes, day hospitals and day centres. By the late 1970s and early 1980s, financial and other pressures made it politically expedient to move back towards the older definition.[8] In 1980, the Conservative Secretary of State for Social Services justified cuts in the social services as follows:

'The personal social services provide only a small part of the totality of care in the community for... the elderly, the old and frail, the physically handicapped and the mentally ill...When one is comparing where one can make savings one protects the Health Service because there is no alternative, whereas in personal social services there is a substantial possibility and, indeed,probability of continuing growth in the amount of voluntary care, of neighbourhood care, of self help'.[9]

This begs the question about the extent to which people are able to obtain informal care. It also ignores the financial, social and emotional costs to the carers and the ability of the health and personal social services to interact and provide an appropriate level of support.

The available statistics do not go far towards tackling these crucial questions.So instead, we start by looking at information about the financial resources available for care outside hospital.

# More money?

Given the lack of a clear definition of community care, it is hardly suprising that government spending on hospital and community health services cannot be easily subdivided into the two categories. Despite this, certain broad trends can be seen in the 'programme budget' for England provided each year to the House of Commons Social Services Committee.

Extracts from this given in Table 3.15 show that the proportion of current spending on the hospital and community health services in England which was devoted to acute hospital services declined only very slightly between 1975-76 and 1984-85. Meanwhile spending on community services, which include health visiting, district nursing, community midwifery, prevention, birth control and school health increased from 8.4 per cent to 9.4 per cent over the same period.[10] Spending on outpatient departments rose from 21.0 per cent of the acute hospital total in 1976-77 to 23.4 per cent in 1984-85. This is a rise from 9.9 to 10.8 per cent of the overall total.[11]

Within the so called 'priority groups', spending showed very different patterns. While, perhaps appropriately, there was very little increase in spending on hospital outpatient services for people with mental handicaps, spending on mental illness out patients and psychiatric day patients rose from 8.5 per cent of the cost of services for mentally ill people in 1976-77 to 12.0 per cent in 1984-85.[11] Spending figures for geriatric services are difficult to interpret, as many elderly people are cared for by other parts of the health service. To add to the confusion, some community care projects work from a hospital base.[12]

Of course, the health service is not the only provider of care outside hospital. Other services are provided by local government and the voluntary and private sector, and many people using them claim social security benefits.

New initiatives in statutory community care are often undertaken in projects funded jointly by health authorities and local authorities. Spending on these has grown since this first started in the mid 1970s, but it still only reached 2.7 per cent of the total English Social Services budget in 1984-85.[11]

Although it is subject to much local variation, social services current expenditure in England as a whole, excluding joint finance, grew by 17.1 per cent in 'input volume' terms between 1976-77 and 1984-85 compared with 9.6 per cent for the hospital and community health services. While the growth rates were similar up to 1979-80, the growth rate from then until 1984-85 was 6.9 per cent for local authority social services compared with 4.5 per cent for hospital and community health services.[11] In recent years, however, some social services departments have been affected by rate capping.

In addition, while the Greater London Council and the metropolitan counties were not responsible for social services, they gave considerable grant aid to local community projects and voluntary organisations developing new initiatives in health and community care. It is not clear how many of these lost their funding when the authorities were abolished on April 1 1986, and how many will continue to be funded by the successor bodies.

In England, DHSS sets some funds aside centrally to fund specific categories of project which are listed in the Social Services Committee's reports on expenditure on the social services. These include schemes such as 'Helping the community to care', which are frequently mentioned in ministers' speeches. In fact the sums of money involved are relatively small. The total amount for England is £10 million spread over 3 years.[11]

Transfers from hospital to community care and earlier discharge after acute care has almost certainly increased the workload of the family practitioner services. For example, a study in one general practice showed that people with mental handicaps discharged from hospital to a hostel made more visits to GPs than a control group matched for age and gender.[13] There is no way, however that any resulting increase in spending on these services in general or on drugs prescribed in general practice can be identified.

**Other sources of finance.** People moving out of NHS hospitals and homes to local authority, voluntary or private homes and hostels or returning to private households are entitled to claim higher levels of social security benefit. Total expenditure on all cash benefits for long term sick and disabled people in 1985-86 was estimated to be over £5 billion. According to a parliamentary reply given by the Prime Minister, 'This represents an increase in real terms of over 50 per cent since 1978-79 of which some £380 million is due to real improvements in the average value of benefits paid.'[14] Some of this is likely to be due to the increase in supplementary benefit paid to people in private old people's homes. The amount paid to people in all types of private and voluntary residential care and nursing homes rose from £102 million in 1983 to £200 million in 1984.[15] Not surprisingly at a time of high unemployment, job opportunities for people recovering from illness or with mild mental handicaps is severely limited, as evidence given to the Social Services Committee's enquiry into community care showed.[16]

Community care may rely indirectly on funding from the housing budget. Some local authorities allocate council houses for use as group homes for former residents of long stay hospitals, while housing associations can use funds from the Housing Corporation to provide houses or flats. It was estimated that in 1984   3 per cent of the people housed by associations were mentally ill and a further 3 per cent were mentally handicapped.[17]

Some community care schemes are funded wholly or partly by voluntary organisations and charities, but although costings may be available of the money contributed by the organisation, it is impossible to estimate the value of the time given by volunteers either to raise the funds or to contribute to the working of the schemes.

**Costs to carers.** Even more hidden costs are incurred by the relatives and friends who provide the major part of care for disabled ill and elderly people outside hospital. For example, a study done in 1980 by the Policy Studies Institute tried to assess the cost to households with a wife, husband and an elderly handicapped relative of the wife's caring activities. It estimated that the cost to the family of providing an equivalent amount of help would have averaged £2,500 per annum at 1980 prices. In addition it was estimated that the average earnings foregone by wives not in employment was £4,500 per annum and the average earnings foregone by wives in employment working less than full time was £1,900.[18]

Six years later, in June 1986, when the Invalid Care Allowance was extended to married women after a case was brought before the European Court, it was worth £23 per week or about £1,200 per annum. Yet it is intended for people who have given up their job to care for a severely disabled relative for at least 35 hours a week. DHSS estimated the net cost of extending the benefit to married women to be £55 million in a full year.[19] When asked by the opposition why he had previously quoted higher figures, Norman Fowler admitted, 'The gross cost is about £80 million but the extension of ICA to married women means that some entitlement to dependency additions will cease'.[19] In other words, the women concerned would lose other benefits totalling about £25 million a year.

**Comparative costs of home and hospital care.** Given the implicit assumption that relatives will bear the brunt of both explicit and hidden costs, it is hardly surprising that community care is assumed to be a cheap option, compared with hospitals. DHSS reviewed comparative costs, in its 1980 study on community care and stated 'that the "cost-effectiveness" of a package of community based services often depends greatly on the presence of informal care'.[20] What happens though, if there are no relatives around, or the person concerned is too disturbed or disabled for them to cope?

It is often tacitly assumed that residential places outside hospital cost the same to provide as in-patient care in long stay institutions, but this begs questions about the quality of care. The Minister of Health told the Social Services Committee, 'If you have some hospital facility in the past which has been underfunded, if you transfer the function to community care, the cost will go up'.[16] The Committee itself concluded 'A decent community based service for mentally ill or mentally handicapped people cannot be provided at the same overall costs as the present service. The proposition that community care could be cost neutral is untenable'.[16] Unfortunately, though, the Committee produced no costings in support of these conclusions.

Some comparative costings were produced by the Audit Commission in its report on community care.[21] These are summarised in Table 4.3 and show that the costs increase with the level of dependence implied by each pattern of care. A

**Table 4.3**
Two examples of comparative long term costs to the state of different types of care, 1986 prices

(a) For a frail elderly single person

|  | Total public cost £ per week |
|---|---|
| Own home | 97 |
| Own home and day centre | 135 |
| Local authority sheltered housing and day centre | 152 |
| Local authority Part III home | 133 |
| Private or voluntary residential home | 138 |
| Private or voluntary nursing home | 184 |
| NHS geriatric ward | 295 |

It is assumed that the person is on a state pension, has no substantial savings, became disabled after retirement and qualifies for Attendance Allowance at the lower rate.

b) For a mentally handicapped adult

|  |  |
|---|---|
| Own home alone | 133 |
| Local authority group home with three other people | 119 |
| Supplementary Benefit supported lodging | 133 |
| Local authority residential home | 190 |
| Private and voluntary residential home | 209 |
| Mental handicap hospital | 255 |

It is assumed that the person has no savings or other income and qualifies for Severe Disablement Allowance, but not Attendance Allowance. It is also assumed that, unless living in hospital, they attend an Adult Training Centre.
Source: Audit Commission[21]

more detailed version of Table 4.3 is given in the Audit Commission's report and shows the extent to which the costs would fall on the NHS, social services and social security. In-patient care would largely come from NHS funds, care in private and voluntary homes from social security, while the cost of care in other settings would be shared to a varying extent by social services and social security.

Although the Audit Commission discussed the problems of shifting funds away from hospitals, it did not allow for these in its costings. As the number of people in a hospital goes down, the cost per person goes up, as facilities such as catering, laundry and boiler houses are shared between smaller numbers of people and cannot be closed before the hospital as a whole.

A study which compared the costs of small NHS units for people with mental handicaps with those of hospital wards for people with similar degrees of dependency found that the costs per person per day of children's units were on average 28 per cent higher than those of wards in long stay hospitals. The costs in adults' units were on average 22 per cent higher. When costs in the units were compared with the marginal savings to the hospital of closing a ward, however, they were on average 98 per cent higher for children and 75 per cent for adults.[22]

It follows from what was said earlier that this additional cost will not necessarily all fall on the NHS. As the North West Thames Regional Policy Statement on mental handicap policy put it, '... it is clear that this new way of life — living in small groups in houses rather than in hospital wards — is bound to cost more. The Regional and district health authorities are committed to putting more money into mental handicap services, but the most significant input of additional cash will come from social security payments for which people living outside hospital will become eligible.'[23] This may well be a little optimistic, given the growing constraints on spending on social security.

All that can be deduced from this confused picture is that while there has been some increase over the last ten years in spending by central and local government and also by other organisations on care in places other than hospitals, the extent is difficult to assess. It is even more difficult to find how this has been translated into staff and facilities, but we look at the available information before trying to relate it to measures of need.

# More facilities?

**Homes and hostels.** The most prominent trend in the numbers of places in homes for elderly and physically handicapped people in England is the expansion of the private sector,as Figure 4.1 and Tables 4.4 and 4.5 show. Over the period 1974 to 1979, the number of places in private homes rose by a third while during the next five year period, the numbers nearly doubled and rose even more steeply in 1985.[24,25] Not surprisingly, by 1985, the numbers of places in local authority and voluntary homes had started to decrease.

Although private and voluntary homes are often grouped together in statistics such as those shown in Table 4.5, they have different mixes of residents and voluntary homes cater for proportionately more younger people. In 1984, 19 per cent of people in voluntary homes were aged under 65, compared with 4.5 per cent

**Table 4.4**
Places in homes for elderly and disabled people, England

|      | Local Authority<br>Authority | Voluntary | Private | Total |
|------|------------------------------|-----------|---------|-------|
| 1976 | 110,796 | 32,789 | 26,412 | 169,997 |
| 1979 | 113,592 | 33,912 | 31,998 | 179,502 |
| 1984 | 116,430 | 38,242 | 63,072 | 217,744 |
| 1985 | 116,080 | 37,446 | 80,041 | 233,587 |

Source: D.H.S.S. Personal Social Services statistics[25]

**Table 4.5**

Residents in accommodation for elderly and physically handicapped people, United Kingdom

Number of people, thousands,

| | Number in homes provided by local authorities | | People, thousands, in voluntary and private homes | |
|---|---|---|---|---|
| | Under 65 | 65 and over | Under 65 | 65 and over |
| 1981 | 5·4 | 121·7 | 8·4 | 65·3 |
| 1984 | 5·0 | 120·9 | 9·2 | 87·9 |
| 1985 | 4·6 | 120·5 | 9·1 | 102·2 |

Source: Social Trends 1987[26], Table 7.34

of those in both local authority and private homes.

The numbers of places in local authority homes and hostels for people with mental handicaps increased fairly rapidly during the late 1970s, but more slowly after 1978, as Figure 4.2 and Table 4.6 show. The totals for voluntary and private homes may be incomplete, but until very recently did not show the sort of expansion in the private sector seen in Figure 4.1.[27]

A similar picture can be seen in the much smaller numbers of places in homes and hostels for mentally ill people, shown in Figure 4.3 and Table 4.7, although here, the voluntary sector has always played a larger role.[27]

In grouping together all residential places in homes and hostels, DHSS' statistics not only mask the varying degrees of dependency of their residents, but also the differences between and within the different categories of home and

**Figure 4.1 Places in homes for elderly and disabled people, England.**

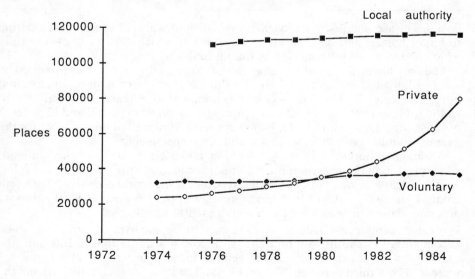

Source: Derived from DHSS personal social services statistics.[25]

**Table 4.6**
Places in homes for people with mental handicaps, England

| | Local Authority | | Voluntary | Private | Total |
| | Staffed | Unstaffed | | | |
|---|---|---|---|---|---|
| 1976 | 8,356 | 347 | 1,933 | 1,137 | 11,773 |
| 1979 | 10,453 | 928 | 2,120 | 1,653 | 15,154 |
| 1984 | 12,803 | 1,544 | 3,996 | 2,275 | 20,618 |
| 1985 | 13,395 | 1,757 | 3,991 | 3,105 | 22,248 |
| Average Number of places, 1985 | 19·7 | 3·9 | 17·2 | 13·4 | |

Source: DHSS Personal Social Services Statistics[27]

**Table 4.7**
Places in homes for people with mental illnesses, England

| | Local Authority | | Voluntary | Private | Total |
| | Staffed | Unstaffed | | | |
|---|---|---|---|---|---|
| 1976 | 1,913 | 825 | 1,149 | 473 | 4,360 |
| 1979 | 2,310 | 1,282 | 1,360 | 655 | 5,607 |
| 1984 | 2,523 | 1,719 | 1,693 | 865 | 6,800 |
| 1985 | 2,563 | 1,800 | 1,952 | 1,219 | 7,534 |
| Average number of places, 1985 | 16·4 | 4·6 | 13·2 | 12·0 | |

Source: DHSS Personal Social Services Statistics [27]

hostel. The accommodation ranges from small homes providing a domestic setting to larger hostels and residential homes, some of which may have a way of life which is just as institutionalised as that in long stay hospitals.[28]

The only distinction made is between staffed and unstaffed homes provided by local authorities. As Figures 4.2 and 4.3 show, the numbers of places in unstaffed homes grew steadily in the late 1970s and continued to increase in the early 1980s. In 1985, 41 per cent of local authority places for mentally ill people and 12 per cent of those for people with mental handicaps were in unstaffed homes in which the average numbers of places were 4.6 and 3.9 respectively.[27]

Although differences in data collection make direct comparisons difficult, similar trends in the provision of residential accommodation were seen in Wales, Scotland and Northern Ireland. One exception is the marked rise by 57 per cent from 447 in 1979 to 703 in 1985 in the number of people living in local authority accommodation in Wales for people with mental handicaps.[30]

**Day centres and meals.** Day centres are used by people living in both residential accommodation and private households. Figure 4.4 shows that in England, the numbers of places in adult training centres for people with mental handicaps increased by a third between 1974 and 1979. The increase then tailed off and the numbers of places increased by only a further 13 per cent between 1979 and

**Figure 4.2 Places in hostels and homes for people with mental handicaps, England.**

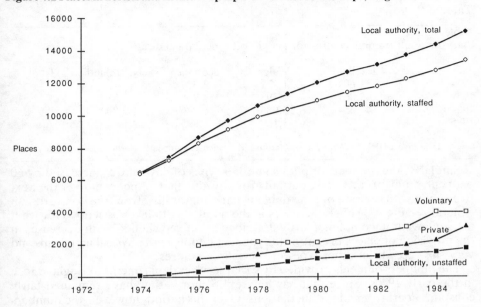

Source: Derived from DHSS personal social services statistics.[27]

**· Figure 4.3 Places in homes for mentally ill people, England.**

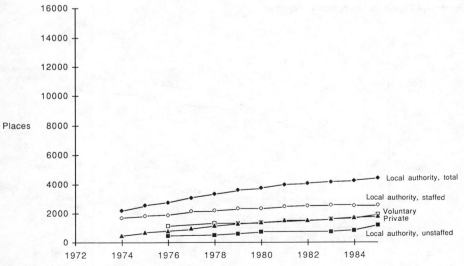

Source: Derived from DHSS personal social services statistics.[27]

1984.[24,31] This levelling off occurred in other countries of the United Kingdom as Table 4.8 shows.

**Table 4.8**

Places in adult training centres for people with mental handicaps

|      | England | Wales | Scotland† | N. Ireland | Total |
|------|---------|-------|-----------|------------|-------|
| 1974 | 31,604  | 1,971 | 3,379     | 495        |       |
| 1979 | 42,061  | 2,493 | 4,705     | 817        |       |
| 1984 | 47,464  | 3,083 | 6,476     | 2,000      |       |
| 1985 | 48,824  | 3,189 | 6,895     | 1,900*     |       |

Source: Data from DHSS[24,30], Welsh Office[30], Scottish Education Department[32], Northern Ireland Office[33]

Similarly, the numbers of places in other types of day centres increased by 60 per cent, from 1974 to 1979, but only rose by a further 13 per cent over the next five years ,with the rate of growth being particularly slow from 1981 onwards. In general, Figure 4.4 shows increases in the numbers of places in centres for what are somewhat uncomplimentarily described as 'mixed clients', with decreases in the provision of places in centres for younger people with physical handicaps and very slow growth in other types of specialised centres.

The numbers of meals provided by social services departments in England rose in the early 1970s. Since then, as Figure 4.5 shows, they have remained fairly constant, apart from minor fluctuations. Over this period, however, the numbers of meals served in recipients' homes have risen and the numbers served in clubs and day centres has fallen.[24,34] Table 4.10 shows the pattern in all four countries of the United Kingdom.

**Figure 4.4 Places in day centres, England.**

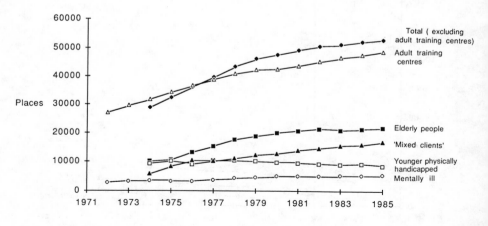

Source: Derived from DHSS personal social services statistics.[31]

**Facing the Figures**

**Figure 4.5 Numbers of main meals provided, England.**

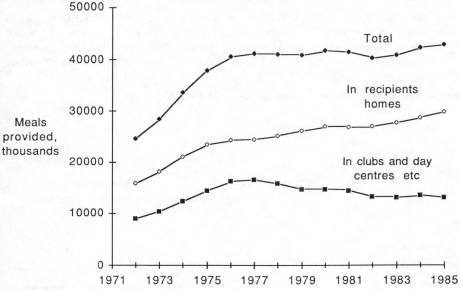

Source: DHSS Derived from DHSS personal social services statistics.[34]

---

**Table 4.9**

Places in day centres for mentally ill, physically handicapped and elderly people

|      | England | Wales | Scotland† | N. Ireland |
|------|---------|-------|-----------|------------|
| 1974 | 26,598  | 2,436 | 3,201     | 463        |
| 1979 | 46,293  | 4,355 | 4,782     | 1,537      |
| 1984 | 52,175  | 5,149 | 5,894     | 1,848      |
| 1985 | 52,945  | 5,515 | 6,863     | 1,843*     |

† Both local authority and voluntary registered
* Provisional
Source: Data from DHSS[24,30], Welsh Office[30], Scottish Education Department,[32], Northern Ireland Office[33]

---

**Table 4.10**

Main meals provided, thousands

|      | England | Wales | Scotland | N. Ireland† |
|------|---------|-------|----------|-------------|
| 1974 | 33,575  | 1,614 | 3,875    | *           |
| 1979 | 40,949  | 2,372 | 4,044    | 572         |
| 1984 | 42,373  | 2,615 | 3,798    | 519         |
| 1985 | 42,931  | 2,650 | 3,805    | 495         |

† In recipients' homes only
* not available
Source: Data from DHSS[24,] Welsh Office[30], Scottish Education Department[32], N. Ireland Office[33]

---

**Facing the Figures**

# More staff?

Over half the staff of local authority social services departments work in residential care, day centres, or day nurseries. The two main groups who work outside these facilities are social workers and home helps. Trends in their numbers since the early 1970s are shown in Figure 4.6 and comparative figures for other United Kingdom countries are shown in Tables 4.11 and 4.12.

**Figure 4.6 Home helps and non-residential social workers, England.**

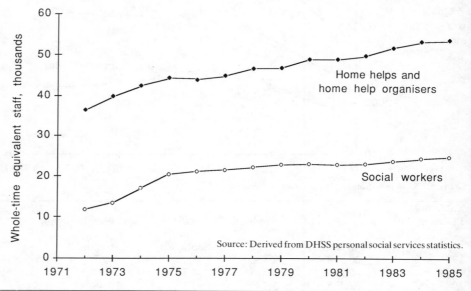

Home helps and home help organisers

Social workers

Source: Derived from DHSS personal social services statistics.

**Table 4.11**
Home helps, whole time equivalent

|      | England | Wales | Scotland | N. Ireland |
|------|---------|-------|----------|------------|
| 1974 | 42,388  | 2,798 | 8,416    | *          |
| 1979 | 46,714  | 2,914 | 9,405    | 3,189      |
| 1984 | 53,145  | 3,573 | 9,485    | 3,186      |
| 1985 | 53,400  | 3,686 | 9,502    | 3,213      |

* not available
Source: Data from DHSS[24], Welsh Office[30], Scottish Education Department[32], Northern Ireland Office[33]

In England, the whole time equivalent numbers of social workers, who include trainees, welfare workers and welfare assistants increased by only 15 per cent over the eight years 1975 to 1983.[24] The numbers of whole time equivalent home helps increased by 17 per cent over the same period.[24,34]

Turning to NHS staff, data about the numbers of whole time equivalent nurses working in the community over the last ten years are difficult to interpret for two

**Table 4.12**
Social workers

|  | England† | Wales† | Scotland | N. Ireland |
|---|---|---|---|---|
| 1974 | 17,042† | 806† | 1,665☆ | * |
| 1979 | 22,733 | 1,202 | 2,714☆ | 1,217 |
| 1984 | 24,292 | 1,416 | 3,129 | 1,273 |
| 1985 | 24,790 | 1,424 | 3,359 | 1,297 |

† Excludes senior social workers
☆ Excludes welfare rights and community workers
* Not available
Source: Data from DHSS[24], Welsh Office[30], Scottish Education Department [32], Northern Ireland Office[33]

reasons. The first is the reduction in 1980 in the length of the working week, to which we referred earlier. At the same time, changes were made in the way data about nurses working in the school health service were collected and classified and this affected the data about other community nurses shown in Figure 4.7. Some attempt has been made to allow for this in Figure 4.8 which suggests a levelling off in the overall numbers of community nurses after these changes took place.[24] This effect is particularly marked when the figures are adjusted to allow for changes in the length of the working week as is also done in Table 4.13.

Community mental handicap nurses and community psychiatric nurses (CPNs) were not identified separately before 1981 and data since then are somewhat problematic, although Figure 4.7 shows clearly that there are not very many of them.

**Figure 4.7 Numbers of staff in selected types of community nursing posts, England.**

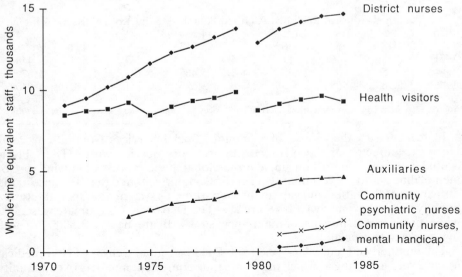

Source: Health and Personal Social Services Statistics for England.[24]

**Figure 4.8 Total community nursing staff, England.**

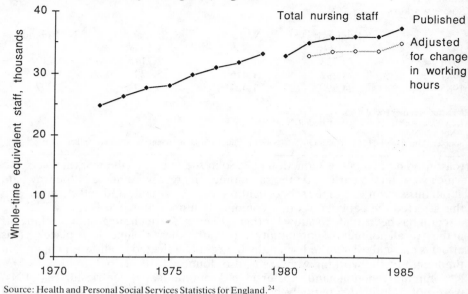

Source: Health and Personal Social Services Statistics for England.[24]

**Table 4.13**
Community nursing staff, whole time equivalent

|      | England | | Wales | | Scotland | | Northern Ireland | |
|------|-----------|----------|-----------|----------|-----------|----------|-----------|----------|
|      | Published | Adjusted | Published | Adjusted | Published | Adjusted | Published | Adjusted |
| 1976 | 26,386    |          | 2,195     |          | 4,135     |          | 1,044     |          |
| 1979 | 29,512    |          | 2,336     |          | 5,013     |          | 1,494     |          |
| 1981 | 34,929    | 32,746   | 2,511     | 2,354    | 5,181     | 4,857    | 1,544     | 1,448    |
| 1984 | 35,845    | 33,605   | 2,648     | 2,483    | 5,465     | 5,123    | 1,791     | 1,679    |
| 1985 | 37,296    | 34,965   | 2,645     | 2,480    | 5,626     | 5,274    | 1,750     | 1,640    |

Source: Data from DHSS, Welsh Office, Information Services Division Scotland and Northern Ireland Office

In evidence to the House of Commons Social Services Committee, Peter Horrocks, director of the NHS Health Advisory Service wrote 'The CPN is probably the most important single professional in the process of moving care of mental illness into the community.' Yet the Committee found that 'Because of the difficulties of definition and gaps in the Department's system of statistical returns, nobody knows how many CPNs there are. The Department's estimate was 2,000 while professional nursing opinion suggested a figure nearer 3,500'.[16] These figures refer to England.

The numbers in Figure 4.7 come from DHSS' Annual Census of Non-medical Manpower, according to which the whole time equivalent numbers of community psychiatric nurses in England rose from 1083 in 1981 to 1883 in 1984.[35] DHSS warns that this is likely to be an underestimate as some nurses who work in the community but from a hospital base may be recorded as hospital nurses. Corresponding sources for other countries of the United Kingdom estimate the numbers of CPNs in Wales and Scotland in 1984 as 140[36] and 223[37] respectively.

A survey done in 1985 by Charlie Brooker for the Community Psychiatric Nursing Association suggested somewhat higher numbers for England.[38] Adjusting his results for non-response resulted in revised estimates of 2441 CPNs in England in 1985, along with 150 in Wales, 224 in Scotland and 136 in Northern Ireland.

This survey collected information about the main working base of CPNs and compared it with the results of a similar survey in 1980. It found a considerable shift away from hospitals. In 1980, an estimated 77 per cent of CPNs worked from a psychiatric hospital or psychiatric unit in a district general hospital, but only 56 per cent did so in 1985. Amongst other things, this change is likely to have decreased the extent to which CPNs were under-reported in DHSS' statistics.

It is likely that statistics about community mental handicap nurses are subject to similar biases. According to DHSS' statistics, the whole time equivalent numbers rose from 233 in 1981 to 765 in 1984, although 49 DHAs apparently still had none in 1984.[35]

**How complete are the statistics?** As with information about finance, statistics about facilities for and staff involved in community care are bound to be incomplete. It is not clear to what extent accommodation in council houses or housing association properties are included. Accommodation for homeless people, whether in hostels or bed and breakfast hotels, is unlikely to be included. Staff of voluntary organisations and private facilities do not appear. It is also unclear how local authority staff providing new patterns of care for example new patterns of home care, are classified. In addition, the statistics do not cover people who might not see providing community care as an explicit part of their job.

For example, in 1978, OPCS' survey of elderly people at home asked respondents about visits received in the last six months by people from statutory or other organisations.[39] A third had been visited by a doctor, 8.9 per cent by a home help, 7.8 per cent by a district nurse and 4.4 per cent by a health visitor. Only 2.7 per cent had been visited by someone from a voluntary organisation and 16.2 per cent by a minister of religion. In contrast to this, 48.2 per cent had been visited by an 'insurance man' and 23.4 per cent mentioned him as the only visitor of this sort.

Even this excludes the people who do the most of the work of caring but are the least visible in official statistics, the unpaid or 'informal' carers.

# Informal care

While there have been changes in the patterns of care provided by health and social services, the main sources of help have always been relatives and, to a lesser extent, friends and neighbours. All too often the brunt of caring falls on one person and, very often this is a woman.[21,40,41]

In 1980, the OPCS 'Women and employment survey' found that 13 per cent of women under 60 had responsibility for sick, disabled or elderly people.[42] This was true for 15 per cent of married women, 12 per cent of widowed, divorced or separated women and only 6 per cent of single women. Comparisons with a similar survey done in 1965 showed that the percentages of women giving care had increased since then. The increase was particularly marked among women in full time paid employment. Nineteen per cent of women with a dependent felt that their paid work had been affected, either in restricting their hours of work, or in preventing them from taking paid employment, or in other ways.

Of course, the caring role is not confined to women, nor to people of working age. For example, a survey of of 783 people aged over 70 in South Wales found that 29 per cent of them needed help with one or more of 15 tasks considered by the researchers to be basic to daily living.[43] Daughters were named most often as the main helper and were mentioned as such by 47 per cent of respondents, while 25 per cent named their spouses. Only 17 per cent named home helps. Thirty six per cent of the main helpers were aged over 65 and 10 per cent were over 75.

Turning to younger age groups, it is not surprising that mothers are usually the main people caring for handicapped children. The picture is more diverse for adults and includes parents, spouses and daughters, depending on the person's age.[44]

It is important not to understate the part played by men in caring for people of all age groups, but the evidence suggests that they are less likely than women to be left to get on with it on their own.[46] For example, a survey of 255 elderly people referred to specialist services in two urban areas in northern England identified and interviewed 157 informal carers, 41 per cent of whom were men.[44] It was found that male carers received more help, both from the services and from informal sources than did women.

These surveys and many other accounts make it clear that the majority of people caring for elderly people and those with mental or physical handicaps or mental illnesses have extremely inadequate help from health and social services.[45] The majority continue to care at considerable expense to themselves. As one of them put it, 'the most hurtful part of caring is the pretence that services exist when clearly they do not.[45]

# The gap between services and needs

The statistics about resources for care show, with some exceptions, a pattern of growth throughout the 1970s with either a slowing up of growth or no further growth in the 1980s. How does this square with the government's claims to be giving priority to community care, on the one hand, and the widespread experience of its absence, on the other? As was explained earlier, there are no global statistics which can answer this question, but it is possible to look at some specific examples.

To start with, a number of the services we have mentioned are used largely by elderly people. Conventionally, the extent of these services is expressed as a rate per 1,000 people aged 65 or over. Yet, as Table 4.14 shows, the use of services, increases with age and is relatively infrequent among people aged 65-74. Use of

**Table 4.14**
Use of some health and personal social services by elderly people in the previous month, Great Britain, 1984

| | 65-69 | 70-74 | 75-79 | 80-84 | 85+ | All aged 65+ |
|---|---|---|---|---|---|---|
| | | Percentage who used service, by age | | | | |
| Home help | 3 | 5 | 12 | 24 | 31 | 10 |
| Lunch provided | | | | | | |
| Meals on wheels | 1 | 1 | 4 | 10 | 5 | 3 |
| Club or day centre | 2 | 2 | 4 | 8 | 6 | 4 |
| Either | 3 | 3 | 7 | 15 | 11 | 6 |
| Day centre | 3 | 4 | 6 | 8 | 7 | 5 |
| Doctor | | | | | | |
| At home | 6 | 9 | 13 | 20 | 25 | 11 |
| At surgery | 25 | 26 | 25 | 20 | 12 | 24 |
| Either | 28 | 33 | 36 | 37 | 37 | 33 |
| District nurse or | | | | | | |
| health visitor | 3 | 4 | 8 | 16 | 23 | 8 |
| NHS Chiropodist | 4 | 8 | 11 | 15 | 14 | 9 |

Source: General Household Survey, 1984,
Tables 8.23 and 8.25

the services is much more common among people aged 75 or over and it is these age groups which are increasing in size. Figure 4.9 shows the difference between relating the numbers of home helps in England to the numbers of people aged 65 and over and to those aged 75 and over. In his pamphlet, 'The care gap', Alan Walker showed similar decreases in other services used by elderly and very elderly people.[47] Table 4.15, which is taken from the Audit Commission's report shows that over the years 1979 to 1984, the numbers of day centre place and meals served scarcely kept pace with the numbers of people aged 75 and over.

Next, there are many distortions resulting from the priority which the government is giving to the closure of long stay hospitals. This is seen as a prime objective, and something for which general managers should be rewarded with extra pay,[48] rather than something which should happen as an inevitable consequence of providing better care elsewhere for the residents. A likely consequence is that people living outside hospitals who come to need long term support have little chance of getting it as the available resources are likely to be directed at people who are currently in institutions. Even these would appear to be inadequate.

A survey by the Campaign for People with Mental Handicaps looked at mental handicap hospitals and units in England which closed between May 1979 and December 1984. It found that, of the people living in them a year before they closed, 68 per cent moved to another NHS hospital and a further 17 per cent moved to an NHS hostel or community unit.[49] Of course, it may be that the people who were easier to place in more domestic accommodation had left earlier, but this still reveals a lack of resources for community care.

**Figure 4.9 Trends in the provision of home help services in England.**

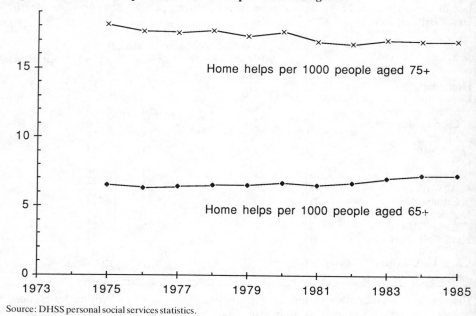

Source: DHSS personal social services statistics.

**Table 4.15**
The balance of care for elderly people, England and Wales

| | Rate per 1,000 people aged 75 or over | | |
|---|---|---|---|
| | 1974 | 1979 | 1984 |
| Geriatric hospitals, occupied beds | 22.1 | 19.6 | 17.1 |
| Local authority homes, occupied beds | 40.0 | 39.3 | 34.5 |
| Nursing homes, long stay occupied beds | 4.8 | 5.0 | 7.6 |
| Voluntary homes, occupied beds | 9.5 | 9.2 | 8.5 |
| Private homes, occupied beds | 7.8 | 9.7 | 17.4 |
| Day patient attendances, per day | 1.7 | 1.8 | 2.2 |
| Local authority day centre places | 5.6 | 10.5 | 10.9 |
| Home help staff, whole time equivalent | 18.3 | 17.9 | 17.9 |
| Meals, thousands per year | 14.3 | 15.6 | 14.2 |

Source: Audit Commission[21]

While we would strongly question the medical type of alternative proposed, there seems to be considerable truth in these observations by a consultant in mental handicap that 'Large mental illness and mental handicap hospitals were established because the community could not cope. If I understand the situation correctly, that the community is again finding it impossible to cope, then we certainly need a new non-political clinically oriented approach to the care of the mentally disordered. Otherwise there will be an enormous waste of resources as well as inferior care.'[50]

The available evidence suggests that pressure to close or reduce the numbers of beds in psychiatric hospitals means that people are increasingly likely to be discharged to inadequate facilities.[51]

A survey of 100 people living in two London boroughs who had recently been discharged from mental hospitals, including 20 living in emergency accommodation, found that two thirds had been given no opportunity to discuss housing possibilities before they were discharged. Only 39 said that their benefit entitlement had been checked before leaving hospital. While some of the 45 people among them who attended day centres were satisfied with what the centres provided, many expressed reservations. In particular, the day centres were not appropriate to the needs of Asian and Afro-carribean people. While 45 of those interviewed wanted a paid job, those who had tried to find one found the stigma of mental illness an extra disadvantage at a time of high unemployment.[52]

This survey was done as part of a research project into the housing problems associated with discharge from psychiatric hospitals. NHS staff reported increasing pressure to discharge people quickly, yet also knew there were other patients who could be discharged if more supported accommodation was available. This was echoed in a report on the housing problems of single homeless people in London, which concluded that there was not enough suitable accomodation for single people discharged from psychiatric hospitals and thus there was little chance of improvement for people outside hospital who may need housing which provides some form of support. In addition, it suggested that the people who were most dissatisfied with their housing were most likely to be readmitted to hospital.[53]

In a letter to the British Medical Journal, it was pointed out that while the numbers of people living in psychiatric hospitals in England and Wales has fallen since 1950, the prison population has risen.[54] The authors admitted themselves that such a statistical association cannot be taken as implying a causal relationship. Furthermore, it has been government policy to close psychiatric hospitals and build more prisons, so the statistics are not unexpected. All the same, the authors quoted research which apparently showed a much higher estimated proportion of people in prison with symptoms of psychiatric disturbance than had been the case in the past. This is a cause for concern which needs to be investigated more fully.

As far as care for elderly people is concerned, Table 4.15 shows that, unlike services which allow people to remain in their own homes, the increase in the numbers of places in residential accommodation has more than offset the rise in numbers of very elderly people. This is particularly true of private and voluntary homes which rely heavily on social security payments.

In part, this is a result of the changes in the social security system which have contributed to the growth in numbers of private old people's homes. After 1983, local DHSS offices set maximum limits on charges to be paid out of social security for elderly people living in private homes. Not surprisingly, homes set their charges at the market rate, which usually, by a not very surprising coincidence, was the same as the local maximum. As a result, the numbers of places and thus also spending mushroomed, from £39 million in 1982 to £105 million in 1983 to £200 million in 1984. In a vain attempt to curb this, DHSS imposed national limits

April 1985. In many places these were lower than the previous local limits. As a result, some people were faced with the choice of being turned out or finding extra money from relatives to make up the difference.[55]

It is far from clear how these payments will be affected in the future by the so called 'reform of social security'. Apparently, the DHSS does not know the answer either. When he was social security minister, Tony Newton said to the Social Services Committee, 'That is something we are intending to give further consideration in the period between now and the implementation of the Income Support Scheme, but the powers that we have in the bill would enable us, should we decide to do so, to continue broadly the present regime under the supplementary benefit board and lodging regulations'.[56]

Meanwhile, there is widespread concern about standards of care in some private old people's homes.[57] What is more, it would appear that sizeable profits have been passed from public funds into private hands, at a time when funds are scarce for expanding the care provided by local authorities, the NHS and voluntary agencies.

A survey of attitudes of people aged over 75 to health and social services found that the majority had no wish to leave their own homes to go into institutional care and were especially antipathetic towards geriatric wards and hospitals.[58] On the other hand, many were unaware of the existence of services such as lunch clubs, day hospitals, incontinence laundry services, bath attendents and sheltered housing.

This, coupled with the patchy provision of many services and the apparently ready availability of social security funds to pay fees may lead elderly people to go into private homes when, potentially they could remain at home. They may also have problems on discharge after hospital stays as caring for people who have just been discharged is a relatively minor part of the work of community nurses. According to OPCS' survey of nurses working in the community only 7 per cent of the time district nurses spend with patients was devoted to this.[59]

# What happened to targets and guidelines?

'Priorities for health and personal social services in England' quoted targets and guidelines for its 'priority groups'. These had been set out in DHSS circulars and in two white papers 'Better services for the mentally handicapped[60] published in 1971 and 'Better services for the mentally ill'[61] which had come out in 1975. These guidelines were endorsed and summarised in 1977 in 'The way forward'.[62]

The 'tentative and provisional basis' for these guidelines was admitted in 'Better services for the mentally handicapped' which said 'Estimating the number of places required — for training or occupation, in residential homes, and in hospitals for day-patients and in-patients — is a matter of judgement. Estimates, therefore, vary considerably even among those who have studied the subject closely... Any estimates made now as a basis for planning services will need to be adjusted in the light of experience and further research'.[60]

In our pamphlet 'Whose priorities?' published in 1976, we estimated that, at the rates of growth quoted in the document, some of the targets would take many

**Table 4.16**
Progress towards White Paper targets
a) for adults with mental handicaps in England and Wales

|  | 1969 | 1984 | Target for 1991 | Percentage of change achieved |
|---|---|---|---|---|
| Hospitals, available beds | 52,100 | 42,500 | 27,300 | 39 |
| Places in all types of home or hostel | 4,300 | 18,500 | 29,800 | 56 |
| Adult training centre places | 24,600 | 50,500 | 74,500 | 52 |

b) for mentally ill people in England

|  | 1974 | 1984 | Target for 1991 | Percentage of change achieved |
|---|---|---|---|---|
| Hospitals, available beds | 104,400 | 78,900 | 47,900 | 45 |
| Places in all types of home or hostel | 3,500 | 6,800 | 11,500 | 41 |
| Day hospital places | 11,200 | 17,000 | 45,800† | 17 |
| Day centre places, local authority and voluntary | 5,400 | 9,000 | 28,200 | 16 |

† The target includes day hospital provision for in-patients, who are not included in the day hospital statistics.
Source: Audit Commission[21]

years to achieve.[63] Table 4.16 shows how the position has changed since then.

It shows that by 1984 despite a marked decrease in hospital places, community services for mentally ill people had made little progress towards the targets proposed for 1991-2. There had been greater increases in services for people with mental handicaps particularly in residential accommodation. Progress towards the target for training centres slackened off progressively from the mid 1970's onwards.[64] As we have seen, among services for elderly people, there were only very modest increases in home helps or in meals served in clubs and day centres or by meals on wheels, and these fell far short of the target. There was however a larger proportionate increase in day centre places.

Similar targets had been adopted in Wales and a different set in Scotland. A comparison of the progress made by 1980-81 in each of the three countries in providing community care for people with mental handicaps found it disappointing, but considered the more positive strategy adopted in Wales offered greater hope for the future.[65]

**Local variations.** 'Whose priorities?' also pointed to the wide differences in the extent to which local authorities provide social services.[63] This has not changed. For example, Figure 4.10 shows the wide variation in the provision of home helps, with only 16 of the 109 authorities achieving the national guidelines of 12 per 1,000 people aged 65 or over.[66]. Similarly, in 1985, 24 of the authorities did not provide any day centres for mentally ill people or any places in centres run by voluntary or other organisations[67] It may be that some of them provided places in 'mixed' centres, but a closer look at day care provided by local authorities and also by the NHS found it very unevenly distributed from place to place.[68]

**Are targets and guidelines any use?** In fact, the guidelines appear to have been abandoned on the grounds that, 'simple single indicators for the provision of individual services are no longer recognised as useful. It is for each social services authority to decide on the level and nature of the home help service to be provided taking into account local need and other factors including the availability of voluntary, private and informal care.'[70] On the other hand the government's reply to the Social Services Committee was more ambivalent when it said, 'National guidelines for provision are intended to help authorities to plan services, but can only provide a broad guide to what is needed.'[71]

It is true that setting statistical targets for many years ahead has many shortcomings. Firstly, the statistics give no indication of the variable quality or the diverse nature of the facilities provided, and the targets do not allow for local variation in need. Furthermore, the statistics do not include new developments in patterns of care during the time period concerned, such as, for example care attendant schemes[71] or supported lodging schemes.[72] In addition, as we pointed out in 'Whose priorities?', the definition of 'client groups', ignores the way people's different problems are interrelated and many of them result from or are made insoluble because of poverty.

**Is this why they were abandoned?** Although these are good reasons for abandoning guidelines, are they the real ones? Could it be that the guidelines are a reminder that facilities for community care have not developed on the scale

**Figure 4.10 Variations in home help provision by English social services authorities.**

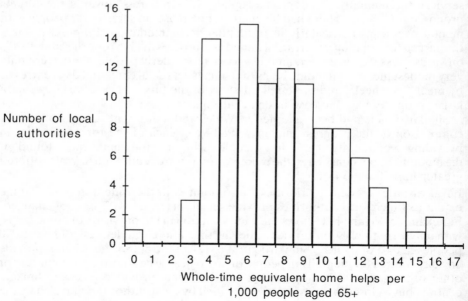

Number of local authorities

Whole-time equivalent home helps per 1,000 people aged 65+

Source: Written parliamentary reply.[66]

thought to be appropriate in the 1970s. It is difficult to avoid the conclusion that as community care is failing to meet these stated objectives, the only course is to abandon them.

# Who cares?

It is difficult to draw any firm conclusions from such a patchy picture. Indeed the very failure to monitor what is happening itself suggests a lack of financial and political commitment to stated policies, apart from the closure of long stay institutions. When questioned by the Social Services Committee about whether the DHSS could measure the effect of community care policies on both sides of its budget, Tony Newton's response was, 'We are not as good as we should like to be, we are conscious of that.'[56]

Commenting on its study of community care in its 1981 policy document, 'Care in Action', DHSS said 'The study suggests that the development of community services has not so far been specifically directed at those groups of people who require a particularly intensive degree of support if they are not to be taken into long term care.'[73]

Since this was published the position has become worse. The numbers of people living in residential accommodation has risen sharply while there has been very slow progress in providing services for people living in their own homes, mainly because of cuts in local authority funds and the threat of rate-capping. There are, of course, wide local variations in the quality and extent of care provided, with a few authorities managing to provide effective care and many more failing to do so.

Commenting on the obstacles they face, the Audit Commission commented 'It is therefore not surprising that joint planning and community care policies are in some disarray. The result is poor value for money. Too many people are cared for in settings costing over £200 a week when they would receive more appropriate care in the community at a total cost to public funds of £100-£130 a week. Conversely, people in the community may not be getting the support they need.

A typical example of the government's attitude to community care was in its handling of the Disabled Persons (Services, Consultation and Representation) Act 1986. This started as a private members bill and was taken on by the government. Amongst other things, it gives disabled people the right to demand from local authorities for an assessment of their needs and the ability of any carer to continue providing care. The local authority has to provide a written statement of their needs and the action it will take to meet them.

The Act was given the Royal Assent on July 8th 1986 but the government took no steps and allocated no money to implement it. When questioned about this by Tom Clarke, the MP who put forward the original Private Members Bill, the Prime Minister replied that the clauses without resource implication could be brought in during 1987 but went on to say that 'The provisions of the Act which have significant resource implications can only be brought into effect as and when these resources can be provided.'[74]

There is only one sense in which the government can claim to be moving towards community care. This is by changing the definition, as it did in its 1981 white paper, 'Growing older',

---

'the primary sources of support and care for elderly people are informal and voluntary. These spring from the personal ties of kinship, friendship and neighbourhood ... it is the role of public authorities to sustain and, where necessary, develop — but never displace — such support and care, care "in" the community must increasingly mean care "by" the community.'[75]

Five years later, the Audit Commission came to a very different conclusion that 'the one option that is not tenable is to do nothing about present financial, organisational and staffing arrangements. Redeployment of the assets released by the rundown of long stay hospitals, combined with the projected increase of 37 per cent in the number of very elderly people over the next ten years presents a "window" of opportunity to establish an effective community-based service to provide the care needed for frail elderly, mentally ill, mentally handicapped and physically handicapped people. If this opportunity is not taken, a new pattern of care will emerge, based on private residential care where appropriate. The results will be a continued waste of scarce resources and worse still, care and support which is either lacking entirely, or inappropriate to the needs of some of the most disadvantaged members of society and the relatives who seek to care for them.'

The government's response to this challenge was to ask Sir Roy Griffith, architect of the NHS management structure to review community care. The announcement that this should be completed by the end of 1987 suggests that one of its purposes is to fend off criticisms of the inadequacy of community care and failure to implement legislation in the pre-election period.

## References

1 DHSS, Welsh Office, Scottish Home and Health Department, Northern Ireland Office. Primary health care: an agenda for discussion. London: HMSO,1986.
2 Fowler N. Hansard, March 14 1986, col 613-614.
3 Pearce D. Population in communal establishments. Population Trends 1983;33;18-21.
4 Acheson E D. From the Chief Medical Officer — 'That over used word community.' Health Trends 1985;17:3.
5 Abrams P. Community care: some research problems and priorities. Policy and Politics 1977;j6:125-51.
6 Ministry of Health. Health and welfare, the development of community care. Cmnd 1973. London: HMSO,1963.
7 DHSS. Priorities for health and personal social services in England. London: HMSO,1976.
8 Walker A. Community care: fact and fiction. In Wilmott P, ed. The debate about community: papers from a seminar on 'Community in social policy'. London:Policy Studies Institute,1986.
9 House of Commons Social Services Committee. The government's white papers on public expenditure: the social services. Vol II HC 702, London: HMSO,1980.
10 Written reply. Hansard, July 25 1986, col 729-732.
11 House of Commons. Fourth report from the Social Servies Committee, session 1985-86. Public expenditure on the social services. HC387-II London: HMSO,1986.
12 Tomalin C. Primary role of hospital. Health Service Journal 1986:483.
13 Goulder T J. Letter. British Medical Journal 1985;290:1826.
14 Written reply. Hansard, February 25 1986, col 383-384.
15 Written replies. Hansard, December 9 1986, col 127.
16 House of Commons. Second report from the Social Services Committee, session 1984-5. Community care, with special reference to adult mentally ill and mentally handicapped people. HC13-1. London: HMSO,1985.
17 Young G. Written reply. Hansard, June 24 1986, col 155.
18 Nissel M, Bonnerjea L. Family care of the handicapped elderly: who pays? No 602. London:Policy Studies Institute, 1982.

19 Fowler N. Hansard, June 23 1986, col 21-26.
20 DHSS. Report of a study on community care. London: HMSO,1981.
21 Audit Commission. Making a reality of community care. London: HMSO,1986.
22 Wright K, Haycox A. Costs of alternative forms of NHS care for mentally handicapped persons. Discussion paper 7. York:Centre for Health Economics, 1985.
23 North West Thames Regional Health Authority. Health services for mentally handicapped people — a policy statement. London:NWTRHA,1986.
24 DHSS. Health and personal social services statistics for England. London: HMSO,various years.
25 DHSS. Local authority personal social services statistics. Series RA(2).
26 Central Statistical Office. Social Trends 17, 1987 edition. London: HMSO,1987.
27 DHSS. Local authority personal social services statistics. Series A/F (11).
28 Hudson B. A revolution, but leading where? Health Services Journal 1986:926.
29 Written reply. Hansard, May 22 1986, col 289.
30 Welsh Office. Health and personal social services statistics for Wales. Various years.
31 DHSS. Local authority personal social services statistics. Series A/F (8).
32 Scottish Education Department, Social Work Services Group.Statistical Bulletins.
33 Department of Health and Social Services. Trends in health and personal social services. Various years.
34 DHSS. Local authority personal social services statistics. Series A/F (18).
35 DHSS. Annual census of non-medical manpower.
36 Written reply. Hansard, April 28 1986, col 289.
37 Written reply. Hansard, April 23 1986, col 173.
38 Brooker C. The 1985 CPNA national survey update. Bristol:CPNA,1985.
39 Hunt A. The elderly at home. SS1078. London: HMSO,1978.
40 Parker G. With due care and attention, a review of research on informal care. Occasional paper number 2. London:Family Policy Studies Centre,1985.
41 GLC Women's Committee, GLC Health Panel. Chance or choice? Community care and women as carers. London:GLC,1984.
42 Martin J, Roberts C. Women and employment, a lifetime perspective. SS1143. London: HMSO,1984.
43 Jones D A, Victor C R, Vetter N J. Carers of the elderly in the community. Journal of the Royal College of General Practitioners 1983;33:707-710.
44 Charlesworth A, Wilkin C, Durie A. Carers and services: a comparison of men and women caring for elderly people. Manchester:Equal Opportunities Commission,1984.
45 Slack P. Life on the receiving end. Community Outlook June 1986:17-18.
46 Anderson R. The unremitting burden on carers. Editorial. British Medical Journal 1987;294:73-74.
47 Walker A. The care gap. How can local authorities meet the needs of the elderly. London:Local Government Information Unit,1985.
48 DHSS. General managers: arrangements for remuneration and conditions of service. Personnel memorandum PM(86)7. London:DHSS,1986.
49 Wertheimer A. Hospital closure in the eighties. London:Campaign for People with Mental Handicaps,1986.
50 Kinnell H G. The hard world outside: some pitfalls to avoid in the community care of the mentally handicapped. Lancet 1984;ii:1202-4.
51 Scull A. The asylum as community or the community as asylum; paradoxes and contradictions of mental health care. In: Bean P ed. Mental illness: changes and trends:John Wiley and Sons,1983.
52 Kay A, Legg C. Discharged to the community. London:City University, 1986.
53 Single Homeless in London Working Party. Single homelessness in London. London:GLC,1986.
54 Weller M P I, Weller B. Crime and psychopathology. British Medical Journal 1986;292:55-6.
55 Counsel and Care for the Elderly. Every solution creates a problem. London:Counsel and Care,1986.
56 House of Commons. Fourth report from the Social Services committee, session 1985-6. Public expenditure on the social services. Volume I. HC 387-I. London: HMSO,1986.
57 McKie D. Standards of care in residential homes. Lancet 1986;i:1509.
58 Salvage A. Attitudes for the over 75s to health and social services. Cardiff:Research Team for the Care of the Elderly, 1986.
59 Dunnell K, Dobbs J. Nurses working in the community. SS1141. London: HMSO,1982.

60 DHSS, Welsh Office. Better services for the mentally handicapped. Cmnd 4683. London: HMSO,1971.

61 DHSS. Better services for the mentally ill. Cmnd 6233. London: HMSO,1975.

62 DHSS. The way forward. London, HMSO, 1977.

63 Radical Statistics Health Group. Whose priorities? London: Radical Statistics,1976.

64 Taylor J, Taylor D. Mental handicap. Partnership in the community. London: Office of Health Economics/MENCAP, 1986.

65 Wistow G. Community care for the mentally handicapped: disappointing progress. In: Harrison A, Gretton J, eds. Health care UK 1985. London:CIPFA,1985.

66 Written reply. Hansard, April 3 1986, col 72-76.

67 Written reply. Hansard, February 21 1986 col, 392-4.

68 Vaughan P J. The disordered development of day care in psychiatry. Health Trends 1983;15:91-94.

69 Whitney R. Written reply. Hansard, January 28 1986, col 495-6.

70 DHSS. Government response to the second report from the Social Services Committee, 1984-5 session. Community care. Cmnd 967. London: HMSO,1985.

71 Hopper C, Roberts J. Care attendant schemes. London:Greater London Association for Disabled People, 1985.

72 Anstee B H. An alternative form of community care for the mentally ill: supported lodging schemes. Health Trend 1985;17:39-40.

73 DHSS. Care in action. London:HMSO,1981.

74 Thatcher M. Hansard, February 10 1987, col 156.

75 DHSS, Scottish Office, Welsh Office, Northern Ireland Office. growing older. Cmnd 8173. London:HMSO,1981.

76 Written reply. Hansard March 4 1987, col 628.

# 5
# Current issues

IN THIS PART of the book we examine current trends in health care and assess where the government's health service policies have taken us. To begin with we compare the NHS with health care systems elsewhere, and in particular examine allegations that the NHS is inefficient, expensive and bureaucratic compared with health care systems in other countries. We then look in detail at the United States, a prime example of a mixed system of private and health care. The US experience is interesting because it provides some evidence of the effects of the privatising policies that the British government has been pursuing for the past seven years.

The following three sections examine the implementation of these privatisation policies in Britain, namely, the extent of private medical care, the effects of the contracting out of ancillary services and increased charges to patients. After this we analyse the lack of employment opportunities in the NHS for women and members of ethnic minority groups.

The next two sections of Part 5 examine in different senses the pressures that various vested interests bring to bear on the provision of health care. We look at the claims that restrictions on drug prescribing lead to patients getting second-best treatment, that limiting the profits of pharmaceutical companies will force them to cut their research, and that better dental health is due to more dental treatment.

Finally, we consider in two related sections the present enthusiasm among professionals for health education, particularly in preventing heart disease and changing diet. We ask whether this is not conveniently ignoring the structural causes of disease, such as poverty, and just blaming the victim.

## The National Health Service: Some International Comparisons

Shortly after the Conservative Government was elected in 1979, the Royal Commission on the National Health Service published its report. The general conclusion of the Royal Commission, partly based on comparisons of health services in other countries, was that 'we need not feel ashamed of our health service and that there are many aspects of it of which we can be justly proud'.[1] At the same time, the Royal Commission recommended more control over the private sector and the abolition of charges to NHS patients in order to strengthen and improve the NHS.

Rejecting these conclusions, the Government greatly reduced controls on the private sector, and greatly increased patient charges. Persisting in its view that something was fundamentally wrong with the NHS, it despatched civil servants in the Department of Health and elsewhere to other countries, to try to find a health care system that might be copied. Without success: the civil servants returned unenthusiastic about what they had seen, and their findings were not published. The Treasury, too, chipped in with its long-held opinion that the NHS was good value for money.

Despite these setbacks, the Government has continued to nudge the NHS towards the goals it favours: more private practice, privatisation of ancillary services, co-operation between the public and private sector, and an increased reliance on charity. It has also continued to allege that the NHS is an inefficient, expensive and bureaucratic system, which bucks health service trends elsewhere. But how does the NHS in its present form compare with health care systems in other countries? Is the NHS really too expensive, or too bureaucratic?

**Expensive?** The best way of measuring how much we spend on the NHS in comparison with other countries is to look at the proportion of our total national wealth allocated to health care: that is, to look at health service spending as a percentage of Gross Domestic Product (GDP).

Table 5.1 shows the proportions of GDP that each country in the European Community devoted to health care in 1982, the most recent year for which comparative statistics are available.

**Table 5.1**
Health care expenditure in the European Community as a percentage share of the Gross Domestic Product, 1982

| Country | Per cent |
| --- | --- |
| France | 9.3 |
| Netherlands | 8.7 |
| Germany | 8.2 |
| Ireland | 8.2 |
| Italy | 7.2 |
| Denmark | 6.8 |
| Spain | 6.3 |
| Belgium | 6.2 |
| UK | 5.9 |
| Portugal | 5.7 |
| Greece | 4.4 |

Source: Written parliamentary reply[2]

These figures were provided in Hansard on 15th April 1986 in response to a question to the Secretary of State for Social Services. As was acknowledged in the written answer, '...the UK spends less on health as a proportion of GDP than most other member states...'[2] In fact, as the table shows, only Portugal and Greece (the two poorest countries in the European Community) spend less than the UK on health care.

In absolute amounts the pattern shown in Table 5.1 is even more striking. In 1982 France spent $996 per person on medical care, the Netherlands spent $851, Germany spent $883, but the UK only spent $539.

Not only does the United Kingdom spend less on health care than most other Western countries; it has increased its spending very slowly over time, while other countries have been increasing their health spending very quickly. In fact there has not been any period since 1950 when health spending in the UK was growing more quickly than the average for other Western countries. In some countries, rapid increases in health costs have been so alarming that they have become major political issues. The health care cost 'explosion' has been a hot topic in America for 15 years; in West Germany there is increasing talk about 'bed mountains'.

Table 5.2 shows by how much the UK has increased its share of GDP devoted to health care between 1960 and 1983, and again makes the comparison with the rest of the European Community.

**Table 5.2**
Changes in the share of GDP devoted to health care between 1960 and 1983

| Country | Per cent |
|---|---|
| France | + 5.0 |
| Netherlands | + 4.9 |
| Ireland | + 4.3 |
| Italy | + 3.5 |
| Germany | + 3.4 |
| Belgium | + 3.1 |
| Denmark | + 3.0 |
| UK | + 2.3 |
| Greece | + 1.8 |
| Portugal | N.A. |
| Spain | N.A. |

Source: Measuring Health Care[3], Table 2, page 12

Only Greece increased its share of GDP devoted to health care by less than the UK over these years. And in the years since 1983 even that has probably changed: Greece began to build a national health service in 1983 and, as a result, devotes considerably more resources to health care.

So, not only does the UK get its health care for a lot less than other comparable countries, but it has also avoided the rapid rises in health care costs which have happened in these other countries. In international terms the NHS is not at all expensive, a fact of which the Treasury, as we mentioned earlier, is very well aware.

**Too bureaucratic?** Bureaucracy and administration are always popular targets of criticism, and the present government has capitalised on this by seeking to imply that cuts in health service spending can be made by reducing bureaucracy, rather than lowering standards of patient care. How realistic is this? The first way of examining this question is to compare administration costs in the NHS with administration costs in other countries' health care systems.

In general, international comparisons demonstrate that the more dependent a health care system is on insurance funding, the higher the administrative costs.[4] The reason for this is a common sense one. Because the NHS is financed centrally, the money to pay for it is simply collected along with other government taxes by the Inland Revenue. Taxes have to be collected anyway for other purposes, so it costs next to nothing to take in what is needed for the NHS and then hand it out through the central departments of health in England and Wales, Scotland, and Northern Ireland to the health authorities.

Because the NHS is basically provided freely to everyone there is no need to have complicated systems of charging people for the use they make of it. The result is a minimum amount of administration or bureaucracy, except of course when patients are charged, as happens with prescriptions, glasses, and dental treatment.

In countries like France, West Germany and the United States, however, much of the money for the health service is collected through insurance schemes. This means that mountains of paperwork are created in assessing each person's insurance premium, collecting subscriptions, checking and updating membership calculating exactly how much to charge people for services they use, and collecting debts.

The result is that in the UK the administrative costs of the NHS are approximately 5 per cent of total NHS expenditure. In France and West Germany the percentage taken up in administration costs is almost twice as big, and in the United States it is at least three times higher, and may be as high as 21 per cent.

Moreover, there is very little evidence that the cost of administration has been going up in the NHS, and quite a lot of evidence that things are well under control. In 1985, for example, the National Association of Health Authorities in England and Wales released the results of their own investigation of NHS bureaucracy.[5] They showed that NHS management costs as a proportion of health authority expenditure had fallen from 5.1 per cent in 1979-80 to 4.4 per cent in 1984-85. The NAHA investigation also showed that expenditure on headquarters administration in health authorities fell by 20 per cent between 1976-77 and 1983-84.

So the government seems to be taking liberties with facts in accusing the NHS of being too bureaucratic. By the standards of most health care systems, the NHS is administered remarkably cheaply and efficiently.

**Out of line?** It has been a major theme of the Government's policy, not only in relation to the economy but also concerning the health service, that we have fallen out of line with other countries and must change to become more like them. This view would suggest that other countries are also trying to increase privatisation in health care and reduce state involvement.

What is the evidence? A survey of policy towards health care in other countries reveals quite the opposite. The general tendency has been for governments to intervene more and more directly in health care. In some countries government involvement has taken the form of legislation to make insurance compulsory, with state benefits available to the less well off. This has happened in Switzerland, Australia, the Netherlands and Canada, for instance. In the United States, as we have seen, the government has been obliged to provide the services which the private companies weren't interested in by introducing its Medicaid and Medicare schemes for the poor and the old in the mid-1960s. As a result, the government financed share of health care spending has risen to almost 50 per cent of all health care expenditure.

In addition, health care costs in private health insurance systems have been rising so quickly that many governments have had to introduce a whole range of compulsory checks and controls to regulate the private insurers. Finally, some countries have simply decided that the best answer to their health care problems is to emulate our system. Italy and Greece have recently set up their own national health services, and Portugal is seriously considering this move.

So, while our Government is trying to expand private medicine and dismantle the NHS, the experience of most other countries is leading them in precisely the opposite direction.

In this very brief look at international comparisons of health care systems we have only examined a few major issues. Even so, the evidence is quite clear that the NHS cannot be accused of excessive bureaucracy or of costing too much. The fact that other countries are moving away from reliance on private health insurance shows how far ahead of its time the NHS was and how big an achievement it still is.

There are, of course, many other reasons why the NHS is a good way of organising health care. Central funding makes it possible, for instance, to try to even out regional inequalities in health services, and to direct money into priority areas such as mental illness, mental handicap and long-term geriatric care. But it seems that even on the grounds which the Government has chosen, there is no evidence to support its desire for a change in health policy.

### References

1. Royal Commission on the National Health Service. Report. Cmnd 7615. London: HMSO, 1979.
2. Written reply. Hansard, April 15 1986, col 361-362.
3. Organisation for Economic Co-operation and Development (OECD). Measuring health care, 1960-1983: expenditure, costs and performance. Paris: OECD, 1985.
4. Maxwell R. Health and wealth: an international study of health-care spending. Lexington: DC Heath, 1981.
5. National Association of Health Authorities in England and Wales (NAHA). Too much bureaucracy in the NHS? NAHA's response to the critics. Birmingham: NAHA, 1985.

# Health services in the USA

Press leaks before and after the 1983 general election gave more than a suspicion that the the Conservatives were again thinking of a fundamental change in the way the NHS is funded.[1] They seemed particularly interested in the American system, so we take a more detailed look at what has happened in the United States.

There are many systems of providing and paying for health care in the United States. Doctors have traditionally sold their services to patients directly on a 'fee for service' basis. Most hospitals are private, being either voluntary 'not-for-profit' or commercial 'for-profit' institutions. Few public hospitals exist. Private insurance schemes exist to cover hospitals' and doctors' fees. The only publicly funded cover is Medicare, for elderly people, and Medicaid for some categories of people on low incomes.

In other words, the private sector provides the greater part of health services in competition, while charity and private hospitals provide a safety net for the people who are least able to pay. This arrangement would obviously appeal to the Conservative Party on ideological grounds but what about the services it provides?

A health service can be judged by its effectiveness and efficiency. Effectiveness refers to the extent to which the aims of health care are met and efficiency to the use of available resources to meet those aims. How far do American health services perform in terms of access to care, meeting health needs and the costs of the system?

**Equal access to care?** In the United States, some people are covered by medical insurance schemes run by their employers, while others have individual policies, which usually cost them more. Medicare and Medicaid were introduced for elderly and poor people. Does this mean that everyone has access to medical care?

Medicaid is intended for people who are below an official poverty line set by the federal government. In practice, individual states are free to decide who is eligible. This has led to regional inequalities. In 1970, eight states excluded over 80 per cent of people below the official federal poverty line. Nine years later, it was estimated that in the country as a whole, between 40 and 67 per cent of people below this poverty line were excluded from Medicaid.[2]

Many large employers provide medical insurance schemes, but small employers are less likely to do so. This means that a substantial minority of the population have no cover at all. This can happen if they do not qualify for Medicaid, are not covered by their employers and cannot afford an individual private insurance scheme. The number of people in this position is not known exactly, but it was estimated in 1982 to be 49 million out of a total population of 211 million.[3]

Even having Medicaid and Medicare does not guarantee access to care. Some people who are covered have difficulty in being accepted as patients because the reimbursements are lower than private fees. It has been estimated that a fifth of doctors see no Medicaid patients and only about half accept people covered by Medicare.[4]

Hospitals are selective too. Fewer than 9 per cent of hospitals account for 40 per cent of care given to people who are on Medicaid or Medicare, or are charity patients or are unable to pay for their care.[5] These are either voluntary 'not-for-profit' hospitals or public hospitals. Compared with private hospitals, these same hospitals care for more people who are either under Medicaid or Medicare or have no cover at all and from whom no fees are recoverable.

Medicare does not provide comprehensive cover. Many of the common problems of elderly people are excluded, as the schemes do not cover hearing aids or dental and opthalmic services. Additional premiums have to be paid to cover doctors' fees and elderly people pay most of the cost of their medicines. The procedure for claiming reimbursement of fees is too complicated for some elderly people who, therefore, miss out. It has been estimated that 70 per cent of applications for Medicare do not lead to full reimbursement because they are incorrect. Other problems are lack of knowledge about entitlements and failure to understand correspondence.[4]

It can be seen, therefore, that in the United States, considerable numbers of people are either partially or almost totally excluded from access to health care.

What about the health care which people do obtain?

**Meeting health needs?** There is no doubt that the best health care in the United States is very good, but is it universally available? Is the care people receive appropriate to their needs?

The type of insurance cover people have undoubtedly influences the type of care they receive. If the doctor is paid on a fee for service basis and the patient pays part of the cost, the doctor is likely to take fewer measures of a preventive nature.[6] A study sponsored by the federal government allocated people at random to one of two insurance schemes, either receiving free care at the time of use or having to pay part of the cost of each item of service. In the paying group, people being treated for high blood pressure had worse control of their blood pressure, and the difference was large enough to reduce their life expectancy.[7]

Unfortunately this research, known as the Rand Health Insurance Experiment, concentrated on a relatively healthy group of the population and followed it over relatively short periods of three to five years. It therefore missed the opportunity of studying the effects of payment systems on those, such as elderly people, whose needs are greater, and of following them over a longer period of time.

This is important as there are considerable inequalities in health within the United States. For example, in one Californian county, the mortality of black people was 58 per cent higher than that of white people.[8] For deaths to which conditions considered to be treatable or preventable contributed, the rates were 77 per cent higher among black people. Another report estimated that the life expectancy of black people in some parts of Georgia is lower than in Kenya.[9]

Competition between several independent sources of care severely restricts the scope for rational planning. The private sector has a poor record in providing care for charity patients and people under Medicare and Medicaid and is more unlikely to provide the less profitable services.

While there is underprovision in some areas, there is overprovision of the more profitable types of care. For example, the numbers of tests and procedures, each of which attracts a fee, is higher in the 'for-profit' hospitals.[10] While some 'not-for-profit' hospitals have a tradition of providing care for uninsured people and a few have a large commitment to people on low incomes, many voluntary hospitals have a similar pattern of work to the profit making hospitals.[11,12] Increasingly, economic developments are forcing many voluntary hospitals to mimic the 'for-profit' sector.[3,13]

There is evidence that financial considerations can have a higher priority than medical needs. For example, eighty three per cent of transfers from the casualty departments of private hospitals to the Cook County, a public hospital in Chicago, were purely for economic reasons. In a quarter of these cases, the patients were medically unstable during transfer. Not surprisingly, they had more complications and fatalities than people admitted directly to the Cook County Hospital.[14]

A national survey of over 6,000 people in 1982 showed that 14 per cent of low income compared with 7 per cent of high income families received their care from outpatient or casualty departments rather than having a personal doctor. People with low incomes were also less likely to have consulted a doctor or to have received preventive care.[15] Two per cent of families in another sample had been refused care because of their inability to pay.[15] All this seriously calls into question the ability of the American system to provide appropriate care to all its citizens.

**Does competition encourage efficiency and keep down costs?** There has been a rapid growth in expenditure on health care in the USA. Americans themselves have recognised that certain aspects of the system of finance have encouraged both inflation and waste in medical spending.

In medicine it is usual for the people who provide the service to decide what the people who use it need. When, in addition, the providers have been paid on an item of service, or piecework, basis but the fees have been charged to a third party in the form of an insurance company or public programme rather than the user, this has encouraged a generous provision of services to people covered by the schemes in question. For example, although its payments are relatively low, certain operations are profitable under Medicaid. As a result, people covered by it have been found more likely to have these operations than the population in general.[3] In another study where all patients waiting for non-emergency operations were referred for a second opinion, a fifth of them were considered not to be in need of the surgery.[16]

As medical care became more profitable, the for-profit commercial hospital sector grew, particularly the chains of hospitals owned by large corporations. Does their greater profitability mean that these hospitals are more efficient? Comparative studies of matched hospitals have shown that the running costs of the 'for-profit' sector were higher than those of public and voluntary hospitals[11,12] and the 'for-profit' hospitals were no better at keeping down costs.[12]

The administrative costs of the 'for-profit' hospitals were higher than those of the voluntary and public hospitals.[12] Overall, administration costs in the United States represent higher proportion of health care spending than they do in our National Health Service. It has been estimated that the costs of administration reached 22 per cent of total US health care spending in 1982, compared with approximately 6 per cent for the NHS.[17]

As the 'for-profit' hospitals charge more for their services and provide a wider range of services,[11,12] it is not surprising that their incomes are higher. It may be that their different medical practices lead to unnecessary treatment. For example, one study found that visits to casualty departments were more likely to lead to hospital admission in 'for-profit' hospitals, compared with other hospitals.[11]

A belief that rising medical costs were propelled by a combination of item of service payments and third party cover has led to alternatives. Prominent among these are Health Maintenance Organisations (HMOs), which have been encouraged by federal government financial policies. HMOs vary in detail, but the feature they have in common is the prepayment of subscriptions to an organisation which contracts in return to provide a range of services to their subscribers on demand. Various devices were later introduced to temper this demand, such as 'co-payments', which in any other country would be called charges. Thus, in contradiction to the traditional systems of payment, the economic incentive is for the doctor to restrict services in order to maximise profits. HMOs are discussed more fully in our next section, in response to the suggestion that they would be a desirable way of organising family practitioner services in the United Kingdom.

Returning to the United States, the 'for-profit' sector adds to its profitability through what has been termed 'cream skimming'. This means concentrating on patients who are able to pay for their services fully and avoiding loss making services. While it is widely recognised that this happens, there are few assessments of the extent of the problem. The concentration of care for poor people into a relatively small number of hospitals is likely to be a reflection of the problem, however.

These hospitals have been particularly badly hit by the recession and recent public spending policy. The rise in unemployment has meant that fewer people are covered by private insurance. At the same time, changes in public policy have reduced the numbers of people covered by Medicaid. A growing number of people are turning to voluntary hospitals for charity care at a time when their resources are threatened by cuts in payments under Medicare and Medicaid. As a result, many of the voluntary hospitals with a history of serving poor people are cutting back on their charity work and even reducing their work under Medicaid.[3,13] The National Association of Public Hospitals records an increase in the 'dumping' of unprofitable cases onto public hospitals.[18] These same public facilities are being curtailed as part of general public expenditure cuts, further damaging the access to and the quality of care provided for many people.

**The American Way.** For all its wealth and its higher spending on health care, the United States has a health care system that is both ineffective and inefficient. It is ineffective in providing access to health care for a large proportion of the people, in meeting health needs and in providing a safety net for people on low incomes. It is inefficient in administrative costs and the use of services. So a move towards the American pattern, whatever the government might claim, is likely to make our health care less not more effective, and less not more efficient.

This brief look at the health care system in the USA gives us some idea of what might be in store if the government pursues its present policies towards the NHS. We now go on to some of the effects these policies have already had by describing recent trends in commercial medicine, privatisation and charges to users of the services.

### References

1. Where health is the way to make a big killing. Guardian. June 4 1983.
2. Brown ER. Medicare and Medicaid: the process, value and limits of health care reforms. Journal of Public Health Policy 1983;4:335-366.
3. Guest DB. Health care policies in the United States. Lancet 1985;2:997-1000.
4. Wattenberg SH, McGann LM. Medicare or 'Medigap'? Dilemma for the elderly. Health and Social Work 1984;9:229-237.
5. Feder J, Hadley J, Mullner R. Poor people and poor hospitals: implications for public policy. Journal of Health Politics, Policy and Law 1984;9:237-250.
6. Manning WG, Leibowitz A, et al. A controlled trial of the effect of a prepaid group practice on use of services. New England Journal of Medicine 1984;310:1505-1510.
7. Brook RH, Ware JE, Rogers WH et al. Does free care improve adults' health? Results from a randomised controlled trial. New England Journal of Medicine 1983;309:1426-1434.
8. Sullivan LW. The status of blacks in medicine. New England Journal of Medicine 1984;309:807-808.
9. Woolhandler S. Medical care and mortality: racial differences in preventable deaths. International Journal of Health Services 1985;15:1-22.

10. Relman AS. Investor-owned hospitals and health care costs. New England Journal of Medicine 1983;309:370-372.

11. Pattison RV, Katz HM. Investor-owned and not-for-profits hospitals. New England Journal of Medicine 1983;309:347-353.

12. Watt JM, Derzon RA, Rogers WH et al. The comparative economic performance of investor-owned and not-for-profits hospitals. New England Journal of Medicine 1986;314:89-96.

13. Salmon JW. Profit and health care: trends in corporatisation and proprietisation. International Journal of Health Services 1985;15:395-418.

14. Schiff RL, Ansell DA, Schlosser JB et al. Transfers to a public hospital. A prospective study of 467 patients. New England Journal of Medicine 1986;314:552-557.

15. Aday LA, Andersen RM. The national profile of access to medical care: where do we stand? American Journal of Public Health 1984;74:1331-1339.

16. McCarthy EG, Finkel ML, Rouchlin HS et al. Second opinions on elective surgery. The Cornell/New York Hospital Study. Lancet 1981;1:1352-1354.

17. Himmelstein DU, Woolhandler S. Cost without benefit. New England Journal of Medicine 1986;314:441-445.

18. Article on publication of survey conducted by National Association of Public Hospitals.Guardian. August 5 1985.

# Commercial Medicine

**'...the Government believes that a thriving private sector strengthens the NHS by relieving some of the pressure on it and by providing an alternative way of developing good practice and improved forms of treatment.'**
**Conservative Research Department, 1986.[1]**

As well as increasing its activities in providing residential accommodation for elderly people and for people with mental illnesses, mental handicaps and other disabilities, the private sector has been playing an increasingly prominent role in providing acute medical care. In this section we describe trends in facilities, involvement by doctors and private medical insurance on which it relies, as well as looking at the patchy information about the type of care provided. It is perhaps as a result of this that more statistics are now available about the activities of the private sector than was the case in the past. These statistics have been used in books written from overtly promotional,[2] mildly approving[3] and critical[4,5] perspectives, as well as in a series of briefings and other reports by NHS Unlimited. All these publications give more detailed information about the recent trends we describe here.

Before 1982, DHSS statistics about numbers of beds in private nursing homes did not distinguish between nursing homes catering for elderly and long stay patients and those which were acute hospitals. DHSS' SBH212 return, introduced in 1982, makes a distinction by identifying 'registered nursing homes with operating theatres' separately.

The Association of Independent Hospitals (AIH) has also started to collect its own statistics and it is these which are shown in Table 5.3. They include information about some private hospitals which are incorporated by royal charter and are not obliged to complete DHSS' returns.

The AIH statistics show that the number of acute private hospitals in the United Kingdom increased from 150 in 1979 to 199 in 1985, with 19 hospitals closing and 68 hospitals opening.[2] The numbers of beds increased by 3281 as a result of building new hospitals and expanding existing ones. A further 11 hospitals and 721

**Table 5.3**
Numbers of beds in acute private hospitals, United Kingdom, 1979-86

| Year | Number of hospitals | Number of beds |
|---|---|---|
| 1979 | 150 | 6,614 |
| 1980 | 154 | 6,978 |
| 1981 | 167 | 7,810 |
| 1982 | 180 | 8,602 |
| 1983 | 187 | 9,245 |
| 1984 | 199 | 10,007 |
| 1985 (July) | 201 | 10,155 |
| (December) | 199 | 9,895 |
| 1986 (October) | 198 | 9,938 |

Source: Association of Independent Hospitals[2,6]
N.B.: There are minor discrepancies between figures quoted by William Laing[2] and those quoted by AIH in 1986[6]

beds were planned to open in 1985-6,[2] but because of closures the total had fallen to 9,938 beds in 198 hospitals by October 1986.[6]

Statistics about pay beds in NHS hospitals are less clearcut as in many cases there are no identifiable beds reserved exclusively for private patients. In fact, health authorities are allotted quotas for the numbers of private patients they can take. As Table 5.4 shows, the quota increased over the years 1979-83 but the average number occupied daily decreased as did the numbers of in-patient stays.[7]

**Table 5.4**
Declining use of pay beds, England, 1979-85

| Year | Authorised quota | Average number occupied daily | Bed occupancy percent | Discharges and deaths |
|---|---|---|---|---|
| 1979 | 2,405 | 1,508 | 62·7 | 91,128 |
| 1980 | 2,405 | 1,514 | 63·0 | 98,565 |
| 1981 | 2,677 | 1,469 | 54·9 | 97,739 |
| 1982 | 2,919 | 1,259 | 43·1 | 80,686 |
| 1983 | 2,987 | 1,264 | 42·3 | 82,938 |
| 1984 | 3,019 | 1,156 | 38·3 | 77,489 |
| 1985 | 2,967 | 1,062 | 35·8 | 70,782 |

Source: DHSS, SBH 212 returns[7]

The growth in numbers of private hospitals between 1979 and 1985 is largely a consequence of 'for profit' organisations entering the market. In 1979, 72 per cent of private beds in the U.K. were in hospitals owned by religious and charitable organisations, and a further 20 per cent were in independent hospitals in many of which local consultants and business people have financial interests.[2,6]

Over the years 1979 and 1986 the growth was in 'for profit' hospitals owned by American groups such as American Medical International (AMI) and Humana, and British groups such as British United Provident Association (BUPA) and

Community Hospitals PLC. Four hospitals run by religious organisations closed between 1979 and 1985,[2] and four more did so from 1985 to 1986 when there was also a contraction in other types of charitable hospital.[6] The numbers of hospitals and beds in each type of ownership are shown in Table 5.5 and Figure 5.1.

**Table 5.5**
Ownership of private acute hospitals, United Kingdom, 1979, 1985 and 1986

| Type of hospital | Number of hospitals | | | Number of beds | | |
| --- | --- | --- | --- | --- | --- | --- |
| | 1979 | 1985 | 1986 | 1979 | 1985 | 1986 |
| Charitable | | | | | | |
|   Religious | 33 | 29 | 25 | 1879 | 1725 | 1508 |
|   Charitable | 21 | 28 | 28 | 1,664 | 2,040 | 1,945 |
|   Charitable groups | 33 | 38 | 37 | 1,149 | 1,555 | 1,483 |
|   Total | 87 | 95 | 90 | 4,692 | 5,320 | 4,936 |
| For profit | | | | | | |
|   American groups | 3 | 24 | 29 | 366 | 1,924 | 2,151 |
|   British groups | 4 | 30 | 34 | 156 | 1,319 | 1,441 |
|   Independent | 56 | 52 | 45 | 1,400 | 1,592 | 1,408 |
|   Total | 63 | 106 | 108 | 1,922 | 4,835 | 5,000 |
| Total | 150 | 201 | 198 | 6,614 | 10,155 | 9,936 |

Source: Association of Independent Hospitals [2,6]

**Figure 5.1 Ownership of private acute hospitals, United Kingdom, 1979 and 1986.**

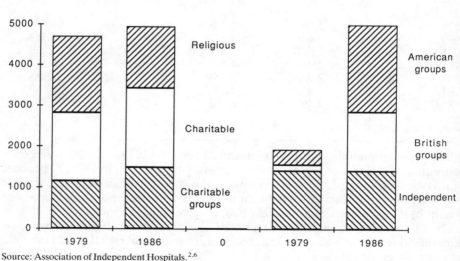

Source: Association of Independent Hospitals. [2,6]

Both NHS pay beds and private hospital beds are very unevenly spread geographically. In 1986, the 4,760 private hospital beds in the four Thames regions accounted for 51.5 per cent of all such beds in England and 47.9 per cent of those in the UK as a whole.[6] Within the Thames regions the beds are concentrated in central London health districts.[4] Pay beds show a similar regional distribution with 46.8 per cent of authorised beds in England in 1983 being in hospitals in the Thames regions or run by Special Health Authorities.[7] The latter are single specialty hospitals linked to London postgraduate institutions.

As Table 5.6 shows, the private medical industry has noticed this uneven distribution. Some of the biggest growth in acute private beds between 1979 and

**Table 5.6**
Private acute hospitals by region and country, 1979 and 1985

| | Number of beds | | Percentage | |
|---|---|---|---|---|
| Region/County | 1979 | 1985 | 1979-85 | 1985-86 |
| Northern | 30 | 144 | 380 | 0 |
| Yorkshire | 341 | 535 | 57 | 6 |
| Trent | 286 | 524 | 83 | − 9 |
| East Anglia | 151 | 332 | 120 | − 3 |
| N. W. Thames | 837 | 1,225 | 46 | 6 |
| N. E. Thames | 1,347 | 1,704 | 26 | − 7 |
| S. E. Thames | 615 | 893 | 45 | 9 |
| S. W. Thames | 762 | 1,001 | 31 | − 10 |
| Wessex | 191 | 630 | 230 | − 8 |
| Oxford | 232 | 470 | 103 | 4 |
| South Western | 346 | 425 | 23 | 0 |
| West Midlands | 336 | 606 | 80 | 0 |
| Mersey | 273 | 312 | 14 | 0 |
| North Western | 283 | 616 | 118 | − 9 |
| England | 6,029 | 9,416 | 56 | − 2 |
| Wales | 202 | 239 | 18 | − 21 |
| Scotland | 265 | 414 | 56 | 0 |
| Northern Ireland | 82 | 86 | 5 | 0 |
| United Kingdom | 6,578 | 10,155 | 54 | − 2 |

Source: Association of Independent Hospitals[2,6]
Population estimates from OPCS Monitor PPI 86/2, General Register Offices, Scotland and Northern Ireland

1985 took place in regions with relatively few pay beds or private beds. Despite this, as Table 5.7 shows, by 1985 there were still considerable regional disparities in the provision of private beds, expressed both as a rate per head of the population and as a percentage of all acute beds in each region.

**Table 5.7**

Private and NHS acute beds by region, 1985

| Region | Private | | | | | |
|--------|---------|---|---|---|---|---|
| | Private Hospitals | NHS Pay bed quota bed quota | Total | Beds per 100,000 population | NHS acute average available daily | Private as percentage of total |
| Northern | 144 | 95 | 239 | 7.8 | 9,698 | 2.4 |
| Yorkshire | 535 | 193 | 728 | 20.2 | 11,168 | 6.1 |
| Trent | 524 | 138 | 662 | 14.3 | 11,665 | 5.6 |
| East Anglia | 332 | 108 | 440 | 22.4 | 5,204 | 7.8 |
| Thames and SHAS | 4,823 | 1,222 | 6,045 | 43.8 | 41,258 | 12.8 |
| Wessex | 630 | 116 | 746 | 26.1 | 7,409 | 9.2 |
| Oxford | 470 | 183 | 653 | 26.8 | 5,863 | 4.4 |
| South Western | 425 | 102 | 527 | 16.7 | 8,672 | 9.8 |
| West Midlands | 606 | 273 | 879 | 17.0 | 13,967 | 5.9 |
| Mersey | 312 | 123 | 435 | 18.0 | 7,092 | 5.8 |
| North Western | 616 | 243 | 859 | 21.5 | 12,472 | 6.4 |
| England | 9,416 | 2,967 | 12,383 | 26.3 | 134,468 | 8.4 |
| Wales | 239 | 49 | 288 | 10.2 | 8,053 | 3.4 |
| Scotland | 414 | 109 | 523 | 10.2 | 20,373 | 2.5 |
| Northern Ireland | 86 | 141 | 227 | 14.6 | 7,105 | 3.1 |
| United Kingdom | 10,155 | 3,266 | 13,421 | 23.7 | 169,999 | 7.9 |

Source: Association of Independent Hospitals. Other data derived from DHSS, Welsh Office, Information Services Division and Northern Ireland Office.

**Doctors and private practice.** Both the regional variations and the changes over time in numbers of private beds are related to the extent to which consultants work in the private sector, but there are no accurate data about the extent to which they do so. It has been estimated that 85 per cent of NHS consultants do at least some private practice and that 200-300 doctors work solely in the private sector.[5]

Some evidence of trends and regional variations in opportunities for private practice can be seen in Tables 5.8 and 5.9. Although in 1983 only 52.1 per cent of consultants employed by the NHS had whole-time contracts, this was considerably higher than the 30.5 per cent who did so in 1970. Even this trend is deceptive, however. Under the conditions of a DHSS circular issued in 1979,[9] NHS consultants with whole-time contracts are now allowed to augment their NHS income by up to 10 per cent through private practice.

This circular also changed the terms of 'maximum part-time' contracts, under which consultants are expected to give 'substantially the whole of their

Table 5.8

**Table 5.8**
Types of contracts held by consultants, England

| Year | Total number | Paid by the NHS Percentage who were | | | Honorary | | Total Total |
|---|---|---|---|---|---|---|---|
| | | Whole time | Maximum part-time | Part time | Number | Percentage of all consultants | |
| 1970 | 9,994 | 30·5 | 65.6 | | 1,258 | 11·2 | 11,202 |
| 1975 | 10,955 | 43·0 | 57.0 | | 1,344 | 10·9 | 12,299 |
| 1980 | 11,774 | 47·8 | 37·1 | 15·1 | 1,712 | 12·7 | 13,486 |
| 1983 | 12,341 | 52·1 | 35·6 | 12·3 | 1,862 | 13·1 | 14,203 |
| 1985 | 12,345 | 52.6 | 36.8 | 10·5 | 1,657 | 11·8 | 14,002 |

Source: DHSS Annual Census of Medical of Medical Manpower. Data for 1970-83 supplied in connection with written parliamentary reply. Hansard July 20, 1984. Data for 1985 in Hansard November 24, 1986, col 130.

professional time' to the NHS, but earn less than the whole time salary. In return for this, no limits are set on the sums they make from private practice. The circular increased the proportion of the full-time salary they earn from 9/11 to 10/11. The much smaller numbers of 'other part-time' consultants are not necessarily heavily involved in private practice. Many hold part-time contracts in more than one region. This is particularly likely to be true of the consultants employed by Special Health Authorities, 65 per cent of whom had part-time contracts in 1985.

Consultants with honorary contracts are, by and large, university employees. While some are employed almost exclusively on research and teaching, many have very full NHS workloads. Although some university consultants do private practice, they are not allowed by the terms of their contracts to profit personally from it. Instead, the proceeds are paid to their institution and usually help fund their research work.

Even when these factors are taken into account, the marked regional variation in the percentage of consultants with whole-time contracts shown in Table 5.9 shows a strong negative relationship with the regional variations in the existence of facilities for private practice shown in Tables 5.6 and 5.7.

**Paying for private care.** Private practice is largely underpinned by the private medical insurance industry. It has been estimated from information in the General Household Survey that about 60 per cent of private in-patient stays and half of private out-patient attendance by residents of Great Britain in 1983 were covered by insurance.[10] This is probably an underestimate. A survey of all stays in private hospitals in 1981 found that 69 per cent were covered by some form of health insurance.[11]

Although for-profit medical insurance companies have made inroads in recent years, the market is still dominated by the 'big three' provident associations, BUPA, Private Patients Plan (PPP) and Western Provident Association (WPA). Of the 4,857,000 people in the UK covered by private medical insurance in 1983, BUPA covered 62.1 per cent, PPP 19.6 per cent, WPA 7.2 per cent, and another five provident associations accounted for 3.5 per cent. In the for-profit sector, Crusader covered 3.2 per cent of those insured and another six companies a further 4.4 per cent.[12]

**Table 5.9**
Types of contracts held by consultants, 1985

| Region | Paid by the NHS | | | | Honorary | | Total |
|---|---|---|---|---|---|---|---|
| | Number | Percentage who were | | | Number | Percentage of all consultants | |
| | | Whole time | Maximum part-time | Part time | | | |
| Northern | 894 | 73.9 | 20.7 | 5.4 | 60 | 6.3 | 954 |
| Yorkshire | 890 | 54.2 | 39.6 | 6.3 | 62 | 6.5 | 952 |
| Trent | 1,013 | 61.2 | 34.0 | 4.8 | 141 | 12.2 | 1,154 |
| East Anglian | 504 | 56.8 | 37.5 | 5.7 | 45 | 8.1 | 554 |
| N W Thames | 959 | 40.8 | 35.8 | 23.5 | 197 | 17.0 | 1,156 |
| N E Thames | 1,262 | 37.8 | 36.0 | 26.2 | 322 | 20.3 | 1,584 |
| S E Thames | 1,036 | 42.4 | 40.9 | 16.7 | 184 | 15.1 | 1,220 |
| S W Thames | 803 | 29.8 | 35.7 | 12.0 | 117 | 12.7 | 920 |
| Wessex | 698 | 52.6 | 41.8 | 5.6 | 62 | 8.2 | 760 |
| Oxford | 599 | 48.4 | 44.6 | 7.0 | 87 | 12.7 | 686 |
| South Western | 750 | 54.4 | 39.2 | 6.4 | 96 | 11.4 | 846 |
| West Midlands | 1,272 | 57.3 | 38.5 | 4.2 | 92 | 6.7 | 1,364 |
| Mersey | 622 | 60.1 | 33.8 | 6.1 | 79 | 11.3 | 701 |
| North Western | 1,137 | 57.1 | 37.6 | 5.3 | 112 | 9.0 | 1,249 |
| Special Health Authorities | 368 | 35.3 | | 64.7* | 286 | 43.7 | 654 |
| England | 12,345 | 52.6 | 36.9 | 10.5 | 1,657 | 11.8 | 14,002 |
| Wales | 750 | 69.6 | 28.3 | 2.1 | 91 | 10.8 | 841 |
| Scotland | 1,764 | 84.1 | 12.9 | 3.0 | 324 | 15.5 | 2,088 |
| Northern Ireland† | 592 | 70.1 | | 17.2 | 75 | 11.2 | 667 |

† 1986   * See text for explanation
Source; Written parliamentary replies, Hansard, April 14, col 289-292, November 24, 1986, cols 29-30, 93-94, 67.

The numbers of subscribers to BUPA, PPP and WPA rose from 632,000 in 1964 to 1,096,000 in 1974, and 2,010,000 in 1984. The corresponding percentages of the UK population covered were 2.3 per cent in 1964, 4.2 per cent in 1974, and 7.8 per cent in 1984.[2] A 'boom' took place between 1979 and 1981 when the numbers of subscribers rose from 1,292,000 to 1,863,000.

The bulk of this growth came not from individual subscribers but from people joining through company schemes. The number of subscribers to 'employee purchase' schemes, in which companies organise schemes for which employees pay, rose from 200,000 in 1979 to 447,000 in 1981, and then fell to 431,000 in 1983. Subscribers enrolling in 'company purchase' schemes in which the employees' subscription, but not necessarily that of their dependents, is paid by the company increased from 625,000 in 1979 to 886,000 in 1981, rising marginally to 968,000 in 1983.[5,13]

Despite these increases in subscriptions and coverage, private medical insurance is still concentrated in the more affluent parts of the country and the social spectrum. Information about private medical insurance was collected in 1982 and 1983 in the General Household Survey.[10,14] This is based on 'standard' economic planning regions rather than NHS regions, so the information in Table 5.10 cannot be compared directly with that in Tables 5.6, 5.7 and 5.9. All the same, the two maps in Figure 5.2 make the geographical association only too evident.

People with private health insurance by no means always use it. In 1983, 42 per cent of in-patient stays and 77 per cent of out-patient attendances by people with

**Table 5.10**
Private medical insurance by standard region, Great Britain, 1983

| | Percentage of people aged 16 and over | |
|---|---|---|
| Standard region | a) who were policy holders | b) who were covered by private insurance |
| England | | |
| North | 2 | 3 |
| Yorkshire and Humberside | 3 | 5 |
| North West | 3 | 6 |
| East Midlands | 4 | 7 |
| West Midlands | 4 | 7 |
| East Anglia | 4 | 7 |
| Greater London | 5 | 8 |
| Outer Metropolitan Area | 8 | 14 |
| Outer South East | 6 | 10 |
| South West | 4 | 8 |
| Wales | 3 | 5 |
| Scotland | 4 | 7 |
| Great Britain | 4 | 7 |

Source: General Household Survey, 1983[10].

Figure 5.2 Private beds in NHS and private hospitals per 100,000 population by NHS region, 1985. Percentage of population aged 16 or over covered by private health insurance, 1983.

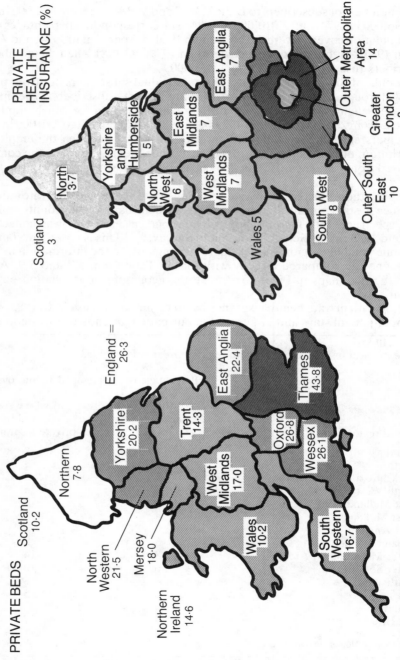

PRIVATE HEALTH INSURANCE (%)

Scotland 3

North 3·7

Yorkshire and Humberside 5

North West 6

East Midlands 7

East Anglia 7

West Midlands 7

Wales 5

Greater London 8

Outer Metropolitan Area 14

South West 8

Outer South East 10

PRIVATE BEDS

England = 26·3

Scotland 10·2

Northern 7·8

North Western 21·5

Mersey 18·0

Northern Ireland 14·6

Yorkshire 20·2

Trent 14·3

East Anglia 22·4

West Midlands 17·0

Wales 10·2

Oxford 26·8

Wessex 26·1

Thames 43·8

South Western 16·7

N.B.: On left hand map, there is a single figure, 43·8, for the four 'Thames' regions combined insurance took place under the NHS.[10]

Despite attempts to extend private insurance coverage among manual workers, Table 5.11 shows that in 1983 it was very low outside the ranks of professional and managerial workers and their dependents. Questions about private medical insurance were asked again in 1986, so it will be possible to see if this position has changed.

**Table 5.11**
Private medical insurance by social economic group, Great Britain, 1983

|  | Percentage of people aged 16 and over | |
| --- | --- | --- |
| Socio economic group | a) who were policy holders | b) who were covered by private insurance |
| Professional | 13 | 23 |
| Employers and Managers | 13 | 22 |
| Intermediate and junior non-manual | 5 | 8 |
| Skilled manual own account non-professional | 2 | 3 |
| Semi-skilled manual and personal service | 1 | 1 |
| Unskilled manual | 1 | 1 |
| All persons | 4 | 7 |

Note: Married women living with their husbands were tabulated according to their husbands' occupations
Source: General Household Survey, 1983[10]

**Care given in private acute hospitals.** It is impossible to comment on trends in surgery in private hospitals. No information is collected routinely on the subject. In an attempt to fill this gap, the DHSS commissioned a survey by the Medical Care Research Unit at Sheffield University who obtained data from 148 of the 153 acute hospitals in England and Wales in 1981.[11,15]

Of the estimated 344,008 patients treated during the year, 28 per cent were having terminations of pregnancy, 92 per cent of which were done in just 15 clinics. A third of the women having terminations came from abroad, mainly from Eire and other parts of Europe. Ninety per cent of people having all other operations taken together came from England and Wales. A few exceptions to this pattern were found: 'residents of England and Wales accounted for only 78 per cent of the women undergoing sterilisation, and, more remarkably, only 22 per cent of the small number of patients receiving major heart surgery, the remainder coming from overseas'.[11]

The study found that 'most of the operations performed on residents of England and Wales were fairly typical of those that characterise NHS waiting lists'[11] apart from the terminations, and also cosmetic operations which accounted for 7 per cent of operations in the survey.

The age structure was, however, different from that of people treated in NHS non-psychiatric hospitals. Excluding women having terminations or using maternity beds, 76 per cent of private hospital patients were aged 15 to 64, compared with 63 per cent of those having in-patient or day case treatment under the NHS.

Information about people using NHS pay beds was included in the Hospital In-Patient Enquiry (HIPE) from 1979 to 1985 and is also included in the new Hospital Episode System.

Data collected in the Sheffield study were combined with those from HIPE to look at the contribution of the private sector to elective, that is non-emergency, surgery to residents of England and Wales,[15] and to compare lengths of stay.[16] It was concluded that the estimated 219,000 people treated in the combined private sector accounted for 13.2 per cent of elective operations on in-patients. Within a selected group of eight operations, the percentage done in the private sector range from 11 per cent for cholecystectomy (removal of the gallbladder) to 26 per cent for total hip replacement.[15]

The percentage of operations done in the private sector ranged from 5.2 per cent in the Northern Region to 21.7 per cent in South West Thames and 21.8 per cent in North West Thames. There was a tendency for people living in regions with fewer private facilities to go for treatment in other areas. It was commented somewhat ominously that 'one of the unresolved issues in health care delivery in the United Kingdom is the extent to which the availability of private facilities should bear on the local distribution of NHS resources'.[11]

Evidence of trends over time was found in eight general practices in and around Oxford in which 6,000 people were asked to list histories of surgical operations they had undergone.[17,18] This found that an increasing proportion of operations were being done privately and marked social class differences in the extent to which this happened. After making statistical adjustments for these and other differences it was found that in the period 1980-83 people were nearly five times more likely to have surgery privately than in 1950-54 and over twice as likely to do so than in 1970-74.[18]

**The privatisation of general practice?** So far the private sector has made few inroads into primary health care, apart from dentistry. It has been estimated that, across the board, ten per cent of all dentists' time is taken up with private practice, but this is decreasing.[2] On the other hand, the emphasis on Health Maintenance Organisations(HMOs) and 'health care shops' in the green paper 'Primary health care, an agenda for discussion'.[19] suggests that the government is interested in them as a move towards privatisation.

Appendix 1 of the green paper compares primary care services here with those in other developed countries. A quarter of the space in its two pages is given over to HMOs. This is completely out of proportion to their importance in the United States, where they cover only 7 per cent of the population, let alone in the world.

It is not surprising that the Conservative Party finds HMOs attractive. In the United States, they are private enterprises selling health services in competition with each other, other private health organisations, and the public sector. At the same time, they can and do contract with the state to provide services. In addition, they have been successful in cutting costs in America.

As a result it is difficult to ignore the suspicion that the proposals made in the green paper for changing the way general practice is financed are intended to make practices more like HMOs. The position of doctors, dentists, pharmacists and opticians as independent contractors to the NHS would make it feasible to graft HMOs onto our primary care system.

At present, GPs are paid in a mixture of ways. These include a basic allowance, a yearly 'capitation' fee for each patient registered and fees for a few specific services such as vaccinations. Additionally, some of their expenses, including rent and staff salaries are reimbursed. Thus a GP's NHS income is the difference between all the allowances and fees, on the one hand, and the costs of running a practice on the other.

The Green Paper suggests alterations which would bring to bear on GPs the market forces experienced by HMOs. These include moving away from direct reimbursement of expenses, increasing the proportion of revenue from capitation fees while decreasing the proportion from allowances and increasing competition for patients between practices. The Green Paper also speculates about the possibility of 'health care shops', which sound like mini HMOs. Privately owned by companies or individuals, they would aim to provide all the services currently divided among doctors, dentists and others.

The government's interest in HMOs is shared by some economists, administrators and doctors.[20,21,22] A report on a British Medical Association seminar on the subject was titled 'Better care — and cheaper'.[22] It is time that the supposed efficiency of HMOs was put into better perspective.

In the United States, HMOs are growing and taking a bigger share of the market because they provide care more cheaply than traditional fee for service institutions.[23] Unlike these, HMOs have an incentive to restrict services because their income is fixed in advance. Thus they save money through lower hospitalisation rates,[23] fewer referrals to surgeons and fewer laboratory tests.[24]

As we have shown in the previous section, American fee for service systems are wasteful and over-provide services. Thus HMOs compare very favourably with them.[25] Similar comparisons may apply within the private sector in the United Kingdom. The conclusions cannot, however, be assumed to apply to comparisons with the NHS which, as we showed earlier is much more economically run than conventional American health care systems. Thus there is not the same scope here for saving money by introducing HMOs. It is likely that savings could only be made by damaging the services provided.

**Other types of private health care.** The private sector makes a varying contribution to other types of health care, as William Laing's review of the market, 'Health Care 1985', shows.[2]

Although, as we have shown in the section on community care, it is providing an increasing number of residential places for people with mental handicaps, the private sector plays a very small role in the care of people with mental handicaps and mental illnesses. More recently, however, there are some signs of commercial interest in providing acute psychiatric care.

In parallel with the increasing numbers of private old people's homes, there has been an increase in the numbers of private nursing homes. Statistics collected since 1982 show increasing numbers of beds designated for elderly people. It is notable that of 38,054 beds in registered private nursing homes in England in 1983, only 8,238 or 22 per cent were in nursing homes with operating theatres.[2,26]

Very little maternity care takes place outside the NHS. Only 1.1 per cent of births in 1985 were in non-NHS hospitals,[27], and a considerable but unknown proportion of these took place in military hospitals. In 1980 only 0.53 per cent of women delivering in NHS hospitals used pay beds, and a further 0.39 per cent used amenity beds.[28] It is likely that this is influenced by the fact that private insurance does not cover normal deliveries.

**Commercial medicine, the NHS ... and health?** 'Co-operation with the independent sector' is a frequently repeated theme in ministerial statements and annual reports of the NHS. In the 1985 report the government expressed the view that 'It makes sense to use the spare capacity in the private sector to tackle the perennial problems of long waiting lists for non-urgent operations'.[29] Health authorities are under increasing pressure to do so in the run-up to the next General Election. Yet when Bath Health Authority used the private sector for children's ENT operations it found that this cost more than treating them under the NHS, and it is likely that other authorities would be in the same position.[30]

The government also wishes to encourage the use of private facilities by NHS patients on a contractual basis. Thus facilities such as the lithotripter provided by BUPA for use by both private and NHS patients at St. Thomas' Hospital are often mentioned with approval.[29]

Pay beds are often praised as a useful source of revenue for NHS hospitals. For example, former health minister Barney Hayhoe claimed that pay beds provided the NHS in England with a revenue of 61 million in 1985-86.[31,32] This statement was, however, made in response to a report by the National Audit Office which concluded that the DHSS' system of setting levels of payment led many health authorities to under-charge private patients.[32,33]

In addition, many health authorities fail to collect all the fees due from private patients. Reports by the National Audit Office have found that this arose either because consultants had not passed payments on to health authorities, or because patients had not paid them, or because patients had not been fully billed for all the relevant items.[34] A survey of 37 health authorities found that 13 of them had a total of uncollected income of £317,000 in 1983-84.[35] In 1986 just one health authority, Bloomsbury, had uncollected debts totalling £318 million, of which £470,000 was owed by foreign residents, embassies and insurance companies.[36]

The role of the private sector in providing types of care not yet available under the NHS is often mentioned. What is less commonly acknowledged is that many private hospitals regularly borrow NHS equipment. Although theoretically they should be charged for it, this does not always happen.[34]

Even when the rules are kept, the 'independent' sector is still heavily dependent on the NHS. In particular, doctors and nurses working in the private sector receive their training in the NHS.

The market forces in the private sector also have a distorting effect on the overall pattern of health care. As we have shown here, private facilities tend to divert health care resources towards the more affluent regions of the country and, more importantly, the upper socio-economic groups. Yet these are the people who are less likely to experience ill health.

Of course, as we pointed out in our pamphlet, 'In Defence of the NHS',[25] more medical treatment is not automatically better than less. A more recent example of this was found in maternity data from the Hospital In-Patient Enquiry.[28] In 1980, 32 per cent of women having their babies in NHS pay beds were induced, compared with 20 per cent of NHS patients. Twenty-four per cent of women in pay beds had instrumental deliveries, and 8 per cent had emergency caesareans, compared with 13 per cent and 5 per cent of NHS patients.

Whether the quality or otherwise of clinical care influences people's decision to go private is a moot point. A survey of patients in two private hospitals asked them what they saw as the principal advantage of private treatment. The most common one, mentioned by about half of the people, was to avoid the NHS waiting list.[37] Yet the waiting time for NHS treatment does not appear to have lengthened particularly in the period just before the boom in the private sector.[38] The ability to choose their own consultant was mentioned by 29 per cent in one hospital and 13 per cent in the other. Perceptions about the quality of care were not frequently mentioned. Indeed, until recently, care under the NHS has been generally considered better than that in the private sector, although recent pressures on the NHS may have meant that this is less true than in the past. A 'Which?' survey in 1984 found little evidence that the private sector compares unfavourably with the NHS in terms of effectiveness or efficiency.[39]

Altogether, there is no evidence to suggest that the growth of the private sector since 1979 has strengthened the NHS. Furthermore, the question of its impact on health has not even been raised.

## References

1. Conservative Research Department. The National Health Service. Politics Today 1986;14:262-280.
2. Laing W. Private health care 1985. London: Office of Health Economics, 1985.
3. McLachlan G, Maynard A (eds). The public/private mix for health. London: Nuffield Provincial Hospitals Trust, 1982.
4. Griffith B, Rayner G, Mohan J. Commercial medicine in London. London: GLC, 1985.
5. Griffith B, Iliffe S, Rayner G. Banking on sickness: commercial medicine in Britain and the USA. London: Lawrence and Wishart, 1987.
6. Association of Independent Hospitals. Survey of acute hospitals in the independent sector, July 1986. London: AIH, 1986.
7. DHSS. SBH211 returns.
8. DHSS. Annual census of medical manpower.
9. DHSS. Pay and conditions of service. Contracts of consultants and other senior hospital medical and dental staff. Personnel memorandum PM (79)11. London: DHSS, 1979.
10. Office of Population Censuses and Surveys, Social Survey Division. General Household Survey 1983. Series GHS No. 13 (SS 457L). London: HMSO, 1985.
11. Williams BT, Nicholl JP, Thomas KJ, Knowelden J. Analysis of the work of independent acute hospitals in England and Wales, 1981. British Medical Journal 1984;289:446-448.
12. Maynard A. The market for private medicine: growth, patterns and constraints. Paper presented to a Financial Times conference, March 1985.
13. BUPA, PPP, WPA. UK private medical care. Provident Association Statistics. London: BUPA, PPP, WPA, 1984.
14. Office of Population Censuses and Surveys, Social Survey Division. General Household Survey 1982. Series GHS No. 12 (SS 457K). London: HMSO, 1984.

15. Nicholl JP, Thomas KJ, Williams BT, Knowelden J. Contribution of the private sector to elective surgery in England and Wales. Lancet 1984;ii:89-92.

16. Williams BT, Nicholl JP, Thomas KJ, Knowelden J. Differences in the duration of stay for surgery in the NHS and private sector in England and Wales. British Medical Journal 1985;290:978-980.

17. Coulter A, McPherson K. Socio-economic variations in the use of common surgical operations. British Medical Journal 1985;291:183-187.

18. McPherson K, Coulter A, Stratton J. Increasing use of private practice by patients in Oxford requiring common elective surgical operations. British Medical Journal 1985;291:797-799.

19. DHSS, Welsh Office, Northern Ireland Office, Scottish Office. Primary health care: an agenda for discussion. Cmnd 9771. London: HMSO, 1986.

20. Enthoven A. Reflections on the management of the National Health Service. Occasional paper 5. London: Nuffield Provincial Hospitals Trust, 1985.

21. Maynard A, Marinker M, Gray DP. The doctor, the patient and their contract III. Alternative contracts, are they viable? British Medical Journal 1986;292:1438-1440.

22. Rice J. Better care and cheaper. BMA News Review. June 1986:29.

23. Manning WG, Leibowitz A et al. A controlled trial of the effect of a prepaid practice on use of services. New England Journal of Medicine 1984;310:1505-1510.

24. Arnould RJ, Debroc LW, Pollard JW. Do HMOs produce specific services more efficiently? Enquiry 1884;21:243-253.

25. Radical Statistics Health Group. In defence of the NHS. London: Radical Statistics, 1977.

26. DHSS. Independent sector hospitals, nursing homes and clinics in England.

27. Office of Population Censuses and Surveys, Birth Statistics 1985. Series FM1, No. 12. London: HMSO, 1986.

28. DHSS, OPCS, Welsh Office. Hospital In-Patient Enquiry Maternity Tables 1977-81. Series MB4 No. 19. London: HMSO, 1986.

29. DHSS. The health service in England. Annual report 1985. London: HMSO, 1985.

30. Deitch R. How much does it cost to cut NHS waiting lists by calling in the private sector? Lancet 1985;i:354.

31. Consultative paper on charges for private patients in NHS hospitals. DHSS press release 86/184. June 10, 1986.

32. McKie D. How badly is the NHS doing out of private practice? Lancet 1986;ii:1451-1452.

33. Comptroller and Auditor General. National Health Service: level of charges for private resident patients. HC 432. London: HMSO, 1986.

34. NHS Unlimited. Private practice: the abuse and neglect of the NHS. London: NHS Unlimited, 1986.

35. Comptroller and Auditor General. Report on 1983/84 accounts of the NHS. London: HMSO, 1985.

36. Sherman J. Unpaid bills top £1 million in London HA. Health Service Journal 1986;96: 1007.

37. Home DA. A survey of patients in the private sector. Hospital and Health Services Review 1984;80:70-72.

38. Coulter A, McPherson K. Waiting times and duration of hospital stay for common surgical operations: trends over time. Community Medicine 1987;9:

39. Timmins N. Private treatment not necessarily best, survey says. Times, June 7, 1984.

# The Contracting Out of Ancillary Services in the NHS.

In 1983 the government issued a circular requiring all health authorities to contract out their catering, laundry and domestic services.[1] A few weeks later the government abolished the Fair Wages Resolution of the House of Commons 1946 which meant that private contractors did not have to pay their employees Whitley Council rates of pay and conditions. Since then health authorities have been instructed by ministers not to include fair wages clauses in their contracts.

In its first term of office the government had issued draft circulars on contracting out, but the slow progress of health authorities in this direction brought the government under increasing pressure from a number of groups. First, the UK proponents of the free market, the Adam Smith Institute, Aims of Industry and the CBI, urged the government to privatise, claiming that this was a superior form of service provision.[2] Secondly, in 1982, the Institute of Directors published a paper which advocated privatization as 'the obvious and most desirable' strategy of breaking the strength of the public sector unions, by reducing union membership and making bargaining arrangements more localised.[3] Thirdly, the contracting companies themselves considered that contracting out in the NHS would provide them with ready and profitable markets, around £175 million a year according to the PR firm of Forsyth.[4]

Fourthly, pressure also came from a parliamentary lobby consisting of some 30 MPs who had shares in the private companies or who were directors or consultants to the firms.[5] Fifthly, contracting out was an attractive policy to a government committed to reducing public expenditure and public employment and weakening the strength of the public sector unions which were considered to be outside the market discipline that had affected the private sector unions. Staffing cuts in the NHS in 1983 were also an impetus to privatisation since contracting out provided a means whereby health authorities could keep within their staffing limits. Lastly, the public administration professional association had also given its approval to the contracting out of ancillary services.[6]

Hence, the political compulsion for health authorities to contract out, despite the lack of evidence that contracting out is cheaper in the long term that the direct production of services. In some cases health authorities have been instructed to award contracts to private companies even when their own in-house bids have been lower.[7]

The government claim that the policy of contracting out leads to 'savings' which can then be spent on 'improvements in services to patients'. However, to date the amount of money saved by contracting out has only been a very small proportion of the total NHS revenue allocation. In 1985, the House of Commons Social Services Committee[8] noted that savings of £9.4 million had been made but thought 'that rather slight, just over 1 per cent of the (annual ancillary) budget', and when compared to the cost of a VAT refund of £27 million made by health authorities to the contractors, 'the savings were hardly a startling success'. The committee concluded that

'This whole exercise, which has been underway for around four years has involved a considerable amount of management time and effort, has caused disruption and discontent not exclusively amongst NHS staff directly employed in these services; and to date has not brought home the bacon.'

In the face of these criticisms the government has hastened the tendering programme and health ministers were given until September 1986 to show substantial savings in the contracting out programme. By the end of September 1986 the Secretary of State for Social Services claimed that over two thirds of services in England had been put out to tender and that £72.7 million had been 'saved' compared with £29 million 12 months before.[9] He also claimed that 'the resources released are now making a substantial contribution to the improvement of patient care'. The total 'savings' at this time represented 0.8 per cent of total

NHS revenue expenditure, and since private contractors had won only 18 per cent of the contracts their contribution was only around 0.27 per cent of this expenditure.

Data obtained from the DHSS by Frank Dobson MP shows a trend for more and more contracts to be won by in-house tenders. For example, between May and November 1985, 78 per cent of cleaning contracts had been won by in-house tenders. Between November 1985 and April 1986, however, 85 per cent of cleaning contracts had been won in-house.[10] The tendering programme has proceeded more rapidly for domestic services for as they are more labour intensive than either catering or laundry there is a greater margin of profit for private companies, or cost reductions by health authorities. 'The margin of cost reduction is the contractor's ability to increase the intensity of labour and cut real wages'.[11]

Private contractors have experienced a number of problems in the tendering process, lack of success in winning tenders, and therefore less profits than initially anticipated, termination of some contracts in mid-term, and others have experienced financial difficulties. A number of companies have found that their tenders were too low and have either withdrawn from the contract (for example Spinneys Ltd at Queen Elizabeth Hospital, Birmingham) or pushed up the costs to the health authority (for example OCS at Addenbrooks Hospital Cambridge [12]). Although there were initially some 40 companies tendering for NHS services, this number is now down to about 16, as several companies have withdrawn from tendering for NHS services altogether (eg Blue Arrow, Reckitts Sunlight and OCS) and others have been subject to takeovers. It is now difficult to apply the term competition to the tendering process, since two companies BET and Hawley dominate the contract cleaning market, holding about half of all government and NHS cleaning contracts, and two thirds of local government cleaning contracts.[13]

These difficulties have led the contractors association, the Contract Cleaning and Maintenance Association, to put pressure on the government to change the rules in favour of the contractors. Accordingly, in January 1986, new instructions which do favour the contractors were issued to health authorities by the DHSS and in a letter to regional chairs by the General Manager of the NHS. The new rules include advice to districts not to investigate the projected workloads, or the terms and conditions of service for employees, nor the expected profit margins of the contractors, the rules have also made it more difficult for districts to terminate a contract when companies fail to provide an adequate service.[14]

After the Griffiths Report in 1983, the new general managers in the NHS were appointed on short term contracts to make 'major improvements in savings', and indeed are now to be paid discretionary additions to salary for the extent to which they achieve change.[15] This is an effective means of ensuring that the tendering programme is complied with and deadlines met, for the general managers'future careers and possible salaries depend on showing they have been successful in this respect. Managers, however, dislike the political compulsion behind the tendering. They dislike the loss of control over their own staff, the loss of commitment and trust of ancillary managers and staff, and the breakup of the ancillary team. These conflicting pressures can be reconciled though by winning an in-house bid, and as we have seen above, the in-house tenders have been increasingly successful in winning the contracts. In order to gain the contract, however, managers have to undercut the unknown bids of the contractors. Trade unions have also found themselves in a dilemma for to preserve their members' jobs and Whitley conditions of pay and bargaining they have often had to be involved in the preparation of the in-house tender.

The government's claim that the contracting out programme contributes cash 'savings' to the NHS and therefore to 'improvements in patient care' can, however, be challenged, for contracting out also generates increased financial and social costs which are not taken into account in claims of short term 'savings'. Financial costs are increased, first, by the hidden costs of administration and staff time involved in the transition process, in the continuous monitoring and evaluation that is required and in emergency measures for contractors' inadequate standards. Secondly, financial costs are increased for other public agencies through higher unemployment and higher health costs. Social costs are generated which are borne by health workers, whose pay and conditions are reduced and by patients through reduced levels and quality of service. Lastly, social costs are also borne by the public through reduced levels of public accountability and a reduction in the social welfare function of the NHS.

**Hidden financial costs.** The amount of money 'saved' by contracting out does not include the direct costs of administrative work in drawing up the specifications and preparing the in-house tender, nor time spent by managers negotiating and consulting with staff and the unions. Neither are the indirect costs of loss of managerial effectiveness during this period included in the savings. Management and other staff time involved in the contracting out period is considerable, and even the accounting firm of Coopers and Lybrand, appointed by the government to find ways of making the terms of contracting more favourable to the contractors, admitted that 'very high levels of staff resource ... have been consumed on the different facets of competitive tendering. This has resulted in a major hidden cost to competitive tendering'.[16]

Contracts can be more inflexible than direct labour and overruns on budgets can increase costs to health authorities. The nature of health care work means that it is difficult to include all contingencies of ancillary work in the specifications. Ancillary managers also recognise that for certain patients there will always be additional but unpredictable amounts of work, but as these are outside routine work they cannot be costed or included in work study data. Any additional work to the contract is then charged to the health authority, again a hidden cost which is not included in the 'savings'.

The principle behind contracting out is that competition is continuous, the contract is only for a limited period of time at the end of which it must be retendered. This assumes that performance during the contract is continuously monitored and evaluated. Evidence from the USA suggests that contracting out, instead of reducing the state's administrative responsibilities and costs, as the free marketeers claim, rather increases these costs. The costs to the public sector shift from that of providing and managing a service to that of monitoring and evaluating a service.[17] Monitoring, supervision and evaluation of contracts, required of both in-house or private contracts, are further costs not included in the 'savings'.

In addition, there have been a high number of instances of contractors failing to provide an adequate service.[18] There are then high administrative costs involved in short term emergency measures which must be taken by health authorities to provide continuity of service. These emergency measures may involve existing NHS staff, assistant managers, supervisers, and nurses working extra hours to get areas up to the required levels of cleanliness.[19] Short term measures may also involve the appointment of additional NHS staff to secure the fulfillment of the contract. For example, Addenbrooke Hospital in Cambridge has had to supply at 'significant additional cost' its own expertise to secure adequate performance from 'the biggest private sector company in the field'.[20] When contracts are terminated because of inadequate performance there are then additional extra costs of retendering and interim arrangements of cover also attract high extra costs.[21]

Additional costs can also arise from redundancy costs when contractors withdraw from a contract prematurely or the contract is terminated by the health authority. Any redundancy costs which occur when a private contractor wins a contract are offset by the health authority from the 'savings' generated by contracting out. If the contract is terminated however the health authority is, under the Wages Act 1986, now responsible for 100 per cent of redundancy costs but has no 'savings' from which to offset them. In one recent case a health authority had to pay £70,000 in redundancies although the contractors pulled out of the contract just five months after it had started.[22]

In those services which are more capital intensive, such as laundry, contracting out to a company means the selling off or closing down of NHS capital equipment. Under the new rules issued in January 1986, companies can now tender for NHS equipment and plant on a lease basis, and at no extra investment cost, companies can hire out laundries equipped at public expense. Should the firm fail to provide an adequate service the facility for the health authority to return to direct labour has been lost, the ancillary team disbanded, and the health authority 'cannot get either the necessary capital allocation from the region or national agreement to rebuild the laundry and the publically owned infrastructure'.[23]

**Costs to other public agencies.** The 'savings' made by health authorites through contracting out ignore the costs to other public bodies through increased redundancies and unemployment. The loss of jobs through contracting out is difficult to quantify as many of the contractors employ part time workers, and reemploy existing NHS staff to varying degrees with rapid turnover of staff. A survey carried out by Michael Meacher's office found that in 1985, in 97 districts where private companies were used, nearly 3;000 health workers had been made redundant. 'The estimated saving for each employee made redundant was 3,400, the net cost to the public through loss of tax and social security benefits was 7,000'.[24]

A privatisation Audit carried out by Sheffield City Council Employment Department in 1985[25] calculated the direct and indirect costs to the public sector caused by contracting out of services in the local authority. Although the Audit was directed to the loss of council jobs, the methods used for calculating the costs of jobs lost apply equally well to the NHS. The calculations included;

Redundancy payments

Loss to the government of income tax and national insurance

Loss of VAT and indirect taxation

Increased unemployment benefits

Increased housing benefits and rate rebates

Increased costs of health care caused by higher unemployment

Increased costs of implementing policies at local and national levels to mitigate the effects of unemployment

Increasing use of social services and other council services

There are also wider social costs to the unemployed and to the community which are difficult to quantify.

Contracting out can also increase the financial costs to the NHS by increasing health costs in a number of ways. Some of these increased health costs are discussed more fully below, they include firstly, increased risks of cross infection from inadequate cleaning, laundry and unhygenic catering. Secondly, contracting out can impose unhealthy and unsafe conditions of work on ancillary and nursing staff, and thirdly, contracting out removes the contributions which ancillary workers have traditionally made to patient care.[26]

**Costs to health workers.** Since ancillary services are labour intensive, costs can only be reduced by intensifying work and lowering the wages and working conditions of staff. This applies to contracts won by in-house tenders as much as the private contractors. As London Health Emergency has said, for ancillary workers the choice is 'heads they win — tails you lose'. The costs of contracting out are, therefore, borne by ancillary workers who suffer redundancies, reduced pay, reduced conditions of work, loss of bonus payments, loss of overtime and shift payments, excessive use of part time work, increased workloads, and reduced access to union protection, although grave abuses of these are more prevalent in the private companies.[27] Although most of the private contractors pay the bottom grade Whitley Council rate, ancillary workers still suffer reduced pay through cuts in their hours of work. The employment of contract workers on a part time basis (one report[28] suggests that 75 per cent of contract cleaners are women working less that 16 hours a week) means that those working under 16 hours a week are not entitled to sick pay, holiday provision, pensions and maternity benefit.

Ancillary work is predominantly work done by women (67 per cent of ancillary staff are women), and in some parts of the country many come from ethnic groups. Women ancillary workers are concentrated on Grades 1-3 of the NHS pay scale, full time workers earning between £72-75 a week in 1985-6. The trade unions argue that 80 per cent of female ancillary workers earn less than 'official'levels of poverty (that is, supplementary benefit levels).[29] So even before a service is contracted out ancillary workers are amongst the lowest paid groups in the country. The effect of contracting out then reduces even more the terms, conditions and security of forms of work carried out by women. At the same time ancillary workers who live in tied hospital accommodation have, under a Rayner 'efficiency' scrutiny which recommended that NHS accommodation be sold, lost their right to that accommodation. If their jobs are privatised as well ancillary workers could find themselves out of both a job and accommodation, a fate which has already occurred to many women in Birmingham and London health authorities.[30]

The government and the private contractors have anticipated that high levels of unemployment will help them to recruit staff at the lower rates of pay and work conditions in the contracts. However, the experience of health authorities working to a contract is one of difficulty in recruiting staff, and this is exacerbated in areas where there are similar, but higher paid, jobs and higher costs of living such as London and the South East of England. As a consequence, turnover of staff is high, there are problems in retaining and training staff and continuity and quality of service are reduced. In Croydon DHA, for example, in the first five months of a cleaning contract by Crothalls, 87 people held 25 jobs.[31]

The process of tendering also has the effect of lowering the trust and morale of staff, so that even if an in-house tender wins a contract, the commitment of health workers to health care and patient orientated tasks is damaged or undermined. If a private contractor wins a tender, the experience and dedication of the workforce built up over many years is lost as the ancillary team is broken up. Ancillary managers are made redundant or are taken on as monitoring officers with no career prospects or pay progression. Once a contract is in operation it becomes socially divisive for the health workers, irrespective of whether it is in-house or private. Ancillary workers are no longer part of the health care team, but become isolated and separated by the factory-like regime of work imposed by the contract which conflicts with the patient care values and priorities of other health care workers. The workloads of nurses are also intensified as they have to take on additional work which the ancillary workers cannot do in the times allowed. A National Audit Office Report on Nursing Manpower found that nurses now spend a considerable proportion (21 per cent) of their time on catering and domestic duties.[32]

**Costs to patients.** The government claims that 'savings' from contracting out are used to improve patient services. But patients also bear the costs of contracting out, for as we have seen, high turnover of staff, the loss of the caring contribution of ancillary workers to patients and additional work for nurses have reduced the continuity and quality of health care. 'Savings' are also made however, by reducing the contract specifications below the previous service standards. Even private contractors claim that cleaning specifications have been drastically revised and reduced to unacceptable levels.[32]

Lower cleaning, catering and laundry standards leaves patients at risk from hospital induced infections. Lowered standards and increased workloads also increases the risks to health workers of skin hazards and other infections, as well as injury and physical strains from heavy manual work. In turn unsafe and unhealthy conditions of work for staff increase risks to patients. In some hospitals private contract standards of cleaning have been so unhygienic that services have not been provided in particular instances, operations, for example, have had to be cancelled because of dirty theatres.[34]

**Costs to the Public.** The limited public accountability that exists at present in the NHS could be further eroded by privatisation. The decentralisation of service provision and the fragmented nature of private sector companies means that these companies are less open to public opinion, political requirements and public policy about the ways in which the NHS should operate.

The criteria applied by the government in its policy of contracting out are narrow economic ones of efficiency, least costs and competition, criteria that are applied by profit seeking organizations. These criteria, however, ignore the different logic of public welfare provision, where, for instance, public policy decisions have to be made on the basis of social welfare criteria orientated towards needs, as well as budgetary constraints. By introducing market criteria into the NHS, multiple social welfare aims are ignored and self interst, profits and competition promoted. Ignoring the longer term social costs of contracting out may ultimately be more costly to society, as public health care is impoverished and health standards of the population decline. In the long term the impoverishment of the NHS could lead to increased social inequality as those who can afford it will buy private health, leaving a residual public health sector for poorer and more vulnerable people in the community.

**Conclusion.** The evidence discussed above has suggested that the government's policy of contracting out has not so far, and will not in the long term, make substantial 'savings' to the total NHS revenue allocation. The amounts 'saved' to date have been a small proportion of the NHS budget. Moreover, cash 'savings' achieved by contracting out generate increased public expenditure through hidden administrative costs, increased monitoring and evaluation costs, through contractors' failures and cost overruns, as well as increased costs to other public agencies. By presenting contracting out as a process that can contribute improvements to patient care, the government is obscuring the real reductions in standards of service and health care and the lowering of the terms and conditions of work for staff. The costs of contracting out are borne by patients and health workers, and women in particular bear the brunt of the costs as ancillary workers and the main users of the services. Contracting out has also caused disruption, uncertainty, and loss of morale and trust of NHS staff. The introduction of market criteria into the NHS has reduced social welfare by conflicting with and adversely affecting the continuity and quality of health care.

**References.**
1. DHSS Circular HS(83) 18. Sept. 1983.
2. M. Forsyth, 'Reservicing health', The Adam Smith Institute 1982. CBI 'Report of CBI Working Party on Government Expenditure', 1981; London.
3. Institute of Directors 'Some thoughts on the tasks ahead' 1982.
4. The Guardian 5.7.84.
5. The Tribune Group, 'The welfare state under the tories' 1985. See also the COHSE survey cited in The Health Service Journal 5.6.86 p.745.
6. R.I.P.A. 'Contracting out in the NHS' 1977.
7. Labour Research May 1984, also The Guardian 7.9.83.
8. House of Commons Social Services Committee 1985 p. xix-xx.
9. Hansard 25th Nov 1986 cols. 214-230.
10. The Health Service Journal 24.4.86 p.549.
11. P. Morris 'A union's view of privatisation' Health Service Manpower Review 1984; 8-10.

12. HSJ 31.7.86 and Labour Research Aug 1986.
13. Labour Research Nov 1986.
14. DHSS 'Competitive tendering. Further advice for health authorities' Dec, 1985. Also 'Patients or profits' London Health Emergency June 1986.
15. DHSS 'NHS Management Inquiry Report' (Griffiths Report), 1983 and DHSS 'General managers: arrangements for remuneration and conditions of service', May 1986.
16. Coopers and Lybrand Associates, Health management update file, 1986.
17. M. Schlesinger, R. Dorwart and R. Pulice 'Competitive bidding and states purchase of services' Journal of Policy Analysis and Management, 1986; 5:2:245-263.
18. Labour Weekly 21.6.85. See also TUC 'Contractors' failures: the privatization experience', 1985, and 'More contractors failures' 1986. Also NUPE Privatization Fact Sheets Series E No. 3 (5.7.84), No. 8 (6.6.85) and No.9 (10.3.86).
19. Public Service Action No.22 May 1986.
20. The Health Service Journal 20.6.85 p.773.
21. Public Service Action, 1986; 22:1986.
22. HSJ 31.7.86.
23. Hansard 14.3.86, col. 1365.
24. The Guardian 11.6.85.
25. Public Sector Team, Sheffield City Council Employment Department 'The public cost of private contractors', 1985.
26. NUPE Privatization Fact Sheet, No.18, 13.5.85.
28. Key Note Publications, 'Contract Cleaning', 1986. Also Bargaining Report Labour Research Department BR No. 53 July 1986.
29. Ancillary Staffs Council Trade Union Side 'Health workers pay, time for action', Nov. 1985.
30. The Guardian 24.10.86 and Public Service Action, 1986; 25.
31. The Guardian 13.3.86.
32. House of Commons, 14th Report, Committee of Public Accounts 'Control of nursing manpower' 1985-6.
33. NUPE Privatization Fact Sheet No. NHS10 7.11.86. Also T. Paklett of Price Waterhouse 'Competitive tendering — the view from no-man's land', Health Manpower Review, 1986; 11:4:16-8.
34. The Guardian 2.4.85.

# Increased charges to patients

Another form of privatisation, which could be termed 'back door' privatisation, is the frequent increases in the real value of charges to patients since the Conservative Party took office in 1979. In this section, we look at the extent of charges, who pays and who is exempt and, finally, arguments for and against making direct charges to users of the health services.

One of the original aims set out in the 1944 white paper, 'A national health service' was 'to provide the service free of charge (apart from certain charges in respect of appliances)'.[1] This was the position when the NHS came into being in 1948, but it did not last for long. In 1949, legislation was passed permitting charges for prescriptions, but it was not implemented.

Further legislation in May 1951 enabled charges to be made for dentures and glasses. It was put into effect straight away, with charges of a guinea (£1.05) for dentures and ten shillings and sixpence (52.5p) for glasses. Aneurin Bevan, who had been Minister of Health at the start of the NHS and was now Minister of Labour, resigned from the cabinet in protest, along with Harold Wilson.

In 1952, the Conservative government imposed the prescription charges which had been made possible by the 1949 legislation. Apart from a brief period in the mid 1960s when a Labour government dropped charges for prescriptions, charges have, as Aneurin Bevan predicted, remained in force under both Conservative and Labour governments.

The contribution of charges to the total cost of the NHS has, however, tended to rise when the Conservative Party has been in office and fall under Labour, as Figure 5.3 shows.[2] This is an updated version of a graph in the Open University book, 'Caring for health, dilemmas and prospects', which contains a fuller description of what happened.[3] As can be seen in Figure 5.3 and Table 5.12, in the

**Figure 5.3 Percentage of the total cost of the NHS in the United Kingdom derived from patient charges 1949-85.**

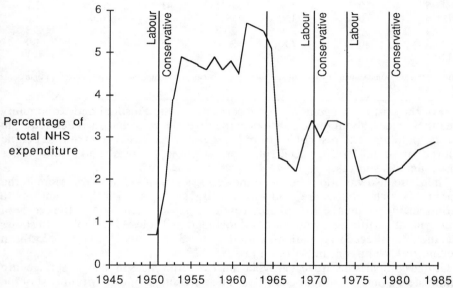

Source: Central Statistical Office. Annual abstract, various years (Prior to 1974, cost of community health services is not included).

1980s, the Conservative government's policies ran true to form. The percentage of the total cost of the NHS in the United Kingdom which is derived from charges rose from 2.0 per cent in 1978-79 to 2.8 per cent in 1983-84, and 2.9 per cent in 1984-85.[4]

Data from the Dental Estimates Board published by the British Dental Association showed a continuing rise from 27.6 per cent in 1983-84 to 30.7 per cent in 1985-86, of the percentage of the total cost of general dental service treatment in Great Britain which came from charges.[5]

**Who pays?** The contribution of charges is not evenly spread across the services. In 1984-85, only 0.77 per cent of current spending on the Hospital and Community Health Services came from charges, compared with 8.8 per cent of spending on the Family Practitioner Services. Within these services, income from charges accounted for 7.8 per cent of the cost of the pharmaceutical services and 25.2 per

**Table 5.12**
Percentage of expenditure on the NHS derived from charges to users, United Kingdom.

| | | Income from charges as a percentage of spending on service | | | | |
|---|---|---|---|---|---|---|
| | | Family practitioner services | | | | |
| Year | Hospital and community health service (current) | Pharma- ceuticals | Dental services | Opthalmic services | Total | NHS Total |
| 1974-75 | 0.75 | 7.3 | 19.1 | 41.2 | 8.2 | 2.7 |
| 1978-79 | 0.65 | 3.2 | 19.7 | 33.3 | 6.0 | 2.0 |
| 1983-84 | 0.78 | 7.6 | 26.3 | 26.7 | 8.8 | 2.8 |
| 1984-85 | 0.77 | 7.8 | 26.4 | 25.2 | 8.8 | 2.9 |

Source: Derived from Annual abstracts of statistics[2,4], and personal communication giving corrected figures for 1983-84 and 1984-85.

cent of the cost of the general dental services. In the Hospital and Community Health Services, about three quarters of the revenue from charges is derived from private patients. The rest comes from charges to overseas visitors and to people injured in road traffic accidents, prescription charges and from other miscellaneous sources.

There are also variations between the countries of the United Kingdom in the extent to which services are paid for by charges to users. Table 5.13 shows the variation in payments for pharmaceutical services, including the cost of prepayment certificates, which are not included in Table 5.12. Table 5.13 shows that the total direct cost to patients varied from 5.3 per cent of the cost in Northern Ireland to 8.4 per cent in Scotland in 1985-86.[6]

Global comparisons are less easy, because of differences in the way services are administered in the different countries. The percentage of the current cost of the Hospital and Community Health Services which came from charges in 1983-84 was 0.85 per cent in England, compared with 0.25 per cent in Wales. This could reflect differences in the amount of private practice.

The extent to which the cost of social services is met from charges is even more variable, as it reflects differences between local authorities both in the provision of services and the levying of charges. In England as a whole, the percentage varied from 10.6 to 11.8 per cent between 1975-76 and 1979-80. It then rose to a higher level and between 1980-81 and 1984-85, it ranged from 13.9 to 15.5 per cent.[7] Much of the income was derived from charges in respect of users of residential accommodation. This accounted for 82 per cent of receipts in 1984-85.[8] Charges for home helps and meals on wheels made up a further 6 and 4 per cent respectively.

**Who is exempt?** Exemptions from charges for prescriptions and dental treatment and eligibility for vouchers for glasses are determined nationally. The categories of people who are entitled to free prescriptions, free dental treatment and

**Table 5.13**
Number and cost of prescriptions dispensed under the NHS in 1985-86

|  | England | Wales | Scotland | Northern Ireland | United Kingdom |
|---|---|---|---|---|---|
| Prescriptions dispensed, millions | 341.4 | 25.8 | 35.9 | 12.9 | 416.0 |
| Percent exempt from charges† | 81.1 | 85.8 | 80.5 | 87.7 | 81.5 |
| Average gross cost, £ | 4.89 | 4.62 | 5.11 | 5.03 | 4.90 |
| Total cost £ million | 1669.4 | 119.0 | 183.4 | 65.0 | 2036.8 |
| Payment from public funds, £ million | 1540.2 | 111.0 | 167.9 | 61.6 | 1880.7 |
| Direct charges to patients, £ million | 115.7 | 6.9 | 14.0 | 3.2 | 139.8 |
| Revenue from sale of prepayment certificates, £ million | 13.5 | 1.1 | 1.5 | 0.26 | 16.4 |
| Total direct cost to patients | 129.2 | 8.0 | 15.5 | 3.4 | 156.2 |
| Percentage of cost paid by patients | 7.7 | 6.7 | 8.4. | 5.3 | 7.7 |

†Includes those covered by prepayment certificates
Source: Hansard, written parliamentary replies[6]

vouchers for glasses are set out in DHSS leaflets P11, D11 and G11 respectively. While there are some differences in detail between the three, they all apply to children and school students, people on supplementary benefit or low incomes and women who are pregnant or who have had a baby within the past year.

The vouchers were introduced in July 1986 to replace National Health glasses, to which some people had been entitled free of charge. It is claimed that the maximum voucher will cover the cost of a pair of glasses, but it remains to be seen whether the value of vouchers keeps pace with prices.

Everyone of pensionable age is entitled to free prescriptions. The increase in the numbers of elderly people and people on supplementary benefit have led to increases over time in the percentage of prescriptions exempt from charges. In England, this rose from 60.3 per cent in 1974 to 64.8 per cent in 1979 and 79.2 per cent in 1984.[7] There are also regional differences, ranging from 74.4 per cent in the Oxford Region to 82.3 per cent in the Mersey Region in 1984.[9] These figures do not include prescriptions for people with prepayment certificates. These accounted for 5.0 per cent of prescriptions in 1980 and 5.5 per cent of of those in 1984.[7] Thus it can be seen that increasing amounts of money are being collected from decreasing numbers of people. This has been done through the large increases in prescription charges shown in Table 5.14.

The numbers of people exempt from dental charges decreased as the age limit was dropped from 21 to 16. This more than offset exemptions on grounds of low income, as Table 5.15 shows. In 1984, 42.4 per cent of courses of dental treatment were exempt from charges and a further 17.5 were free check ups for people who

**Table 5.14**
Selected patient charges in the NHS 1979-86, £

| Date | Prescription charge (per item) | | Dental treatment charge (maximum per course of routine treatment) | |
|---|---|---|---|---|
| | Nominal | Real* | Nominal | Real* |
| May 1979 | 0.20 | 0.20 | 5.00 | 5.00 |
| July 1979 | 0.45 | 0.42 | 7.00 | 6.60 |
| April 1980 | 0.70 | 0.58 | 8.00 | 6.62 |
| December 1980 | 1.00 | 0.78 | 8.00 | 6.26 |
| April 1981 | 1.20 | 0.89 | 9.00 | 6.65 |
| April 1982 | 1.30 | 0.88 | 13.00 | 8.78 |
| April 1983 | 1.40 | 0.91 | 13.50 | 8.77 |
| April 1984 | 1.60 | 0.99 | 14.50 | 8.95 |
| April 1985 | 2.00 | 1.18 | 17.00 | 9.99 |
| April 1986 | 2.20 | 1.20 | | |
| April 1987 | 2.40 | | | |

* Calculated by deflating the nominal charge by the Monthly Retail Price Index.
From April 1985 patients are charged 40 per cent of any excess of the cost of treatment over £17 in addition to the full cost of treatment up to £17, up to a maximum of £115.
Sources: York Family Practitioner Committee personal communication. Annual Abstract of Statistics.[2] DHSS leaflets, Birch S, Health Services Journal.[15]

---

**Table 5.15**
Courses of dental treatment exempt from charges, England and Wales, 1977 and 1984.

| | 1977 | | 1984 | |
|---|---|---|---|---|
| | Number | Per cent | Number | Per cent |
| Courses exempt | | | | |
| Low income | 556,840 | 2.0 | 2,106,170 | 6.5 |
| Expectant and nursing mothers | 765,760 | 2.7 | 945,550 | 2.9 |
| Still at school | 12,085,880 | 42.7 | 10,791,140 | 33.1 |
| Total exempt | 13,408,480 | 47.4 | 13,842,850 | 42.4 |
| Check up only for people not exempt | 3,698,460 | 13.1 | 5,714,670 | 17.5 |
| Total courses of treatment | 28,276,860 | 100.0 | 32,608,200 | 100.0 |

Source: Annual reports of Dental Estimates Board, 1977 and 1984.[10]

---

were not exempt.[10] Given the extent of unmet need for dental treatment among elderly people,[11] it is disturbing to find that in 1984, only 12.2 per cent of courses of treatment for people aged 65 and over were given to people who claimed exemptions of the grounds of low income.[10]

**Could we afford to abolish charges?** The Conservative government justifies the principle of keeping and increasing charges on two grounds. Firstly, it says it cannot afford to abolish them. This ignores the possibility of making savings in other ways, which would also improve the services.

In the case of pharmaceuticals, savings could be made through generic substitution, which is discussed in some detail later. Estimates of possible savings from this range from 100 million to 200 million, depending on the extent to which generics are substituted for branded drugs and whether new generics are introduced to replace branded products which are out of patent.[12] A further 200 million could be saved if action was taken against the hidden profits produced by transfer pricing.[13] As we show later, there would be benefits in extending the selected list principle to other classes of medicines. This would produce savings even if, unlike those introduced by the present government, the lists were drawn up with the interests of patients as the prime consideration.

Changes in and affecting the dental services would need to have a longer time scale. There are some tasks which dental auxillaries could do as well as dentists at lower cost. Dental auxillaries are licensed to do dental health education, apply preventive agents such as pressure sealants and fluoride, and scale and polish teeth as well as filling them. Dental therapists can do fillings after two years of training.

The DHSS has already called for a ten per cent reduction in the numbers of dental students and the British Dental Association has called for a 10 to 15 per cent cut.[14] The suggestions for cuts have been made because some dentists are underemployed. If more auxillaries are used and dental health continues to improve, we will need fewer dentists than at present. A reduction of 50 per cent in the numbers of dentists in training would still result in an overall increase as more dentists would qualify than retire each year.

Employing more dental health educators and policy changes in other areas could contribute to a shift towards preventing the need for dental treatment. Introducing food policies, in line with British Medical Association and NACNE guidelines, to reduce sugar consumption by half, and fluoridating water supplies would both lead to signifigant improvements in dental health.

The second argument used against abolishing charges is that this would help the people who are better off. This ignores the fact that charges fall on those people who are prescribed medicines, use the dental service, or wear glasses without distinguishing between people who are just above the exemption level and those who are much better off. While we support the principle that people's contribution towards the costs of the NHS should be related to their ability to pay, this can be achieved much more effectively and fairly through the tax system than by making charges at the time when the services are used.

In contrast to this, the Conservative Party's intentions for a sizeable increase in charges after the general election are set out very clearly in the 1987 public expenditure white paper.[16]

### References

1. Ministry of Health, Department of Health for Scotland. A national health service. Cmd 6502. London: HMSO, 1944.

2. Central Statistical Office. Annual abstract of statistics. London: HMSO, various years.

3. U205 Course Team. Caring for health: dilemmas and prospects. Milton Keynes: Open University Press, 1985.

4. Central Statistical Office. Annual abstract of statistics 1987. London: HMSO, 1987, and personal communications giving correct data for 1983-84 and 1984-85.

5. British Dental Association. Dental health services: an opportunity for change. Response of the British Dental Association to the government's green paper on Primary Health Care. London: BDA, 1987.
6. Written replies. Hansard, December 12 1985, col 743-744, January 19 1987, col 395-396, 421-424, February 23 1987, col 134-136.
7. DHSS. Health and Personal Social Services Statistics for England. London: HMSO, various years.
8. House of Commons. Fourth report from the Social Services Committee, Session 1985-86. Public expenditure on the social services, volume II. HC 387-II. LOndon: HMSO, 1986.
9. Central Statistical Office. Regional Trends 1986. London: HMSO, 1986.
10. Dental Estimates Board. Annual reports 1979 and 1984. Eastbourne: Dental Estimates Board.
11. Smith JM. Oral discomfort — a necessary feature of old age? Age and ageing 1979; 8 :25-31.
12. Collier J, Macfarlane AJ, Shulman J. Prescription charges. Lancet 1986; i: 967.
13. Shulman J, Rentoul J. Profits of sickness. In: Who cares? New Statesman report 8. London: New Statesman, 1984.
14. British Dental Association Manpower Committee. Second report 94/86, London: British Dental Association, 1986.
15. Birch S. Prescription for privatisation. Health and Social Services Journal 1985: 576-577.
16. The government's expenditure plans, 1987-88 to 1989-90. Cm 56-II. London: HMSO, 1987.

# Equal Opportunities For NHS Staff?

Marked inequalities are to be found in the employment patterns of women and members of black and ethnic minority groups in the NHS. The DHSS publishes statistics on the proportion of women who are doctors, dentists and nurses and for place of birth of doctors, but for other occupational groups we have to rely on special studies of employment patterns. One such study[1] of a London Hospital (Table 5.16) shows considerable occupational segregation for men and women and by place of birth. As the report observed, 'Each occupation is clearly dominated by one group, delineated according to sex and ethnic origin'. This also happens within occupational groups.

That the NHS does show clear discrimination in employment patterns was also clearly highlighted in a survey of 2,000 doctors carried out by the Policy Studies Institute (PSI) in 1980, the results of which were published in the book 'Overseas Doctors in the National Health Service'.[2] This discrimination displays itself at all levels. DHSS figures show that overseas doctors formed about 28 per cent of the total of all hospital doctors in 1985.[3] About 76 per cent of overseas doctors were

**Table 5.16**
Occupational group of workers at a London hospital, by place of birth and sex

|  | Ancillary & Maintenance | Clerical | Professional & Technical | Nurses & Midwives | Doctors |
|---|---|---|---|---|---|
|  | % | % | % | % | % |
| Male British born | 11 | 5 | 17 | 1 | 43 |
| Male overseas born | 23 | 4 | 12 | 2 | 22 |
| Female British born | 11 | 75 | 54 | 28 | 25 |
| Female overseas born | 55 | 16 | 17 | 69 | 10 |

Source: L. Doyal et al 'Migrant Workers in the National Health Service' Report prepared for the SSRC by the Department of Sociology, Polytechnic of North London, June 1980[1].

from the New Commonwealth. However this 28 per cent were not equally distributed across the grades of the profession, as table 5.17 indicates, and table

**Table 5.17**
Overseas doctors as a percentage of hospital medical staff, England, 1975 and 1985

| | Percentage of doctors who were born outside the United Kingdom and Irish Republic | |
| --- | --- | --- |
| Grade | 1975 | 1985 |
| Consultant | 14.4 | 18.9 |
| Senior Registrar | 28.1 | 18.3 |
| Registrar | 57.2 | 44.4 |
| Senior House Officer† | 59.0 | 36.4 |
| All hospital medical staff | 35.2 | 28.0 |

† For 1975, includes post-registration House Officers
Source: Health and personal Social Services Statistics for England, 1986[3]

**Table 5.18**
Percentage of overseas doctors in selected specialities, 1981

| | Percentage of doctors from overseas | | | |
| --- | --- | --- | --- | --- |
| | Geriatrics | Mental illness | General surgery | Anaesthetics |
| Consultant | 43.4 | 24.3 | 8.6 | 16.2 |
| Senior Registrar | 47.3 | 37.0 | 11.7 | 19.6 |
| Registrar | 83.6 | 58.1 | 43.2 | 53.3 |
| Senior House Officer | 62.4 | 46.6 | 58.9 | 52.4 |

Source: Commission For Racial Equality, 1974, 1987[4]

5.18 highlights that overseas doctors tend to be concentrated, when they do reach the higher levels, in the less popular branches of the profession.

In the PSI study 38 per cent of the sample were found to be born overseas. However 45 per cent of UK born doctors were consultants compared with only 9 per cent of Asians. The study also showed that a comparison of doctors of similar age, qualifications and language skills, still showed a gross disparity between British and overseas qualified doctors. As Steve Watkins says 'The medical profession clearly uses black doctors as pairs of hands to do the work which white doctors do not want to do. It measures the status of an hospital by the proportion of its staff who are white, the status of a speciality by the extent to which it can fill its posts without resorting to the use of black doctors, and the status of a job by the number of white applicants it receives. It barely conceals these criteria for judgement'.[15] More recently, and on the subject of selection of students for London medical schools, a study of names of undergraduate students showed that for each school there was a relatively fixed proportion of non-European students over the period 1982 to 1984 and that there were marked differences between the schools (varying between 5 per cent and 16 per cent). The authors went on to state that 'The results suggest that racial and sexual discrimination operates when students are selected for medical education'.[16]

**Doctors.** DHSS statistics show that in 1985, 23.6 per cent of all hospital medical staff were women.[3] As Table 5.19 shows, however, only 13 per cent of consultants are women, whilst nearly a third of senior house officers are women.

The proportion of women in different specialities varies widely (Table 5.20). At consultant level women account for 0.6 per cent of general surgeons but form a higher percentage in the less powerful and less prestigious specialities. For example, women account for 18.8 per cent of consultants in anaesthetics, and 16.9 per cent of consultants in mental illness. Over the last five years, 40.3 per cent of newly appointed consultants in Child and Adolescent Psychiatry were women.[7] As the DHSS points out this speciality involves less night and on call work (and therefore fits better with childcare responsibilities) 'but may also reflect a realistic appraisal by women doctors of their prospects for progression in certain of the acute specialities'.[7]

In most specialities at most grades women are still in a minority. However the

**Table 5.19**
Women as a percentage of hospital medical staff, England 1975 and 1985

| Grade | Percentage of doctors who were women | |
| | 1975 | 1985 |
| --- | --- | --- |
| Consultant | 8·8 | 13·0 |
| Senior Registrar | 17·7 | 24·9 |
| Registrar | 17·0 | 22·3 |
| Senior House Officer† | 20·6 | 32·3 |
| All hospital medical staff | 16·6 | 23·6 |

† For 1975, includes post-registration House Officers
Source: Health and Personal Social Services Statistics for England, 1986[8]

**Table 5.20**
Percentage of women in selected specialities, England and Wales, September 30, 1985

| | Percentage of doctors who were women | | | |
| | Geriatrics | Mental illness | General surgery | Anaesthetics |
| --- | --- | --- | --- | --- |
| Consultant | 11·5 | 14·0 | 0·6 | 18·8 |
| Senior Registrar | 23·0 | 31·0 | 2·2 | 25·9 |
| Registrar | 12·9 | 36·8 | 4·7 | 28·8 |
| Senior House Officer | 31·8 | 41·1 | 9·1 | 36·4 |

Source: DHSS Medical 'manpower' statistics[7]

**Facing the Figures**

percentage of women entering medical schools in this country has been increasing over the last 20 years from 24.2 per cent in 1967/68 to 44.3 per cent in 1984-5.[7] It is only very recently though that some medical schools have started recruiting equal numbers of male and female students.

Most people think that there is no longer any evidence for direct discrimination in the selection of women medical students, partly because of the 1975 Sex Discrimination Act. Indirect discrimination still exists, though, particularly in the attitudes of society, schools and families that shape expectations and create pre-selection discrimination before women even think of becoming a doctor.

A BMA publication entitled 'Becoming A Doctor' stated : 'Perhaps most medical schools faced with the choice of giving the last available place to a boy or a girl of equal merit, would give it to a boy — for the only reason that the girl might stop practising as soon as she got married'. This pamphlet was published from 1962 to 1983. Although it was revised five times, the advice quoted above was still in print in 1976.

Many women are unable to comply with the basic entrance qualifications because their schools do not supply adequate teaching in the necessary subjects or, more importantly, because girls are discouraged from studying those subjects. Once qualified, women are unable to comply with the demands of a medical career because these conflict with the demands of their traditional roles of wife and mother. The choice between this and the achievement in traditional male spheres such as science and medicine is what is meant by pre-selection.

A study of women students at King's College Hospital Medical School noted the increasing numbers of women accepted to study medicine. It showed that women students in general had higher qualifications on entry and did significantly better in the final exams. In spite of this, though, only 30 per cent of women acquired higher qualifications after qualifying compared with 42 per cent of men. Female doctors were less likely to be in paid employment because of family commitments, but only 20 per cent of the cohort were not practising at a later follow up.[8]

**Nurses.** A study of overseas nurses in Britain[9] showed that an average of 9 per cent of all NHS hospital nurses in 1971 were 'immigrant' i.e. born in a developing country and arriving in the UK after the age of 16. 'Immigrants' formed 20 per cent of pupil nurses, 15 per cent of midwives and 14 per cent of student nurses. At sister and senior level, however, proportions of immigrant staff dropped to 4 per cent and 1 per cent. It also appears that black nurses are more likely to be found in certain specialities such as geriatrics and mental health. These tend to be less popular careers for which lower academic standards have been set by schools of nursing. Cheryl Hicks' article on racism in nursing makes depressing reading.[10] Quoting General Nursing Council figures she points out that nearly one third of 1982's overseas learners were in psychiatric and mental handicap training. She also points out how overseas recruits are pressurised into SEN, rather than SRN training and that black nurses find it difficult to obtain promotion.

Nurses are the largest category of NHS employees and in 1984 84.7 per cent of full-time and nearly all part-time nurses in England were women.[3] Yet as Table 5.21 shows women accounted for a lower percentage of qualified than enrolled and other nurses. This is perhaps not surprising given the higher percentage of women among pupil than student nurses.

**Table 5.21**
Percentage of overseas workers at a London hospital in each occupational group

| | | |
|---|---|---|
| All nurses | 84.7 | 98.8 |
| Qualified | 78.5 | 98.0 |
| Enrolled | 87.2 | 99.1 |
| Others | 86.2 | 99.1 |
| Students | 89.6 | 98.8 |
| Pupils | 93.2 | 100.0 |

Source: Health and Personal Social Services Statistics for England, 1986[3]

Among qualified nurses the male minority occupies a disproportionately high number of nursing officer posts. A study in one health district revealed that 37 per cent of posts at Nursing Officer and above are held by men, while only 8 per cent of all nurses in the district were men. Moreover men are appointed earlier in their careers than women.[11]

**The distinction between clerical and administrative staff.** A study[12] of administrative and clerical staff found that the majority of clerical staff were women, but there was a marked gap between Higher Clerical Officer (HCO) level, 87 per cent of whom were women, compared with 42 per cent of those on General Administrative Assistant (GAA) grade. While most secretaries were Higher Clerical Officers, the General Administrative Assistant grade is the first rung on the promotion ladder for administrators. As one manager said: 'Managers see GAA as a career post; HCO is just a job... Managers fear that women will go off, get married and have babies, and therefore it is a waste of investment.'

The authors of the study commented:

'It became clear from reading managers comments that women who were spotted at interview as potential mothers, or women already with children were often viewed as liabilities. They were frequently questioned about their domestic commitments at interviews and discrimination was practised against them in favour of candidates with no domestic commitments, for example, women with no children, women with grown up children, and men.'

The authors concluded that the only question that should be discussed at interview is 'Can you meet the requirements of the job?'

Before 1981 there were no women in Chief Administrative posts at district level and following the 1982 reorganisation of the Health Service there were still less than half a dozen women district administrators.[13] Of the General Managers appointed since 1985, only 3 per cent of District General managers were women, and information available for 9 out of the 14 health regions shows that 17 per cent of unit general managers were women.[14]

**Ancillary workers.** The study of a London hospital mentioned earlier found further striking divisions by sex amongst ancillary workers (Table 5.22).

As in other occupations women workers in general and overseas born women in particular are concentrated in ancillary jobs which are similar to those performed, unpaid, in the home, for example, cooking, cleaning and laundry, whilst few or no women, as Table 5.22 shows, are to be found in maintenance or portering. Domestic, catering and laundry jobs are also concentrated in grades 1-3 at the

**Table 5.22**
Ancillary workers at a London hospital, occupation by place of birth and sex

|  | Domestic | Catering | Mainten- ance | Porters | Other Ancillary | All Ancillary & Maintenance |
|---|---|---|---|---|---|---|
|  | % | % | % | % | % | % |
| Male British born | — | 4 | 20 | 37 | 33 | 11 |
| Male overseas born | 6 | 27 | 80 | 63 | 40 | 23 |
| Female British born | 16 | 14 | — | — | 7 | 11 |
| Female overseas born | 78 | 55 | — | — | 20 | 55 |

Source: L. Doyal et al 'Migrant Workers in the National Health Service' Report prepared for the SSRC by the Department of Sociology, Polytechnic of North London, June 1980[1].

bottom of the NHS scale whilst porters and maintenance workers are on Grades 4 and 5 of the scale. Information from two regional health authorities shows that 98 per cent of staff on Grade 1 of the pay scale are women and in grade 2, 83 per cent are women.[15]

In some parts of the country the NHS is highly dependent on overseas workers. The study of a London hospital 'Migrant workers in the NHS'[1] found that in their survey 72 per cent of nurses were from overseas and for ancillary and maintenance workers the figure was 78 per cent (Table 5.23). Thus in these two occupational groups, about three out of every four workers were born abroad.

Even with such high numbers of overseas workers in some hospitals racial discrimination still occurs. A report by the Commission for Racial Equality found

**Table 5.24**
Percentage of overseas workers at a London hospital in each occupational group

| Occupational group | Percentage of workers from overseas |
|---|---|
| Ancillary and maintenance | 78 |
| Clerical | 20 |
| Professional and technical | 29 |
| Nurses and midwives | 72 |
| Doctors | 32 |
| All occupations | 60 |

Source: L. Doyal et al 'Migrant Workers in the National Health Service' Report prepared for the SSRC by the Department of Sociology, Polytechnic of North London, June 1980[1].

'that the hospital service is as vulnerable to unlawful racial discrimination as other employing groups and that specific cases of discrimination have taken place. Nevertheless, employing authorities do not seem to realise that racial discrimination can still take place in organisations which employ substantial numbers of ethnic minority staff. Furthermore such discrimination is not only the result of isolated behaviour of one racially prejudiced manager; it is very frequently the result of the unthinking operation of a system which discriminates against ethnic minority groups'.[16]

**Discrimination against women.** Generalisations about women.are often used to justify treating them differently from men. In many cases these generalisations are used to support discrimination agaist women in the NHS, as in many other places of employment.

Although most women do leave the labour market for a time at the birth of their first child the majority return eventually, although not necessarily to the same job or even the same kind of work. The General Household Survey[17] shows that in 1984 54 per cent of women with dependent children aged 5 or more were working and for those with dependent children aged 10 or over, 68 per cent were working.

More detailed information about changes over time was obtained in the 'Women and Employment Survey'[18] carried out in 1980. In this survey employment histories were collected from a nationally representative sample of 5,588 women of working age. The survey shows that it is now normal practice for women to work full-time until the birth of their first child. Marriage, unless it is associated with an early birth, is now rarely a reason for stopping work, although it was for the oldest women in the survey. Almost all women who have a child have a break from employment. Only 4 per cent of women interviewed had been in the labour market continuously throughout their working lives and some of these were likely to leave subsequently to have a further child.

What is striking is that very high proportions of women return to work after having a child, and that contrary to popular belief this is not a new phenomenon. For example, 87 per cent of women who had a first birth in the early forties had subsequently returned to work, and over 90 per cent of women who had a first birth in the late fifties and early sixties had returned to work at some stage.

There have however been other changes. Compared with women who had their first baby between 1950 and 1954, women who had their first baby between 1974 and 1979 tended to return to paid work sooner, both after their first birth and their most recent birth. There was also an increasing tendency to return to employment between births, this was true of 47 per cent of women whose latest birth had been between 1975 and 1979. Thus the idea that women's paid employment falls into two distinct phases is increasingly inaccurate.

It is widely thought that women change their jobs frequently. The survey showed however that amongst women who have worked for more than 20 years, a third had worked for less than five employers and only a quarter for eight or more. Women changed their jobs most quickly in their first five years of work but this is also true of men. More women leave an employer to change straight to another job than to stop work, and women were more likely to leave an employer for a job-related reason than a domestic reason.

The evidence from the 'Women and Employment' survey suggests therefore that women are a stable and permanent part of the workforce. But many women when they return to work after the birth of their children have to take work (often part-time work) at a lower wage and skill level than their previous work.[18] As our examination of women's employment in the NHS showed, women tend to be concentrated in the lower paid and lower status jobs. As a public employer the NHS could do more to promote equal opportunity policies for women, but the existing pattern of health employment reinforces and perpetuates the wider inequalities that women experience, and which are most acute for black women.

## References

1. Source : L.Doyal, Gee F, Hunt G, 'Migrant Workers in the National Health Service'; Report prepared for the SSRC by the Department of Sociology, Polytechnic of North London, June 1980.
2. Smith D J, 'Overseas Doctors in the NHS', London: Heinemann for the Policy Studies Institute, 1980.
3. DHSS Health and Personal Social Services Statistics for England. London: HMSO, 1986.
4. Commission for Racial Equality, 'Overseas doctors: experience and expectations', London: CRE, 1987.
5. Watkins S, 'Racialism in the NHS' Radical Community Medicine, 1983; 16: 55-60.
6. Collier J, Burke A, 'Racial and sexual discrimination in the selection of students for pre-clinical medical schools', Medicine and Education, 1986; 20:86-90.
7. DHSS Medical Manpower Division, 'Medical and dental staffing prospects in the NHS in England and Wales' Health Trends 1986; 18:49-56.
8. Personal communication, study carried out by medical students at King's College Medical College, London.
9. Thomas M, Williams S, 'Overseas nurses in Britain', A PEP survey for the UK Council for Overseas Student Affairs, Broadsheet No. 539, London: Political and Economic Planning, 1972.
10. Hicks C, 'Racism in nursing', Nursing Times, 5th May 1982, 12th May 1982..
11. Kaye V. 'Can you meet the requirements of the job?' Health and Social Services Journal 1984; XCIV, 736-737.
12. Davies C, Rosser J, reported in Kaye V. 'Can you meet the requirements of the job?' Health and Social Services Journal 1984; XCIV, 736-737.
13. Davies C, Rosser J. 'Gendered jobs in the Health Service' in Knights D, Wilmott H, 'Gender and the labour process', Aldershot, Hants: Gower, 1986.
14. Health Service Journal, various issues 1986.
15. Ancillary Staffs Council Trade Union Side 'Health workers pay: Time for action now' London: Nov.1985.
16. Commission for Racial Equality 'Ethnic minority hospital staff', London: CRE, 1983.
17. OPCS Social Survey Division. The General Household Survey 1984 Series GHS no.14 SS457M. London: HMSO, 1987.
18. Martin J, Roberts C, 'Women and employment: a lifetime perspective' SS1143, London: HMSO, 1984.

# Prescribing and the Pharmaceutical Industry

The actions of individuals in buying medicines, of doctors in prescribing them and the policies of government towards their licensing and marketing are all affected by the barrage of publicity directed at them by the pharmaceutical industry. We shall consider here some recent campaigns waged by the industry and its supporters.

First, we consider two aspects of the argument about the prescribing and availability of drugs. Should the pharmacist be allowed to substitute an unbranded generic equivalent for the more expensive branded drug prescribed by the doctor? Secondly, does a 'selected list' of drugs which may be prescribed lead to a poorer quality of service?

In the second part of this section, we deal with the justification put forward by the drug companies for their huge profits. They claim that these are needed to fund research and development, and that if profits were cut, the companies would be forced to transfer their research facilities elsewhere.

**'Generic drugs and selected lists lead to second best treatment?'** Generic or approved drug names represent the chemicals which go to make up the drug. These names are recognised and used internationally. While they are not particularly easy to remember, they indicate the true nature of the drug as well as the class to which it belongs. The brand name of a drug is the one chosen by the manufacturer and used to advertise the drug to doctors. These names are chosen for their ability to be easily remembered rather than their ability to inform. Brand names used by the same manufacturer for the same drug can differ from country to country and this can lead to confusion.

A generic drug is one sold under its generic name, without any brand name and at a lower price than the branded equivalent. The drug industry claims that a greater use of generic drugs will be detrimental to patients, doctors and the economy, and that patients will be damaged by preparations of inferior quality. On the other hand, pharmacologists claim that having a larger number of similar medicines sold under different brand names obscures awareness of the pharmacological properties and leads to an increasing incidence of drug interactions, morbidity and mortality.

Generic drugs cannot be marketed without a product licence. This is issued by the licensing authority only after the Medicines division of the Department of Health and Social Security and the Committee on Safety of Medicines make the same checks as they give to branded products. These include checks on the purity of the starting materials, the methods used to synthesise them, the source of the additional materials added and the purity, specification and identity of the final medicine. If the margins between safe and toxic doses are narrow, the generic must be shown to act in the same way as the branded drug in terms of the extent and rate at which it is absorbed.

It is now government policy to encourage generic prescribing, and as a result these medicines account for 22 per cent of all prescriptions issues by doctors. There has been no public, professional or industrial outcry against these prescriptions in terms of quality.

Despite this, the proposal that pharmacists should substitute generic products for branded drugs prescribed by general practitioners provoked great protests, even though generic substitution has been practised in all NHS hospitals for at least ten years. In December 1982, when the government was still less than enthusiastic about generic prescribing, it was unable to cite a single case when it had led to problems in hospitals.[1] Most of the arguments against the wider use of generics are based on anecdotes rather than on published data. More recently, however, there has been concern that some manufacturers of generics have not maintained the standards they showed in order to get their licence.[2] In hospitals, there are quality control checks which enable such lapses to be detected. There is therefore an urgent need for similar quality control facilities to be provided for community pharmacies.

A great wave of outrage greeted the proposal announced by the government in November 1984 of a 'limited list' of medicines which could be prescribed within the NHS. The list covered cough and cold remedies, tonics, laxatives, analgesics for mild to moderate pain, antacids, low dose vitamin preparations, benzodiazepine tranquilisers and sedatives. The Secretary of State for Social Services described these as 'medicines prescribed mainly for the relief of symptoms caused by minor and self-limiting ailments, that do not normally call for medical intervention'.[3]

This simple and shrewdly worded proposal brought together the three important principles of generic substitution, a selected drugs list and restrictions on doctors' clinical freedom.

Objections to the limited list were orchestrated by the Association of the British Pharmaceutical Industry (ABPI). They were then taken up by the British Medical Association (BMA), the Association of Scientific, Technical and Managerial Staff (ASTMS), sections of the Conservative Party and Labour spokespeople Michael Meacher and Frank Dobson, supported by a number of other Labour MPs. ASTMS' position was not unexpected, given that it has many members in the pharmaceutical industry, but the Labour spokespeople's position directly contradicted the call in their party's 1983 general election manifesto for 'the introduction of a selected drugs list together with the practice of allowing pharmacists to substitute less expensive generic drugs when overpriced but equivalent brand name drugs are prescribed'.[4] These policies had been set out in an earlier document[5] and reappeared in 1987 in a 'Charter for the family health service'.[6]

A 'selected' drugs list is defined as a list of medicines which are chosen for prescribing on the grounds of need, safety, efficiency and economy. It should ensure that the best quality drugs, either branded or generic, are available and known to prescribing doctors. The list should exclude drugs that are ineffective or unsafe and those which are overpriced versions of other drugs. It should allow for new and more effective drugs to replace those whose usefulness has been superceded by more effective ones. A selected drugs list should therefore be compiled with two objectives, to improve the quality of care for patients and to increase economy in the use of drugs.

How did the government's reasons for introducing what was first described as a 'limited list and later as a 'selected list' relate to these objectives and to the objections put forward by opponents of the list?

**'Clinical freedom must be defended.'** This was put in various ways. The BMA said the list limited doctors' freedom to prescribe what the patient needs. The ABPI claimed in a series of full page newspaper advertisements that doctors would be robbed of the freedom to give their patients the best drugs. When the list was debated in parliament, Labour MP Maurice Miller said 'The doctor's freedom to prescribe what he believes to be best for his patient should be paramount'.[7]

Yet, very different views had been expressed two years before in an editorial in the British Medical Journal. 'Clinical freedom is dead and no one need regret its passing. It should have been strangled long ago, for at best it was a cloak for quackery... it was a myth that prevented true advance and we welcome its demise'.[8] As Joe Collier, Deputy Editor of Drug and Therapeutics Bulletin, put it, 'There is a mistaken belief that patients automatically benefit if doctors have more drugs to choose from. However sensible choice depends on ability to choose, which in turn demands knowledge and information. But most doctors do not have the time, experience, interest or expertise to assess drugs by analysing information from drug trials'.[9]

Most doctors restrict their prescribing to no more than 300 products. A number of these do not conform to either rational or acceptable use of drugs. So, in place of freedom to prescribe badly, a selected list in the main gives doctors a new freedom to prescribe well.

It can no longer be argued that a drug is effective or even needed simply because it is prescribed by doctors. The United Kingdom Joint Formulary Committee considered that 24 per cent of the 2,000 branded drugs which they evaluated were regarded as 'less suitable for prescribing because of uncertain, doubtful or little value'.[10]

The drugs blacklisted by the government all fall into this category. Yet millions of prescriptions were written for them each year. A good example is peripheral vasodilators which are advertised and promoted for the treatment of poor circulation and senile dementia. Despite scientific evidence from the American Medical Association and the UK Joint Formulary Committee suggesting that they do more harm than good, they were still prescribed at a cost to the NHS of 30 million per year. The use of most cough mixtures and tonics on the blacklist can never be substantiated by acceptable published evidence. Yet prescriptions for them used to cost the NHS many tens of millions of pound annually.

**'Blacklisted drugs are needed and are without adequate substitutes.'** This may well have been true with the original version of the limited list which contained only 31 drugs. It does not, however, apply to the final version, which was announced in February 1985, and contained over 100.[11] This followed recommendations made to the DHSS by the Drug and Therapeutics Bulletin. A blacklist was also published, giving 1800 drugs which are no longer prescribable.

It was opposed on the grounds that poor and elderly people would have to put up with less appropriate medicines. Michael Meacher said that the list would 'deprive poorer patients of the drugs they need'.[12] John Griffin of the ABPI claimed that '70 — 80 per cent of people taking drugs do not pay prescription charges. In future they will have to pay or go without. ... It will result in elderly, children and the poor having to take second class medicines, namely less palatable, less convenient and less effective ... adequate substitutes will not be available'.[13]

These opponents inferred that the blacklisted drugs are necessary for good health care, when in fact they are banned from most hospital lists precisely because they are not regarded as acceptable. The drugs on the blacklist are the very ones which the BMA and Pharmaceutical Society representatives on the committee of the British National Formulary have for years advised doctors not to use. This is either because they lacked evidence that they were effective or because they were less suitable or grossly overpriced.

While the government may have done NHS patients a favour by protecting them from these drugs, the fact that it continues to allow them to be prescribed privately calls its motives into question. It also made no serious attempt to inform the public that the blacklisted drugs were not worth having. On the contrary, it pointed out that these drugs were still available on private prescriptions. This is a particularly cynical approach, given that many of the people who used such drugs over long periods were poor and elderly.

While it is difficult to find a clinical need for the categories of drugs chosen that is not met by the limited lists, there are some exceptions. In hospitals, these are dealt with by appeals procedures, but the government made no attempt to set up similar procedures for drugs prescribed in general practice.

The limited list does have the advantage of obliging doctors to use generic names for drugs more frequently. The BMA is on record as favouring generic prescribing rather than brand names to encourage doctors to think about the contents of the medicines they prescribe. The BMA's official handbook, the British National Formulary, lists all drugs by their generic name.

'These proposals are contrary to the founding principle of the NHS — equal health care for all. They will divide the rich from the poor and create a two tier health service.' 'Between 70 and 80 per cent of people taking drugs which Mr Fowler proposed to ban did not pay prescription charges. They will now have to pay or go without.'[13]

The underlying principle of the NHS is the right of patients to treatment at the time of need, without cost being a consideration. This cannot be equated with the dubious right to receive overpriced, inappropriate and ineffective drugs in the mistaken belief that more expensive products are better. The real reason that the drug industry feared the limited list was the concern that introducing it in the United Kingdom might set a precedent for other countries.

On the other hand the fact that the limited list was not extended to the private sector makes it clear that one of the government's reasons for introducing it was to challenge the principle that the NHS should be comprehensive and thus to move towards a two tier service. Ironically, it chose to do this with a policy which actually provided inferior care for private patients compared with the NHS.

**'Jobs will be lost.'** It was claimed that there would be 2,000 job losses out of a total workforce of 70,000,[14] while ASTMS said it was fighting the measures to protect 5,000 white collar jobs. Although some firms made workers redundant after the limited list was introduced, the total job loss was difficult to assess, as some firms started recruiting workers again fairly soon afterwards.

For the unfortunate people who did remain unemployed the real challenge, as in the tobacco and armaments industries, is to create pressure for alternative jobs rather than defend the continued manufacture of harmful or useless products.

'The list poses a severe threat to the UK drugs industry and could destroy it'. 'British research based companies will be badly hit.'

Information compiled by city analysts Greenwell's for the drug industry paper Scrip showed that most companies were likely to lose little of their profits. Boots,

LRC and Smith and Nephew were unaffected, while it was predicted that Glaxo would lose 5 per cent, Beechams 6 per cent and Fisons 8 per cent of their UK sales. While Reckitt and Coleman were likely to lose 50 per cent of their sales of drugs, these form only a small part of their company's business. Wellcome were predicted to lose 15 per cent, mainly from two drugs Actifed and Calpol which were, however, available off prescription. Roche, the Swiss multinational stood to lose 70 per cent of its sales.[13] It should, however, be remembered that across the board, UK sales made up only 4 per cent of the world total.[15] Two years later, in February 1987, a figure of 6 per cent was quoted.[16]

**Did the government achieve its objectives?** The government's original aim in introducing the limited list was to halt the rise in the NHS drug bill by £100 million.[3] This was scaled down to £75 million when the list was expanded.[11] It now claims that these savings have been made and 'form part of the general increase in resources made available to the NHS'.[17] Yet as Table 5.24 shows, although the numbers of prescriptions dispensed fell by £6.6 million in 1985-86 compared with a rise of £10 million in the previous year, the overall cost rose by 6.1 per cent, just ahead of inflation.[18] In any case, the pharmaceutical industry is still one of the most profitable industries in the country.

---

**Table 5.24**
Prescriptions and their cost in the United Kingdom before and after the implementation of the limited drugs list on April 1, 1985

|  | Financial year | | |
|  | 1983-84 | 1984-85 | 1985-86 |
|---|---|---|---|
| Prescriptions dispensed, millions | 412.6 | 422.6 | 416.0 |
| Percentage exempt from charges† | 78.4 | 79.7 | 81.5 |
| Average gross·cost £ | 4.30 | 4.54 | 4.90 |
| Total cost, £ million | 1,773.7 | 1,919.0 | 2,036.8 |
| Percentage of cost paid by patients* | 7.5 | 7.6 | 7.7 |

† Including those covered by prepayment certificates
* Including payments for prepayment certificates
Source: Written parliamentary replies[18]
The information in these was compiled on a slightly different basis from Table 5.12, so there are apparent discrepancies.

---

The government's decision to implement a limited list is in line with recommendations from the World Health Organisation and the Royal Commission on the National Health Service. These both suggested that the numbers of medicines available for prescribing should be subject to restrictions based on safety, efficacy, convenience of dosage and cost.

Although the government's second list met these requirements, the way it was implemented left a great deal to be desired. We should like to see the selected list principle extended to all classes of medicines, but it should apply to private patients and over the counter sales as well as NHS prescriptions. In addition medicines should be chosen after proper consultation procedures, using the criteria described above. There should be an appeals procedure to deal quickly with exceptional cases and a serious attempt should be made to educate the public about why drugs have been blacklisted.

In failing to do any of these things, the government made it only too apparent that saving money and moving towards a two tier health service were high on its list of reasons for introducing its limited list. As a result, very few people became aware of the potential benefits to patients of using selected lists of medicines in general practice as well as in hospitals.

**Drug companies need large profits for research and development?** The Concise Oxford Dictionary defines research as 'the endeavour to discover new facts by scientific study in the course of critical investigation'. True research is therefore aimed at adding to existing knowledge.

Research in the pharmaceutical industry has a more flexible definition. One third of the cost of pharmaceutical research and development (R and D) is spent in the hunt for a 'candidate' drug, and a further third is devoted to clinical studies in patients. Of the remaining third, considerable sums are spent on developing large scale production plants and appropriate pharmaceutical formulations.[19] Other items included under the umbrella of R and D include developing more pleasing colours and tastes, drug packaging, expenses for employees to attend conferences at home and abroad, general market research aimed at improving sales, and purchasing international patents to improve the monopoly position of the firm abroad.[20]

The majority of drugs or medicines produced as a result of R and D are not new, but are 'me-too' in character. In other words, they involve molecule manipulation in order to produce a drug similar in character to a competitor's without infringing their patent.[5] Such drugs add little or nothing to meeting patients' needs. Of 1,087 new drugs investigated by the United States Food and Drug Administration (FDA) in 1980, 2.4 per cent represented a 'possible important therapeutic gain', 8.4 per cent a 'moderate therapeutic gain' and 89.2 per cent 'little or no therapeutic gain'.[22]

The proportion of turnover spent on R and D ranged from 4 to 10 per cent and totalled £250 million in 1985.[23] Worldwide pharmaceutical research over the same period totalled £900 million. Marketing and promotional costs for the same period accounted for from 12 to 18 per cent of turnover.[24] All research is paid for from profits earned from the sale of drugs, and is fully allowed for when profits are fixed. Declared profits, on the other hand, exclude money set aside for R and D, while part of the cost of sales promotion is allowed for against pre-tax profits. For a new product most R and D costs are recouped within two years, leaving eight years of clear profit before the patents expire.

The world's leading drug company is Germany's Hoechst, with sales in 1983 of $2,350 million. This company spends the major part of its research budget on testing rather than discovering new drugs. This same company claimed that it intended cancelling a £10 million plan to double research in the UK because of government action to cut profits by 2.5 per cent and threatened to transfer this facility to Japan. 'The commercial logic of this decision is mystifying, as the Japanese have just slashed drug prices far more heavily'.[25] While Hoechst was making this announcememt, Glaxo announced that it was spending 11 million to extend its manufacturing and research facilities.

The United Kingdom leads the world in developing new drugs, with twelve of the twenty top selling drugs to its credit, including Tagamet, the world's number one. A new and innovative drug may cost up to £100 million to develop. The Committee on Safety of Medicines is known to approve new drugs twice as fast as its American counterpart, the FDA. Because the CSM enjoys world wide confidence, this ensures large international earnings for new drugs developed here and explains why foreign multinationals are keen to establish R and D bases here, R and D costs are lower here than in other western countries, because our scientists are paid much less. In spite of the excellence of our research workers, three scientists with PhDs can be employed here for the same price as one in the USA. It is clear that the threat to transfer R and D investment away from the UK is a ploy designed to frighten the government. At a time of high unemployment it is economic nonsense.

The manufacture and distribution of drugs is international. UK companies export half their production, while foreign multinationals supply 69 per cent of the NHS' drugs. The UK drug market represents only 6 per cent of the global sum,[16] while 5 per cent of world drug manufacture is produced here. Therefore the profit on NHS sales cannot be a factor in deciding to remove R and D facilities and does not pose a threat to the pharmaceutical multinationals. The extent of the cut imposed by the government in 1984 on drug prices was a mere 2.5 per cent, which was minimal in global terms. Stockbrokers de Zoete and Bevan estimated that this would cost ICI £3.5 million in 1984. Worldwide trading profits for ICI in pharmaceuticals in 1983 were £199 million while, despite the cuts, profits were expected to reach £260 million.[26]

The pharmaceutical multinationals have not established research and manufacturing bases in the UK just to earn profits from the NHS. They are therefore not likely to leave or transfer their research facilities to other countries just because of a marginal fall in profits. It is also clear that most of the research in the pharmaceutical industry is devoted to the development and marketing of non-essential duplicative products which are usually used to relieve trivial conditions, rather than those needed to improve health care. This policy is intended to boost market shares and the prices of drugs.

**References**
1. Hansard. Written reply, December 1 1982, col 219.
2. Shulman J. Generics — public protection. Official reference book. London: Proprietary Articles Trade Association, 1986.
3. Fowler N. Statement on the Queen's speech. Hansard, November 8 1984, col 226.
4. Labour Party. Election manifesto. London: Labour Party, 1983.
5. Labour Party. Labour's programme. London: Labour Party, 1982.
6. Labour Party. The best of health. Charter for the family health service. London: Labour Party, 1987.
7. Miller MS. Hansard, March 18 1985, col 720.
8. Hampton JR. Editorial. The end of clinical freedom. British Medical Journal 1983;287:1237-1238.
9. Collier J, Medawar C. Guardian. December 17 1984.

10. British National Formulary. Quoted in: Medawar C, Social Audit. The wrong kind of medicine. London, Hodder and Stoughton,1984
11. Fowler N. Statement on limited list prescribing. Hansard, February 21 1985, col 1219-1229.
12. Meacher M. Letter. Guardian. February 4 1985.
13. Veitch A. Drugs ban will destroy health service, say firms. Guardian. December 4 1984.
14. Veitch A, Erlichman J. NHS drugs curb 'will cost 2,000 jobs.' Guardian. February 5 1985.
15. Griffin J, Taylor D. Pharmaceutical Journal. January 2 1985: 38-39.
16. Fleming R. Scrip. Quoted in: Wyke A. Pharmaceuticals. Economist. February 7 1987.
17. Written reply. Hansard, December 18 1986, col 702.
18. Written replies. Hansard, December 12 1985, cols 699-700, 729-732, 743-744, January 13 1986, col 501-502, January 19 1987, col 395-396, 421-424, February 23 1987, col 134-136.
19. Rawlins MD. Guardian April 6 1986
20. Lall S. The international pharmaceutical industry and less developed countries with special reference to India. Oxford Bulletin of Economics and Statistics 1974;36:143-172.
21. Doyal L. The political economy of health. London: Pluto,1979.
22. Muller M. The health of nations. London: Faber and Faber,1982.
23. DHSS. Press release. June 26 1986.
24. Investor's Chronicle, February 2 1979.
25. Erlichman J. Guardian. March 21 1984.
26. Erlichman J. Guardian. March 6 1984.

# Dentistry and dental health

The Government is proud of the increased levels of dental activity which have taken place under its rule, and increases in numbers of dentists and courses of dental treatment are often mentioned in ministers' statements, press releases and in Norman Fowler's two leaflets on the NHS.

Does this mean that the dental health of the population is better or worse than it was? If there is a change, does it bear any relation to the increased dental activity? Does regular attendance for check-ups, and regular brushing really reduce the level of caries?

**More dentists and more treatment?** For example, the 1986 leaflet 'The Health Service today' pointed to an increase of 20 per cent in the number of dentists in England from 11,919 in 1978 to 14,334 in 1985. Similar increases took place in the other countries of the United Kingdom, but the numbers had been increasing throughout the 1970s and are therefore part of a longer term trend.[1,4]

These numbers refer only to the General Dental Service (GDS), that is dentists who work as independent contractors in the Family Practitioner Services. The numbers of hospital dental staff in England increased from 789 whole-time equivalents in 1974 to 926 in 1978 and 1061 in 1984, an increase of only 15 per cent between 1978 and 1984 compared with 17 per cent between 1974 and 1978.

Meanwhile, the numbers of whole-time equivalent community dental staff increased from 1351 in 1974 to 1,505 in 1978 and then fell to 1,412 in 1984, rising only slightly to 1431 in 1985.[1] Similar changes took place in Wales and Scotland although the decline in total numbers of community dentists was not visible until 1982 in Wales and 1984 in Scotland.[2,3]

Increases in number of courses of dental treatment in the GDS are also frequently quoted, but in each country these increases also go back before 1978.

For example, in England numbers of courses of treatment rose from 24.6 million in 1974 to 27.1 million in 1978 and 31.4 million in 1985. This excludes courses of treatment in hospital, community clinics and in the private sector.

Within the overall rise in numbers of courses of treatment there have been changes in the types of treatment given. Thus, there have been increases in the numbers of check-ups, X-rays, treatments for periodontal (gum) disease, root treatments and crowns, but decreases in the numbers of extractions. In England, the numbers of fillings have fallen,[1] while the numbers have levelled off in Wales and Scotland.[2,3]

**Less caries … is it related?** While these statistics show increases in dentists and the work they do, both expressed as numbers and as rates per 1,000 population, they are entirely unrelated to the people in whose mouths the work is done. To collect information about this, the Office of Population Censuses and Surveys (OPCS) has done a series of surveys of the dental health of the population. The most recent survey showed that between 1973 and 1983 the severity of caries among children in the United Kingdom declined by about 35 per cent.[5]

The most recent survey of adults was done as long ago as 1978. This showed a small decline in the severity of caries among adults over the years 1968 to 1978. There was also a decline in the proportion of adults with no teeth. Data collected in the 1983 General Household survey shows that this trend continued into the 1980s.[7] This raises the question of whether the increase in dental activity is responsible for this decline in caries and improvement in dental health.

The two most effective methods of reducing caries are dietary control of added sugars and use of fluoride. Household sugar consumption decreased by 30 per cent during the 1970s.[8] Sugar confectionery consumption also declined. For example, boiled sweet consumption decreased from 85,695 tonnes in 1975 to 68,045 tonnes in 1982.[9] Breastfeeding increased markedly, and with that change in patterns of infant feeding, the consumption of sucrose in infant and baby foods declined. There is evidence that the increase in the use of fluoride toothpaste has affected the decline in caries.[11,12] In the early 1970s fluoride toothpaste accounted for less than 5 per cent of the toothpaste market. At present 95 per cent of toothpastes are fluoridated.

There is no evidence available indicating that dentists increased their preventive activities during the 1970s. There are no NHS fees for fluoride applications by general dental practitioners, and no routine statistics are collected about any type of preventive activity.

**Do regular check-ups help?** The improvement in dental health, as measured by numbers of sound teeth without decay or filling, was greater in irregular than in regular dental attenders. Irregular attenders are people who only visit a dentist when in pain. They have fewer filled teeth but more decayed untreated teeth than regular attenders. As Table 5.25 shows, however, they also have more sound unattacked teeth than regular attenders. The only group of regular attenders who had significantly more sound teeth in 1978 than in 1968 were the 16-24 year olds.

Although the statistics about check-ups quoted earlier show marked increases in numbers, they do not tell us how often individuals go for check-ups, or whether they comply with advice to go every six months.

Six monthly dental checks have been recommended by the dental profession for over 100 years but there does not appear to be a sound basis for the recommendation.[13] In 1977 when a critical review was carried out, the data were based upon rates recorded before the decline of dental caries. Now there are fewer dental lesions to progress through the enamel to the dentine, when filling becomes necessary.[14] Because caries progresses slowly when it does progress, and many lesions remineralize and heal, an interval much longer than 6 months can safely be recommended for adults. Caries progresses much more slowly in adults than in children.

Frequent dental attenders have fewer untreated decayed teeth but they do receive more fillings than those who attend less frequently. Frequent attenders had almost twice as many tooth surfaces filled in comparison with infrequent attenders.[15]

The evidence suggests that people under the age of 18 need not go for check-ups more than once a year provided they do not have any pain and are not having a course of treatment. A longer interval would be appropriate if no decay was found at the last visit and/or the child has no teeth which have been filled. For example, if a child of 12 has not had any decay the interval between checks could be increased.

The majority of people aged 18 years or over need checks at intervals of two years or longer. If they have a lot of fillings, and fillings are done at each visit, they should ask the dentist why and if they feel the dentist is sound they should go for annual checks.[13,16]

**Does brushing help?** There is some evidence that people may be brushing their teeth more often or more effectively, but this would be unlikely to result in a marked decline in caries. While brushing is useful to keep gums healthy and to transport fluoride in toothpaste to the teeth, there is little evidence to support the view that brushing itself prevents caries.

There are two main reasons why brushing cannot prevent tooth decay in the decay-prone sites. Firstly, the toothbrush bristles cannot get to the bacterial plaque in most pits, fissures and surfaces between the teeth. Secondly, acids are formed within 3 to 5 minutes after eating sugars. So even if the brush could reach the acid-producing bacteria, brushing would have to be done within two minutes of eating.

An extensive review of the literature on clinical trials[17] indicates that there is insufficient evidence to support the view that toothbrushing is effective for caries control. This scepticism was echoed by a WHO scientific group which said that brushing as a public health measure to prevent caries should not be over-emphasised.[18]

**Variations in activity … and in need.** The OPCS surveys of dental health show predictable regional variations with people in the South of England having many more teeth than those in the North of England and in Scotland. Dentists are similarly distributed, within England there are more dentists per head of the population in the South than in the North, ranging in 1984 from 0.23 dentists per 1,000 population in the Northern and Trent regions to 0.44 in North West Thames.[1]

There is little evidence, however, that dental activity has had much to do with the geographical variations or with the improvement in dental health over time. As shown in Table 5.25, the main improvement in adult dental health between 1968 and 1978 was in irregular attenders. The greatest reduction in

**Table 5.25**

Comparison of average numbers of sound teeth in regular attenders at dentists and irregular attenders who go when they have trouble with their teeth, England and Wales 1968 and 1978

| | Average number of sound teeth by age | | | | | | | | | |
| | 16-24 | | 25-34 | | 35-44 | | 45-54 | | 55+ | |
|---|---|---|---|---|---|---|---|---|---|---|
| | 1968 | 1978 | 1968 | 1978 | 1968 | 1978 | 1968 | 1978 | 1968 | 1978 |
| Regular attenders | 14.3 | 16.1 | 12.3 | 12.4 | 11.1 | 11.0 | 9.8 | 10.0 | 8.8 | 8.9 |
| Irregular attenders | 18.6 | 19.0 | 14.7 | 16.1 | 13.7 | 14.3 | 10.7 | 11.3 | 8.6 | 9.0 |

Source: OPCS Survey of Adult Dental Health 1968-78[6]

edentulousness (the absence of any teeth) was in people in Social Classes IV and V in the North of England. This is a group who go less frequently than others for dental treatment.[6]

At the same time there is considerable evidence of unmet need, particularly amongst poorer people who have untreated decay and older people, many of whom have low quality dentures. There is also evidence of much unmet need for dental care amongst people with disabilities. This is a group for whom the community dental service is responsible, yet, as pointed out above, this service is being cut.

**To sum up.** In summary, the increased level of dental activity which has occurred is unlikely to have contributed much to the improvement in dental health. This improvement is more likely to be due to a reduction in the consumption of sugars, and an increase in the use of fluoride toothpastes.

People are told to visit the dentist every six months, yet there is no scientific basis for this recall interval, and evidence suggests that a longer interval would be beneficial.

There is considerable unmet need for dental treatment among elderly, poor and disabled people and an increase in the community dental staff is recommended. At the same time, as the British Dental Association has pointed out, there is currently an 'overproduction' of dental graduates and a reduction in the number of dental students is called for. Instead dental auxiliaries with more appropriate skills are needed to deal with the changing pattern of disease.

**References.**
1. DHSS. Health and personal social services statistics for England. Various years.
2. Welsh Office. Health and personal social services statistics for Wales. Various years.
3. Information Services Division. Scottish health statistics. Various years.
4. Central Statistical Office. Annual abstract of statistics 1986. London: HMSO, 1986.
5. Todd JE, Dodd T. Children's dental health in the United Kingdom 1983.SS 1189. London: HMSO, 1985.

6. Todd JE, Walker AM. Adult dental health, England and Wales Vol. 1., 1978. SS1112. London: HMSO, 1980.
7. Office of Population Censuses and Surveys. General household survey 1983. Series GHS. No. 13. SS457L. London: HMSO, 1985.
8. Buss DH. The resilience of British household diets during the 1970s. J. Human Nutri 1979; 33:47-55.
9. Cocoa Chocolate and Confectionery Alliance, Annual Reports 1979-80 and 1982. CCCA, 11 Green Street, London W1Y 3RF.
10. Martin J, Monk J. Infant feeding 1980. London: OPCS, 1982.
11. Marthaler T.M. Explanations for changing patterns of disease in the Western world. In: Cariology. Ed.B.Guggenheim, Basel: Karger 1984. 13-23.
12. Andlaw RJ, Burchell CK, Tucker GG. Comparison of dental health of 11 yr old children in 1970 and 1979, and of 14 yr old children in 1973 and 1979: Studies in Bristol, England. Caries Res 1982; 16: 257-264.
13. Sheiham A. Is there a scientific basis for six monthly dental examinations? Lancet 1977: ii: 442-444.
14. Schwartz M, Grondahl HG, Pliskin JS, Boffe J. A longitudinal analysis from bite-wing radiographs of the rate of progression of approximal caries lesions through human dental enamel. Arch Oral Biol 1984; 29:529-536.
15. Nuttall NM. General Dental Service treatment received by frequent and infrequent dental attenders in Scotland. Br Dent J. 1984; 156: 363-366.
16. Routine six-monthly checks for dental disease? Drug and therapeutics Bulletin 1985; 23: 69-72.
17. Sutcliffe P. Oral cleanliness and dental caries. In: The Prevention of oral disease Murray J J. Ed. Oxford: University Press 1983; 159-174.
18. WHO. The etiology and prevention of dental caries. Wld Hlth Organ. Techn. Rep Series. No.494., Geneva: WHO, 1972.
19. Smith J M. Oral and dental discomfort — a necessary feature of old age? Age and Ageing 1979; 8: 25-31.
20. British Dental Association, Dental Services: an opportunity for change. Response of the British Dental Association to the Government's Green Paper on Primary Health Care. London: British Dental Association, 1987.

# Health Education: Blaming the Victim?

In Autumn 1986, the Undersecretary of State for Health, Edwina Currie, suggested that the real cause of the poorer health experienced by Northerners is their diet. Ill-health, she implied, has nothing to do with poverty and unemployment, and can best be tackled by 'impressing upon people the need to look after themselves better'. Her predecessor, Ray Whitney, expressed similar views when opening a Health Education Council exhibition in September 1986:

'as a nation we must improve our record in reducing the number of deaths from Coronary Heart Disease. Certainly the government has an important role to play — which it is already playing — but real success can only come from the efforts of each of us as individuals. Experience in other countries shows that the sort of life we lead very often has a direct link with our life expectancy and that, for the great majority of us, our life style is by far the most important factor in maintaining good health.'[1]

Edwina Currie's outburst was merely a less tactful version of a now familiar message echoed by mainstream health education materials. Despite the elaborate theoretical discussions which have taken place about the supposedly new discipline of 'health promotion',[2] the current practice of health education consists of providing information about how the individual's behaviour can harm their health, rounded off with exhortations to behave more responsibly. Discussions about 'community development' and 'self empowerment' emanating from academic departments are largely drowned by the day to day business of relaying information about the need to change life styles, to use the health services more effectively, to bring up children better and generally to smarten up.

**Why health education?** The Department of Health and Social Security publication 'Prevention and health: everybody's business'[3] in 1976 heralded a resurgence of interest in preventive medicine in general and in health education in particular. This stemmed from a recognition that, historically, declining mortality rates are more strongly related to improvements in living standards, in nutrition, in housing, in working conditions and in sanitation than in medical treatment. The implication was that this would remain true in years to come. This assumption was strengthened by the recognition that by and large the major diseases causing death in western societies, coronary heart disease (CHD) and cancers, are not by and large amenable to medical intervention once they have developed.

A further expectation was that prevention would be cheaper than acute medicine and so a shift of resources to prevention would save money. While many health workers were attracted by the potential of health education to democratise and demystify medicine, as well as to improve the nation's health,[4] government agencies were clearly most impressed by the possibility of savings. In 1977, DHSS suggested in 'Prevention and Health' that 'prevention could lead to a reduction of the burden on the services and of the high cost of the drugs bill'.[5]

Health education materials and campaigns are produced by many different organisations, but the Health Education Council (HEC) has been responsible for much of this work. In 1979 it launched the 'Look after yourself' campaign with booklets and 'Look after yourself' classes. Later, in 1983, the start of a major campaign against heart disease was marked by the publication of 'Beating heart disease'. These activities emphasised the need for individuals to alter their diet, exercise patterns and smoking habits. While it was promised that making these changes in life style would improve general health and well being there was a particular emphasis on avoiding heart disease.

In 1985 this focus on heart disease culminated in 'Heartbeat Wales', an HEC heart disease prevention project targetted at the Welsh population. Since then similar programmes have been opened in Glasgow (Glasgow 2000) and Northern Ireland (Change of Heart) leading to an all UK project, 'Look after your heart', launched in April 1987.

**Are healthy lives and healthy life styles synonymous?** The 'Look after yourself' approach to preventing ill-health accepts the reality that smoking, poor diet and physical inactivity can contribute to poor health. By focussing on these issues, however, it ignores other important causes of sickness. Although there is a growing body of research on the social causes of ill-health, much more research has been done on such factors as diet and high blood pressure. The way the Minister of Health, Tony Newton, retreated behind the smokescreen of 'considerable academic debate'[6] when asked about the links between poverty and ill health showed that it is a politically sensitive area.

In Part 2, we showed the association between overall mortality rates and social class as measured by the Registrar General's classification. While these data clearly demonstrate large and increasing inequalities in health there are problems in using social class for such analyses. There is a considerable range of earning power within each social class, and substantial overlaps of occupational wage levels between classes.[7] Social class is therefore a poor discriminator of material well being and may underestimate the true inequalities in health.

Within a single industry, however, there is likely to be a more clearcut relationship between employment grade and economic position. A large study of civil servants found that the overall death rate in a ten year period was three times greater in the lowest employment grade than in the highest.[8] This was true for nearly all causes of death. Furthermore, the greater part of the differences in death rates from coronary heart disease could not be explained by smoking habits, obesity, serum cholesterol, raised blood pressure or reported physical inactivity. Similarly the differences between the grades in the extent of smoking could not explain the steep gradient in lung cancer mortality rates. Clearly the lifestyles are not the only factors which can influence death rates.

Edwina Currie singled out the people in the North of England as being in particular need of her advice to 'look after themselves better'. This is despite the fact that the North of England already suffered higher death rates than most southern areas apart from London when statistics were first compiled in the mid nineteenth century and has continued to have high rates ever since.[9,10] These differences are seen for nearly all causes of death and remain evident even when allowance is made for the age and social class structure of regional populations.[11] Despite this, Edwina Currie implied that these differences are solely due to the bad habits of people living in the North. As it is unlikely that this behaviour relates in an identical way to all the causes of death, her explanation was vastly oversimplified.

Many people feel that the work they do damages their health. Despite the research evidence, however, the association between work and ill health is largely ignored outside discussions of specific occupational hazards, like asbestos. As early as 1958, American researchers reported that overwork was an independent and more important risk factor for heart disease than diet, smoking, lack of exercise and a family history of heart disease.[12] More recently a Swedish report has shown an increased rate of heart attacks in shift workers compared to those with a more pleasant working environment.[13] This difference could not be explained by factors such as smoking. Similar findings came from a larger analysis of deaths from heart disease across all occupational groups within Sweden. Heart disease was found to be the most common in groups of workers who had the least control over what they did at work and when they did it, but who were hardest pressed in terms of the actual demands of their jobs.[14]

This discussion touches only briefly on the importance of social factors in the causation of ill health. Other research has shown the detrimental effects of unemployment and poor housing on health. Britain's Asian community suffers a particularly high rate of deaths from heart disease which cannot be explained by smoking, diet and blood pressure. This raises the possibility that factors such as the stress of living in a racist society are important determinants of ill health.[15]

Clearly, simply attributing the cause of disease to people's lifestyles is inadequate. Suggesting that illness is entirely dependent on individual behaviour focusses our attention away from the broader social determinants of ill health. Acting alone we cannot avoid poverty, stressful work, poor housing, unemployment and racism.

**Looking after our hearts.** Books, leaflets, talks and videos used in health education give no idea of the possible importance of economic, political and social factors in causing ill health. 'Looking after yourself' suggested that the only problem with the modern world is that we have it too easy:

'Although you inhabit an electronic, push-button, high-technology world, you still have a Stone Age body. It took millions of years of evolution for the human body to become adapted for primitive survival — for running, fighting, jumping, lifting, dragging, climbing — in order to hunt, trap and gather food. It simply hasn't had time to adapt to our modern mollycoddled way of life.'[16]

Coping with 'the stresses of everyday life' is best achieved by gentle rhythmic exercise. A photograph of the Medical Officer of the HEC jogging pushes the point home.

The only possible cause of heart disease outside of the classic risk factors considered is 'stress'. The section in 'Beating Heart Disease' on stress starts:

'Most people would put stress at the top of their list of things that are bad for the heart. It seems obvious that worry and anxiety, or frequent crises and rows can make your blood pressure go up and lead to a heart attack. But this is still difficult to prove, partly because stress is almost impossible to measure and define. However, people who have a certain kind of personality — striving, ambitious, competitive, impatient, always pressed for time — seem to be more in danger of having a heart attack than more relaxed, easy-going types. We call the first heart-risk type "Type A".'[17]

Dubious claims are then made that Type A's have higher blood pressure and serum cholesterol levels. There is a higher proportion of people classified as Type A in high status than in low status occupations. Strong competitive drive, hostility and impatience are qualities which help social advancement in a free market economy. Indeed an editorial in the Lancet went so far as to hint that having fewer people with Type A personalities might threaten our economic potential.[18] Yet it is not privileged businessmen but the people at the bottom of the scale who are at the greatest risk of heart disease. Type A personality clearly cannot account for the social class inequalities in heart disease.

Despite this, after briefly advising meditation and deep breathing, 'Beating heart disease' dismisses the environmental determinants of health. This clears the way for advice to stop smoking, eat a better diet and exercise more.

The DHSS book, 'Avoiding heart attacks' gives a detailed account of its views on the causes of coronary heart disease, with a chapter devoted to each life style risk factor. There is no mention of social class inequalities, work, unemployment or any other social factor. Four pages deal with stress and personality, which have 'unproven' status as risk factors. The section on stress concludes:

'Stress cannot be associated with a particular job or way of life but only with the way an individual responds to it... The fascinating aspect of the whole question of stress, however, is how some people seem able to take in their stride "the slings and arrows of outrageous fortune" while others are unable to cope with relatively minor buffetings. The differences between people and their response to life's challenges could be the missing dimension in the risk factors of coronary heart disease'.[19]

The only mention of psycho-social factors deals with them as though they were a problem of the individual and, therefore, yet another personal risk factor. The suggested way of dealing with this one is not by changing eating habits or exerting will power over the urge to smoke but by 'walking the dog'. The possibility that material circumstances work against people's attempts to lead a 'healthy lifestyle' is seldom considered.

Similarly, external social factors are excluded from other health education materials. Stress becomes the catch-all category for everything which cannot be subsumed under the classic risk factors. When stress is mentioned, it is usually to deny that it plays a major part in causing heart disease. The Open University 'Healthy Eating' course includes a section on reducing risks for heart disease. The only mention of non life style factors reads, 'personality and stress are not fully accepted as risk factors and are almost impossible to measure.'[20]

These materials reflect the opinions expressed in the various 'expert reports' on CHD prevention that have appeared over the past few years. The World Health Organisation text 'Primary Prevention of Coronary Heart Disease' devotes only a small space to 'psychological and social factors'. A short discussion of Type A behaviour is followed by the plea that 'the danger is that public and professional misconceptions about stress, whereby it is assigned a primary role in the genesis of CHD, may divert attention from demonstrated needs in prevention.'[21]

The reason why attention is given to stress, if only to deny its importance, is because the lay public consider it an important cause of heart disease. A survey carried out for the HEC revealed that stress was the most frequently mentioned cause of heart disease.[22] This was reported in the HEC's newspaper as demonstrating the crass ignorance of the general public under the headline 'Heart disease risks ignored'.[23] The HEC survey required people to volunteer causes of heart disease, which were then coded according to a preconceived scheme. This had separate categories for various diet related factors, such as bad/wrong diet, too much fat/sugar in the diet, high cholesterol, excessive drinking and being too fat. Dividing up the numbers of factors associated with diet in this way resulted in several separate groups, with relatively small numbers in each. This allowed the public's knowledge of a possible link between diet and health to be underestimated, perhaps for polemical reasons.

In contrast to this, surveys which present possible risk factors to subjects and ask whether they cause heart disease, or ask what change people would make in their lives to avoid heart disease reveal high levels of agreement with conventional wisdom about life-style factors and ill health.[24] Where lay beliefs differ from what health educators hope people believe they tend to reflect reality. Beliefs about the preventability of disease are strongly related to social position, with more fatalistic opinions being held by the poorest people.[25] As we mentioned above, this group has high mortality rates which cannot be explained by lifestyle factors alone. The beliefs therefore describe the situation as it exists.

**Eat yourself fitter?** The over-riding importance attached to smoking, diet and physical inactivity leading to the exclusion of politically embarassing social factors, is one aspect of what has come to be known as victim blaming. Individuals are blamed for having themselves brought about any disease they suffer through irresponsible behaviour.

A second aspect of victim blaming is demonstrated by the assumption that choices about what people eat, how much they exercise, or whether they smoke are freely made. Clearly this is not the case. The choice to indulge in the 'drugs of solace', tobacco and alcohol, is hardly made in a vacuum.[26] Wide ranging social pressures come to bear upon people to adopt such behaviour. Not least of these are pressures generated by organisations with a vested interest in cigarette, alcohol and junk food consumption.

Edwina Currie has claimed that 'the government is playing its part' in the campaign to reduce smoking. Accepting contributions from tobacco companies to Conservative Party funds is only one aspect of how governments play their part. Norman Tebbit told workers at a Rothmans factory that the Conservatives do not want to stop cigarette advertising. 'If we give in to the people who want to stop smoking, then we will have to give in to those people who want to stop drinking, or taking sugar in tea because it is fattening, or skiing because it is supposedly dangerous.'[27] The government also plans to subsidise the production of Skoal Bandits, which are tobacco sachets for sucking, to the tune of £1 million.[28] Yet these can lead to mouth cancer as well as to cigarette smoking via nicotine addiction. The way the full economic and political power of the tobacco companies is used to ensure a continued market for cigarettes belies the myth of freely made choices.[29]

In the next section we describe the forces which constrain people from choosing a healthy diet. The case of the National Advisory Committee of Nutrition Education (NACNE) report, which recommended an unequivocal shift in the British diet, illustrates the degree to which truly free choice is discouraged. The NACNE report was first suppressed, then, at the hands of the food industry advisors to the DHSS and the Ministry of Agriculture, Fisheries and Food, its status was downgraded from that of an official statement to a mere advisory document.

Two years after this, Dr Donald Acheson, DHSS' Chief Medical Officer, gave a presidential address on 'Prevention and Government' at the 1985 annual meeting of the British Association for the Advancement of Science. In it, he said:

'another example of co-operation between Government Departments in the interest of health is the recent report on "Diet and Cardiovascular Disease" — the so called COMA report which makes a number of recommendations particularly in respect of diet with the aim of reducing the incidence of coronary heart disease. Obviously the recommendations have implications for the food industry as well as the general population and it was therefore significant that the report was welcomed by the Ministers in MAFF as well as by the Health Departments. It is hoped that advice which translates science into choices for diet in everyday terms will soon be published.'[30]

The 'guide in everyday terms' referred to by Dr Acheson was the Joint Advisory Council on Nutrition Education (JACNE) report. This was based on the advice of the COMA committee, which was considerably less stringent than that of NACNE. Yet three weeks before Dr Acheson's speech welcoming the JACNE report, the Sunday Times reported that he had put pressure on Dr John Garrow, who chaired the JACNE to change the report in a way which would diminish the negative impact of the committee's advice on the consumption of butter, milk and meat. These are the most important sources of animal fat, which is believed to cause heart disease. Even the Sunday Times was driven to demurely comment that 'the food industry makes major contributions to Conservative Party funds'.[31] The translation of 'science into choices for diet in everyday terms' is clearly not as straightforward or innocent as it sounds.

**Health and government policy.** Exhortations to look after yourself ignore the existence of determinants of ill-health which can only be tackled through changing government policy. This is clearly the case for food, tobacco and alcohol policy. But it is also true of the policies which allow for the existence of mass unemployment, poverty and deregulated working environments. On many occasions, the government makes decisions which have detrimental effects on health and then tries to tackle the consequences through victim blaming health education.

For example, over Christmas 1986 the Department of Transport launched a campaign against drunken driving. In an attempt to persuade people to leave their cars at home, it used the slogans 'don't get a ban get a bus' and 'use a bus for Christmas'. The very same Department of Transport had pushed through legislation deregulating and privatising the bus service earlier in 1986, leading to a situation where unprofitable late night and rural services were not running. In many areas there were no services from before Christmas until January 2nd.[32] The slogans were guaranteed to fall on deaf ears.

A second example is the issue of cold weather payments during the cold spell in January 1987. The DHSS had made the regulations about cold weather payments for old age pensioners more stringent in late 1986. If these regulations had applied in 1986, only £1.8 million would have been paid out rather than the actual figure of £4 million. The average temperature had to be more than 1.5 degrees below freezing for a whole calendar week before applications could be made. There was a public outcry, and amidst this, the government announced payments of £5 per week, based on predicted temperatures. No permanent change has, however, been made in the regulations, so there is no long term commitment to a more adequate system of payment. What is more, after a general election, the government may be less disposed to yield to public opinion in the short term.

Although they were not guaranteed money, old age pensioners were given plenty of advice. An HEC booklet 'Keeping Warm in Winter' suggests things you could do for yourself to save money:

'If it is really cold and you are worried about the amount of heat you are using, move to one room for living and sleeping, and heat only that one ... Do not wash your hands or dishes under running water. Put the plug in or use a bowl... If you have all your blankets in use and are still cold, layers of newspaper between them will help.'[33]

The inconsistency between the actual nature of the cause of ill-health and the attempts to deal with the problem by health education is obvious. Cold related disease amongst badly off pensioners cannot simply be prevented by advice, nor can people take buses that do not run. With other diseases these relationships are less obvious, but they still exist. Changing behaviours cannot occur in a society where the interests vested in maintaining them are strong. Nor can lifestyle changes, by themselves, eradicate premature disease.

The effective prevention of ill-health requires concerted action at the level of public policy. Charles Webster, who was commissioned to write the official history of the NHS, has long argued that there should have been a preventive wing of the NHS from its conception. Seen in this light, the announcement in November 1986 that the HEC was to be replaced, in April 1987 by a Special Health Authority, directly accountable to the DHSS, might have seemed a positive initiative. Agencies promoting health clearly require closer connections with government bodies. Improving health does not seem to be the prime reason for this change, however. The British Medical Journal suggested that a major impetus for the takeover was DHSS' concern that the HEC was becoming too political in its attacks on the alcohol industry.

One of the first people appointed to the new Authority was Anne Burdus, an advertising executive with links with the tobacco and alcohol industries. JACNE is to be wound up. Its chairperson, Dr John Garrow, an influential critic of government food policy, was one of the HEC members not selected to be a member of the new Authority. Other 'food experts' of a different type have been found to be more suitable appointments for the new Authority. They are Carey Dennis, a senior Tesco executive, and Caroline Waldegrave, a managing director of Prue Leith's School of Food and Wine, who is married to junior environment minister William Waldegrave.[35]

The first venture by the new Special Health Authority is the 'Look after your Heart' campaign, to which we referred earlier. This is a classic victim blaming project. It aims to:

'raise people's awareness of the risk factors relating to Coronary Heart Disease, and to put across simple messages about how to reduce the risk. It could be described as a national call to arms to beat heart disease, Britain's number one killer... The rate of premature death and illness can be reduced by simple changes in everyday lifestyles — changing diet, taking regular exercise, stopping smoking. This will be the theme of the new campaign. It will not be focussed exclusively on the prevention of heart disease, but will encourage the adoption of healthier lifestyles in general.'[36]

This 'national call to arms' is being made through a high profile campaign using television, newspapers, radio. Its publicity materials include badges, T-shirts, and booklets and it is seeking positive endorsement by well known personalities, and consumer groups. What is its strategy for tackling social class inequalities in health?

'The "Look After Your Heart" campaign will be aimed at everyone. However some groups, mainly the lower socio-economic groups C2, D, E, are hard to reach with health messages and advice. The prevalence of heart disease is also greatest amongst these groups. Special efforts will be made to reach these groups with the campaign messages... A new easy-to-read guide to healthy living will be widely available from the start of the campaign. It will contain simple messages and will be specifically targetted at those groups most at risk.'[36]

The 'hard to reach' people in the lower social class groups are not so unaware of the victim blaming nature of such materials as the DHSS might like to think.[37] It is not knowledge about the relationship between lifestyle factors and ill health that they lack, but the power to deal effectively with the causes of ill-health.

Opinion polls show that the government's health record is an electoral liability. A publicity campaign claiming that ill-health is caused by irresponsible behaviour absolves the government from guilt. This single thread runs through Edwina Currie's comments and the 'Look After Your Heart' campaign. In an election year it looks as though we will be force fed until we believe that health is only a matter of individual behaviour and not any responsibility of the government. The Director of a pressure group, the Coronary Prevention Group, said on a radio programme that people with heart disease were 'victims of their own ignorance'.[38] It seems we may become victims of our educators.

## References

1. DHSS press release, September 4 1986.
2. Anderson R. Health Promotion: an overview, European Monographs in Health Education Research 1984;6: 1-125.
3. DHSS. Prevention and Health: Everybody's Business. London: HMSO, 1976.
4. Tannahill A. Health Promotion — caring concern. Journal of Medical Ethics 1984;1:196-198.
5. DHSS. Prevention and Health. London: HMSO, 1977.
6. Written reply. Hansard, November 25 1986, col 121.
7. Wilkinson RG. Socio-economic differences in mortality: interpreting the data on their size and trends. In: Wilkinson RG, ed. Class and Health. London: Tavistock, 1986.
8. Marmot MG, Shipley MJ and Rose G. Inequalities in death — specific explanations of a general pattern? Lancet 1984; i: 1003-1006.
9. General Register Office. Ninth Annual Report of the Registrar General of Births, Deaths and Marriages in England. London: HMSO, 1849.
10. OPCS. Area Mortality. Decennial Supplement 1969-1973, England and Wales. London: HMSO, 1981.
11. West R. Geographic variations in mortality from ischaemic heart disease in England and Wales. British Journal of Preventive and Social Medicine 1977; 31; 245-250.
12. Russek HI, Zohman BL, Relative significance of heredity, diet and occupational stress in coronary heart disease in young adults. American Journal of the Sciences 1958; 235: 266-275.
13. Knutsson A, Akerstedt T, Jansson BG, Orth-Gomer K. Increased risk of ischaemic heart disease in shift workers. Lancet 1986; ii: 89-92.
14. Alfredsson L, Spetz CL, Theorell T. Type of occupation and near future hospitalisation for myocardial infarction and some other diagnoses. International Journal of Epidemiology 1985; 14: 378-388.
15. Coronary Prevention Group. Coronary Heart Disease and Asians in Britain. London: CPG, 1986.
16. Health Education Council. Looking After Yourself. London: HEC, 1979.
17. Health Education Council. Beating Heart Disease. London: HEC, 1983.
18. Lancet. Are we killing ourselves or not?. Lancet 1981; ii: 669-670.
19. DHSS. Avoiding Heart Attacks. London: HMSO, 1981.
20. Open University. Healthy Eating. London: Open University, 1985.
21. World Health Organisation. Primary Prevention of Coronary Heart Disease. Denmark: WHO, 1985.

22. Research Surveys of Great Britain. Heart Disease. London: RSGB for the HEC, 1981.
23. Health Education News. Heart disease risks ignored. London: HEC, September 1981.
24. Welsh Heart Programme. The Pulse of Wales. Cardiff: Heartbeat Report No. 4, 1986.
25. Calnan M. Maintaining health and preventing illness: a comparison of the perceptions of women from different social classes. Health Promotion 1986; 1: 167-177.
26. Cameron D, Jones I. An epidemiological and sociological analysis of the use of alcohol, tobacco and other drugs of solace. Community Medicine 1985; 7: 18-29.
27. Wilkinson J. Tobacco. Harmondsworth: Penguin Books, 1986.
28. 'Skoal Bandits' in Health Care. Parliamentary Monitor No. 2, December 8 1986.
29. Taylor P. The Smoke Ring. London: The Bodley Head, 1986.
30. Acheson ED. Prevention and Government. British Association for the Advancement of Science. Annual meeting. August 26-30 1985.
31. Guide to healthy eating blocked.Sunday Times. August 9 1985.
32. Buses put anti-drink drive on the rocks. Guardian. December 8, 1986.
33. Health Education Council. Keeping warm in winter. London: HEC, 1982.
34. Smith R. Long live health promotion. British Medical Journal 1986; 293: 1957-1958.
35. Fowler abandons crusade to fight heart disease with health food. Guardian. March 3 1987.
36. DHSS/Health Education Council. 'Looking After Yourself' campaign. London: DHSS/HEC, September 1986.
37. Farrant, W, Russell J. Beating heart disease: a case study in the production of Health Education Council publications. Bedford Way Paper 28. London: University of London Institute of Education, 1986.
38. Dillon A on BBC Radio 4. October 10 1986.

# Food, health and welfare

Mentions of food and health usually evoke images of brown rice and vegetables on one hand and sausage, chips and an additive-laden instant pudding on the other. It is hoped that this section encourages the reader to see beyond the individual's choice of food to the connections between poverty, diet and health, the food industry and government control of the food supply.

Classic diet-health research of the last thirty years has focused on the diseases of 'over-nutrition'. These studies, for all their weaknesses,[1] support a growing consensus on the ideal nutrient balance of a diet conducive to health and well-being. The BMA's 1986 report 'Diet, Nutrition and Health', for instance, gives dietary objectives regarding intakes of: energy; total, saturated and polyunsaturated fats; salt; fibre; sugar; alcohol and complex carbohydrates. The objectives echo the preoccupations of those who see heart disease, stroke, cirrhosis, large bowel cancer and dental caries as the main diet-related and hence preventable diseases.

Despite reports such as the BMA's, the individualistic approach to disease prevention of our medical and scientific elites still prevails. It is reflected in their reluctance to demand policy changes likely to disturb political forces. It is certainly not merely disagreement about the validity of the evidence linking diet to disease which leads to this conservatism for the evidence here is stronger than that supporting many accepted routine medical procedures.

The powerful campaigning work of a small group of people, including Philip James (Director of the Rowett Nutrition Research Institute, Aberdeen) and Caroline Walker (nutritionist, ex-City and Hackney Health Authority), has forced some policymakers and health professionals to admit that problems exist at a structural level.

An editorial in The Lancet[2] rehearsed the now well-known story of how the 1983 NACNE (National Advisory Committee on Nutrition Education) Report[3] was obstructed by ministerial and food industry tactics. The particular success of NACNE lay in its bid to recommend practical dietary changes, which previous reports had not done. Public concern at the high rate of heart disease had grown massively by that time and in 1984 the COMA Committee Report admitted that a diet-health problem did exist in this country.[4]

So now Government ministers recognise the importance of heart disease prevention, at least when talking to the diet-health lobby. For example, Peggy Fenner, Junior Minister of Agriculture, Fisheries & Food said at the Coronary Prevention Group Annual General Meeting in May 1986: 'Heart disease is a matter of major concern to the government.'

How is this concern translated into action? The main initiatives have involved health education. 'Heartbeat Wales', 'Glasgow 2000' and in 1987, Northern Ireland's 'Change of Heart' and England and Wales' 'Look After Your Heart' campaigns are large projects aimed at reducing the toll of heart disease. Many other local programmes exist. Their strategy has been to intervene in the process considered to lead to heart disease at the level of the individual, namely the lifestyle risk factors of smoking, diet and exercise.

This approach implies that the mass of the population needs to be educated and persuaded to change their way of life. As far as diet is concerned, this means that most of us are eating the 'wrong' food. Social and economic obstacles to health are for the most part ignored; the assumption is that our habits are formed in a vacuum. The risk factor approach is at best a partial explanation for the prevalence of heart disease but again little is spoken of this in the mainstream of health education.

The emphasis on health education/promotion is not the result of some natural and politically neutral evolution of policy. Health promotion campaigns are good propaganda and relatively cheap. They create the appearance of active concern. Most importantly they do not challenge the economic status quo, which supports present social divisions and hence present particularly high rates of degenerative disease amongst the poor. The implication of these health education campaigns is that what we eat is determined purely by personal choice. This is not so.

**Who eats what and why?** There is much evidence of differences in the diet of rich and poor, and these have health implications.

The 1983 National Food Survey shows continuing class differences in foods eaten. Comparison of high and low income households shows that consumption of many foods is related to income — large, poor families eat little fruit, cheese, carcass meat, poultry, fish and fresh and frozen vegetables, and relatively large amounts of nutrient-poor foods such as processed meat products, lard, sugar and jam.[5]

The first report of the nationwide 1983 survey on the diet of schoolchildren confirms and quantifies what had been suspected. More than three quarters of all 10-15 year olds had fat intakes above 35 per cent of dietary energy — the COMA recommended maximum. On average, almost half of this fat came from chips, crisps, biscuits, chocolate and burgers.

The press release accompanying publication of the report advocated simply 'more information and education about healthy eating' to deal with this overconsumption of 'junk' food. Apparently neither the abolition of nutritional standards for school meals in 1980 nor the staggering amounts of money spent on advertising confectionery are considered important here.

Children of unemployed parents were significantly shorter than others. Although the consumption of individual nutrients did not differ significantly between these and other groups, the overall patterns of fat, mineral and vitamin consumption suggest that a composite measure of the quality of the diet would show a statistically significant difference between groups defined by income and social class.[6]

'Jam tomorrow?', a survey of food circumstances, attitudes and consumption of a thousand people on low incomes in the north of England conducted in 1983/4, gives a special insight into the links between financial hardship and diet.[7] A quarter of unemployed respondents reported being short of money for food. Thirty seven per cent of this group said they had missed a meal in the previous year for lack of money. One in eight of unemployed and retired respondents indicated that they did not have use of a fridge.

The survey highlighted an important weakness of health education when it is not accompanied by the necessary policy changes, in this case increased payments for food purchases to enable those on low incomes to follow health advice. A diet recall question revealed that more than a third of unemployed respondents had eaten chips (a 'bad' food) in the previous 24 hours, despite the knowledge that food was important for health (85 per cent said it was "fairly" or "very important"). There cannot be continuity between beliefs, knowledge and behaviour without the necessary cash. It should be noted here that chips are a high energy-value food; whether or not they are to be classed as a food to be avoided depends on the method of preparation.[8]

Between 1980 and 1983 food spending by low income households (bottom 25 per cent) rose by only 6.1 per cent compared with 15.6 per cent for rich (top 25 per cent) households.

Bread is an important source of dietary fibre and many nutrients, among them protein, calcium and iron. Wholemeal bread is superior in most respects in terms of its nutritional value, compared to white. The 1983 National Food Survey shows that households whose head earned over 250 gross per week ate 349g of white bread per person per week and 198g of wholemeal and brown. For households whose head earned 80 or less, white bread consumption was 794g — over double — and brown and wholemeal consumption was only half (96g).[5]

When wholemeal costs more than white, exhortations to switch to a higher fibre diet are clearly unhelpful. How can people on low incomes be expected to be able to eat more wholemeal bread, when food pricing structures encourage them not to?

The last government review of this subject was published in 1981. Unfortunately the expert panel did not support Professor Morris's proposal that

the following be included amongst the report's recommendations:
'over the period of a few years the government makes the necessary arrangements with industry and trade so that the price of the standard brown and standard wholemeal loaf is lowered to that of the standard white loaf'.[9]

An effective food policy must undoubtedly include such measures if the health of Britain's poor is to improve.

**Low income families.** Official statistics published in 1986 paint a grim picture of poverty in the 'eighties. The low income family tables for 1983 show that at that time almost one in three lived on or just above the poverty line.

The tables were published a year after the information should have been available, we must assume because the government wished to conceal the details (see table 5.26), which show that in 1983 16.4 million adults and children were living within 40 per cent of the Supplementary Benefit level in Great Britain. This represents a 42 per cent increase over 1979.

Publication meant placing a copy of the report in the House of Commons library on the last day of the parliamentary session. Hansard reveals that this took place in response to a written question from a little-known backbencher, Edwina Currie.[10]

**Table 5.26**
Estimated numbers of people unemployed or officially defined as in poverty, Great Britain, 1979 and 1983

| People | Thousands | |
|---|---|---|
| | 1979 | 1983 |
| (a)  Receiving Supplementary or Housing Benefits | 3980 | 6130 |
| (b)  Relative Net Resources below 140% (see note) | 7590 | 10250 |
| Total in poverty trap (a + b) | 11570 | 16380 |
| Estimated numbers of people including dependants | | |
| Unemployed | 1240 | 4110 |

Note: The Relative Net Resources (RNR) measure of disposable income is defined as:

$$RNR = \frac{NI - NHC - OEE}{SBSR} \times 100$$

where
NI = net income (net earnings/social security payments excluding housing)
NHC = net housing cost (net rent/mortgage interest, rates)
OEE = other essential expenditure (estimated fares to work)
SBSR = supplementary benefit scale rate (ordinary rate, or for retired, long-term rate)

Source: DHSS, Low Income Families 1983[12] Data derived from Family Expenditure Survey.

The junior Social Security Minister, John Major, in his answer claimed that part of the increase in those classified as poor results from a 6 per cent rise in the real value of Supplementary Benefit between 1975 and 1983. Based on the Retail Price Index, this figure does not properly take into account the actual rise in the cost of living experienced by the unemployed and badly paid. The Low Pay Unit has for several years costed the 'Low Paid Price Index' using a basket of goods based on the buying power of the lowest fifth of households by income.[11] This gives a more valid estimate of 2.7 per cent for the increase in Supplementary Benefit, less than half the government's figure.

The major reason for the increase in those below the Government's own poverty level is not liberalisation in the definition of poverty. Nor is it demographic change, as the age structure of the population changed little between 1979 and 1983. The cause is simple: unemployment and low pay coupled with subsistence welfare payments resulted in an additional 4.8 million people being thrown into the poverty trap.

Having reluctantly been forced to make these estimates public, the government simultaneously announced its plans for action: the method used to set the poverty line (see note to table 5.26) will be changed for the 1987 set of figures. To use the DHSS' phrase, 'a technical review will examine the methods and assumptions at present used in the collation of these tables'.[12]

Though many of its people are poor, taken together the countries of the United Kingdom are not. We have the fourteenth highest gross national product per person internationally. There is no absolute necessity for the extreme divisions in wealth, income, education and social status that exist.

The decline in wealth differentials this century has been halted by monetarist policies. In 1984 the richest 10 per cent owned 52 per cent of marketable wealth (homes, stocks and shares, pension rights, etc.) while the poorest half of the adult population owned only 7 per cent.[13]

The product of these social and economic inequalities for the poor are bad housing, alienation and ill-health; the poor always knew this, and since the Black Report no one is able to deny it.[14] The health costs of economic policies which punish the poor are increasing, as is shown by the new Decennial Supplement on Occupational Mortality for 1979-83 (see earlier).

Food is an important mediator in this situation, and not solely in terms of physical well-being. Access to food for people forced to live in poverty is significant for many reasons. It affects both psychological and physical well being, and just as importantly, helps or hinders plans to work, particularly for women as the main food providers in the home. For all people, but particularly those of non-English origin, the price and availability of traditional foods will influence factors as diverse as amount of time spent on food shopping to feelings of cultural and personal identity.

**Vested interests.** The development of a coordinated food policy will not take place while the government is advised by committees dominated effectively, if not numerically, by industrial vested interests (see table 5.27). The Priorities Board, which advises the Ministry of Agriculture, Fisheries and Food (MAFF) on

**Table 5.27**

Membership of policy committee at the Ministry of Agriculture, Fisheries and Food for composition, labelling, advertising, additives and contaminants.

| | |
|---|---|
| Chair | Government scientist |
| 5 | food industry employees (1 retired) |
| 3 | medical doctors |
| 1 | advertising agency journalist |
| 1 | industry consultant |
| 1 | Local authority scientist |
| 1 | consumer representative |
| 1 | trading standards officer |
| 1 | home economist |

Source: MAFF, 1987

research policy is chaired by Sir Kenneth Durham, chairman of Unilever. These bodies give only a weak voice to consumers; workers in the industry have no representation at all, though it not only produces our food, but is also one of the countries' major employers. In 1986 2.8 million people were in food-related employment, this representing 13 per cent of employees in Great Britain.[15]

Policy-making could be made more democratic by adding food industry trade unionists, who have a special understanding and interest in production processes, as well as dietitians, other health professionals and proper consumer representation to these bodies. At present responsibilty is split between the Department of Health and Social Security (the COMA committee) and MAFF.

Overall responsibility for food and health policy needs to be clarified as part of a review of economic and social policies to tackle the causes of social inequality and the resulting ill-health.

UK food production and consumption is not controlled by either the government and ministers of the day, or the EEC alone. Leaving aside the lack of consumer and non-'expert' consultation that exists in the present statutory framework of Britain's food system, the main determinant of the food we eat is the food industry itself.

There is unprecedented concentration of ownership in many sectors of the industry with five companies controlling two thirds or more of gross output in each of the following sectors: fats and oils, fish products, grain milling, bread, biscuits and flour confectionery, ice cream, sweets and chocolate.[15] Such concentration of ownership implies concentration of decision-making, which cannot be in the interests of consumers.

In 1985 the food industry spent £325 million on advertising and a further £2,400 million on packaging. In that year Rowntree Mackintosh, Mars and Cadbury together spent £66.7 million on advertising their chocolates, whilst the entire HEC budget for promotion of healthy eating was only £750,000.[15] Similar excesses exist in the retailing sector: Sainsbury and Tesco alone have 59 per cent of the packaged grocery business in London.[16] It seems that commercial interests have called the tune in the British food system in recent years. The situation is changing at last, as interest in food policy and healthy eating spreads.

The food industry is conducting a good public relations campaign. For example the nutritional labelling schemes of the large supermarket chains have provoked much admiration, but where are the labels saying 'high added sugar' and 'low in fibre', etc? Such schemes add to the confusion, since the labelling only emphasises the positive attributes of a food ,whilst serving only the retailers interests.

The industry is fighting back. The Food & Drugs Industry Bulletin attacks bodies such as the London Food Commission (LFC) as 'a self-appointed group of activists'.[17] The LFC, established in 1985 to be a consumer and industry voice, when none previously existed, is advised by a council of representatives of statutory, voluntary, and trade union organisations; it was forward-funded by a grant from a local authority.

The LFC can justifiably claim greater financial independence and credibility than several organisations supported by the food industry which project an image of academic rigour whilst peddling what can only be described as gross propaganda.

The 'World Sugar Research Organisation' (wholly funded by the sugar industry), for instance, circulated an apparently authoritative three-page letter to GP's in July 1986 which gives the impression that current sugar intakes are not a dietary problem, provided that tooth decay is seen as a necessary evil: 'Sugars do not have a unique role in the aetiology of obesity'.

Nowhere does this letter remind doctors of the recommendations of the Royal College of Physicians' 1983 Obesity report: 'Food manufacturers should be encouraged...to reduce the fat and sugar content of a wide range of manufactured foods'; 'foods rich in...sugar need to be restricted on a long-term basis' for those who are overweight or obese. This working party also proposed 'a halving of the average UK sugar consumption to increase the nutrient density of the diet' on the basis that 'sugar is an unnecessary form of energy in a community with such a widespread overweight problem'.[18]

**Policy.** The debate about the future of the welfare state has shifted from being largely a defence of existing provision. The welfare state badly needs to be rebuilt (in the case of the NHS, quite literally) in the light of analyses of the failures of the past forty years.[19]

Within this reassessment, food policy plays an important role. Proponents of food-health intervention had to argue for an indiscriminate population approach to coronary heart disease (CHD), for example, in order to drive the issues home. We are told that the population mean of serum cholesterol is too high and the goal of a major reduction of CHD mortality requires us all, rather than just those with high blood cholesterol, to change our diet.

Now it is time to add a more detailed analysis of the structure and conditions within the food system so that future interventions will be effective in tackling the severest problems, namely the poor diet and bad health of unemployed people and those on low incomes. This reassessment must include issues such as food costs, food advertising, agricultural policies and the food subsidy system.

Many health educators tackle the issue of diet and income inequality by asserting that eating healthily is cheap. They do so in the absence of a real comparison of the cost of diets of low income households with that of a diet meeting current nutritional guidelines.

At present we can only assume that the DHSS sets the food cost component of Supplementary Benefit on the basis of Rowntree's 1901 'minimum subsistence diet'. In 1933 a BMA committee defined a physiologically based minimal diet which was used in the setting of benefit levels by Beveridge in 1942. The diet component has not been reviewed since.[20] This reflects very badly on a Government which claims 'major concern' for diet and health.

Neither DHSS nor MAFF have published the costing of a recommended diet, however the 1986 report 'Tightening Belts' shows that in practice a diet meeting the long term NACNE guidelines cost 35 per cent more than the current diet of group D, the lowest of the four income bands, in the 1983 National Food Survey.[21]

The issues now become clearer — for households with a low income lack of money is at the root of many health and often social problems. This lack will undermine attempts to follow nutritional advice to eat a healthy diet. Whilst sound nutritional advice and information should be available for all, at the same time food pricing and promotion should be such that no-one is constrained from choosing good, healthy food.

## References

1. U205 course team. A cautionary tale. In: Caring for health: dilemmas and prospects. Milton Keynes: Open University Press, 1985:166-77.
2. Anonymous, Britain needs a food and health policy. Lancet 1986; 2: 434-6.
3. NACNE. Nutritional guidelines for health education in Britain, A report of the National Advisory Committee on Nutrition Education. London: HEC, 1983.
4. Department of Health and Social Security. Diet and Cardiovascular Disease (the COMA Report). Report on Health and Social Subjects, Number 28. London: HMSO, 1984.
5. MAFF, Household Food Consumption and Expenditure: 1983. Annual Report of the National Food Survey Committee. London: HMSO, 1985.
6. DHSS. The Diets of British Schoolchildren : 1983. Preliminary report of a nationwide dietary survey of British schoolchildren. London: DHSS, 1986.
7. Lang TM et al. Jam Tomorrow? Food Policy Unit, Manchester Polytechnic, 1984
8. Hill J, Mellor J, West A. Low Fat Chips. Nutrition and Food Science July 1984: 8-9.
9. DHSS. Nutritional Aspects Of Bread and Flour. Report on Health and Social Subjects Number 23. London: HMSO, 1981.
10. Written reply. Hansard, July 25th 1986, cols 711-712.
11. Low Pay Unit, Low Pay Bulletin, July-October 1978
12. DHSS. Low Income Families-1983. London: DHSS, 1986. Tables calculated from Family Expenditure Survey data.
13. Guardian, September 23 1986. Based on: Inland Revenue Statistics. London: HMSO, 1986.
14. Department of Health and Social Security. Inequalities in Health. London: DHSS, 1980. Townsend P, Davidson N. Inequalities in Health. London: Pelican, 1982.
15. London Food Commission, Food Facts 1986, free from the LFC, PO Box 291, London N5 1DU.
16. CES/London Food Commission. Food Retailing in London. LFC, 1985.
17. Food & Drugs Industry Bulletin. Oyez Business Studies Ltd. February, 1986.
18. Royal College of Physicians, 'Obesity' report. London: Royal College of Physicians of London, 1983.
19. See for example: Graham H. Health and Welfare. London: Macmillan Education, 1985.
20. Walker CL and Church M. Poverty by administration: a review of supplementary benefits, nutrition and scale rates. J Human Nutrition 1978; 32:5-18. Kincaid JC. The subsistence principle. In: Poverty and Equality in Britain. London: Pelican, 1979.
21. Cole-Hamilton I and Lang TM. Tightening Belts. London Food Commission, 1986.

# 6
# Monitoring the System

IN THIS part, we look critically at the range of ways currently used to monitor the performance of the NHS, and explore some ways of relating these activities more directly to the public's interests in the service.

## What do we mean by monitoring?

The general concept of monitoring the performance of a system consists of firstly measuring the level or value of selected and relevant outputs, then comparing this level with a previously-determined and desired reference level such as a target or objective, and then finally altering the inputs to the process if there is a discrepancy. Monitoring activity can be found in many areas of the NHS, and is essential to the operation of such a complex system, especially when implementing changes.

However, a relatively small amount of this kind of activity involves monitoring performance towards targets set by 'the public' who are variously seen as users of the services, taxpayers and voters. It can be argued that in a democracy, this occurs by broad policies being endorsed by the people who vote for the party which wins a general election. In this case the only practicable way to operate continuous monitoring and evaluation is through the traditional routes of civil service and NHS staff accounting to the Secretary of State who is then accountable to parliament. Quite apart from the fact that election manifestos rarely spell out fine details of the way broad policies will affect the delivery of individual local services, they are open to different interpretations within the NHS, and to change between elections. There is therefore very little sense in which the emphasis of various monitoring activities directly reflects the concerns of the public. At the same time, the level of frustration is growing as the NHS is clearly not performing as well as many people, including staff as well as patients, would wish. Performance monitoring activity is described in more detail below, and ways of improving it are suggested.

## Setting objectives and targets

The 'official' overall objectives of the NHS are little different from the conception in the 1944 White paper. It has been argued that they are unattainable, because demand for health care is insatiable. Therefore, it is suggested that there is little point in seeking more resources for the service. While it is clear that demands for health care are generated by factors outside the NHS, as well as by developments in medical skills and techniques, the above argument only serves to emphasise the need for greater openness and public participation in decisions about priorities for using NHS resources, and about the proportion of a relatively finite sum of public funds to be spent on the NHS. This raises issues of the need to increase the public's awareness of health matters, and their right to a say, and how to make the NHS more democratically accountable, without simply favouring the most articulate or vociferous groups. In terms of the year-to-year operation of the NHS, targets are set by central government relating to its broad aims or objectives, often rather indirectly. These affect its structures and processes throughout the service. For example, the RAWP formula has produced financial targets for regions to operate within; in theory at least measures of progress towards these targets reflect an equalisation of 'access' to equal services on a geographical basis.

Targets and action to achieve them are often only described in terms of structures such as management hierarchies and building programmes, or processes such as the number of operations performed, or the throughput of patients. There is an increasing awareness that achieving targets set in these terms does not necessarily mean that the NHS is improving the nation's health, either in terms of the outcomes of peoples' encounters with these structures and processes, or more widely in terms of preventing ill-health.

A greater attention to outcomes of the service will naturally raise difficult questions about priorities for care. Members of the wider public may view these differently from priorities pursued by, or imposed upon, members of health authorities. Since neither members of district or regional health authorities, nor, for that matter, Community Health Councils are elected to those positions, the priorities and targets to be pursued have always been shaped by central government. This is despite the broad objective, reaffirmed by the Royal Commission of the NHS as a 'national service responsive to local needs'.[1]

# Monitoring structure and process

Monitoring the structure and process of health care tends to be dominated and shaped by central forces, although the data collected may be used locally in short or long term planning as well as being submitted for regional and DHSS scrutiny. For example, the implementation of the Griffiths report, which continues to have a major influence on the shape of health services right down to clinic and ward level, has reinforced monitoring processes which are designed to convey largely quantitative information back to the 'centre', via such means as annual reviews, manpower returns and Rayner-type scrutinies of the use of NHS property and land.

**Performance Indicators.** A recent development is the use of routinely collected health service statistics to produce so called 'performance indicators'. These were first developed by John Yates of the Inter-Authority Comparisons and Consultancy group at the Health Services Management Centre of the University of Birmingham. The DHSS has subsequently produced its own set of Performance Indicators (PIs) which cover manpower, estate, finance and clinical performance.

The DHSS PIs are intended to be used only by NHS managers and are not available in a form that is readily accessible. As the promotional brochure[2] put it, 'If you are a manager or assist one, you will find that PIs provide information which will help you to examine performance, identify scope for improvement and decide whether any action should be taken'. This does not necessarily debar other people from looking at them, but they will have to have access to the right type of computer as PIs are circulated on floppy disk only.

PIs are presented so that any district can examine its own performance in relation to the performance of other districts in England. Figure 6.1 gives an example of the type of information that can be obtained from John Yates' PI package. The graph shows the distribution of values for a selected indicator, percentage bed emptiness in the specialty of gynaecology, for districts in England. A different print-out summarises the data on several indicators to give a district profile for a particular specialty. An example of a profile for gynaecology in the health district of Haringey is given in Figure 6.2. The selected indicators ive measures of:

Demand: waiting list per bed
    percentage non-urgent cases waiting over one year
Inputs: Beds per catchment population (where beds = no.of beds allocated
    to gynaecology and catchment population is an
    estimate of the population served by the district.)
Process: Length of stay, turnover interval, percentage day cases,
    outpatient attendance rate and outpatient clinic size

There are no measures of outcome included in this profile, either medical or in terms of quality of care or patient satisfaction, so it is difficult to judge a district's performance. For example, is it 'good' or 'bad' to have a longer length of stay than the average for England? It might be considered 'bad' if the longer lengths of stay do not result in any benefits for the patient, as shorter lengths of stay would allow more patients to be treated. However, there is very little research on the effects of varying length of stay on outcome. Of course, the success or otherwise of shorter lengths of stay also depends on the availability of adequate community care when the patient is discharged.

The DHSS in their version of PIs have attempted to cover a much wider area of activity. They have begun to tackle the area of quality but as no data is routinely collected on quality, they only provide a checklist of questions for health districts to consider such as these selected from the 13 on the Acute Care checklist:

'Is there a menu choice for main meals?'
'Is there a play area for young children accompanying mothers to antenatal/paediatrics outpatient clinics?'
'Have you a system to inform outpatients when clinics run late?'

PIs are quite often inappropriately used. One of the conclusions that is sometimes drawn from an examination of performance indicators is that the NHS does not need more resources but should make more efficient use of the resources it already has. An example of an indicator often used in this way is percentage bed occupancy, though, in order to use physical resources such as beds more efficiently, it may be necessary to have more staff or financial resources. Thus, for example, one of the reasons beds might not be used efficiently could be a shortage of nursing staff. It may often be cheaper to make 'inefficient' use of physical resources.

Performance indicators are intended to be a management tool and do provide a

**Figure 6.1 Inter Authority Comparisons 1985, per cent emptiness for gynaecology.**

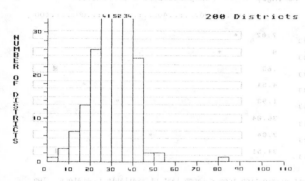

```
           INTER AUTHORITY COMPARISONS 1985

               % Emptiness FOR GYNAECOLOGY

              41 52 34          200 Districts
N
U    30
M
B
E
R
     20
O
F

D    10
I
S
T
R
I     0
C       0  10  20  30  40  50  60  70  80  90  100  110
T
S
```

PERCENTAGE BED EMPTINESS

Indicates : The proportion of available beds that are not used.

Value judgements : High figures suggest inefficient use is being made of allocated resources.

Reservations : 1. This indicator presents a very incomplete picture without analysis of other indicators such as length of stay and throughput per bed. For example, the generally accepted indicators of good practise, such as a short length of stay and high throughput per bed will increase emptiness.
2. The indicator can vary markedly according to clinical work pattern, eg. (a) pressure on resources may lead to low emptiness figures as length of stay is increased to 'protect' bed availability; (b) bed complement must be accurately counted to exclude day case care beds and any 5-day wards, as these will increase emptiness; (c) limited number of theatre sessions will cause an apparent problem of which bed emptiness is but a symptom.
3. Beds 'borrowed' from other specialties are borrowed at 100% occupancy. This may decrease true emptiness.
4. The figures for average emptiness may hide fluctuations even over relatively long periods.

Method of calculation : Number of unoccupied beds (available beds minus average occupied beds) divided by number of available beds expressed as as percentage.

John Yates                                    17 October 1986

Source: Reproduced from Performance Indicators package.

useful starting point for examining activity in a particular district. They are, however, being used for evaluation of a very narrow interpretation of 'performance' and they monitor districts by making comparisons with other districts rather than in terms of outcome, quality, satisfaction, equality of access or success in meeting needs of the population. Even those involved in their development have stated clearly the limited potential of these PIs in measuring the quality of care or its outcomes. They have pointed out that the indicators largely focus on measures which may be regarded as 'good' or 'bad' depending on different people's priorities. To be of any value, PIs must be seen in the wider context of the whole range of local services and conditions.

**Figure 6.2 Inter Authority Comparisons 1985, gynaecology district profile.**

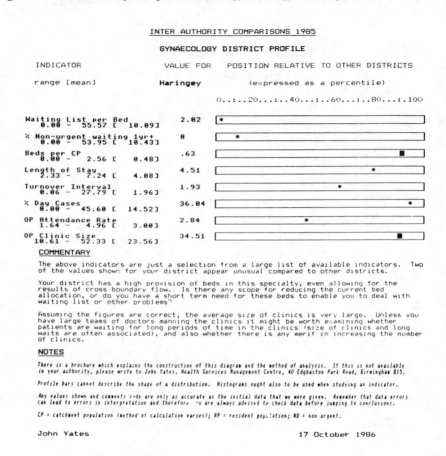

INTER AUTHORITY COMPARISONS 1985

GYNAECOLOGY DISTRICT PROFILE

| INDICATOR | VALUE FOR | POSITION RELATIVE TO OTHER DISTRICTS |
|---|---|---|
| range [mean] | **Haringey** | (expressed as a percentile) |

```
                                             0..:..20...:..40...:..60...:..80...:..100

Waiting List per Bed
  0.00 -  55.57 [  10.09]        2.02      [ *                                        ]
% Non-urgent waiting 1yr+
  0.00 -  53.95 [  10.43]        0         [   *                                      ]
Beds per CP
  0.00 -   2.56 [   0.48]         .63      [                                       ■  ]
Length of Stay
  2.33 -   7.24 [   4.08]        4.51      [                                    *     ]
Turnover Interval
  0.06 -  27.79 [   1.96]        1.93      [                           *              ]
% Day Cases
  0.00 -  45.60 [  14.52]       36.04      [                                      *   ]
OP Attendance Rate
  1.64 -   4.96 [   3.00]        2.84      [                  *                       ]
OP Clinic Size
 10.61 -  52.33 [  23.56]       34.51      [                          ■               ]
```

**COMMENTARY**

The above indicators are just a selection from a large list of available indicators.  Two of the values shown for your district appear unusual compared to other districts.

Your district has a high provision of beds in this specialty, even allowing for the results of cross boundary flow.  Is there any scope for reducing the current bed allocation, or do you have a short term need for these beds to enable you to deal with waiting list or other problems?

Assuming the figures are correct, the average size of clinics is very large.  Unless you have large teams of doctors manning the clinics it might be worth examining whether patients are waiting for long periods of time in the clinics (size of clinics and long waits are often associated), and also whether there is any merit in increasing the number of clinics.

**NOTES**

There is a brochure which explains the construction of this diagram and the method of analysis.  If this is not available in your authority, please write to John Yates, Health Services Management Centre, 40 Edgbaston Park Road, Birmingham B15.

Profile bars cannot describe the shape of a distribution.  Histograms ought also to be used when studying an indicator.

Any values shown and comments made are only as accurate as the initial data that we were given.  Remember that data errors can lead to errors in interpretation and therefore  you are always advised to check data before jumping to conclusions.

CP = catchment population (method of calculation varies); RP = resident population; NU = non urgent.

John Yates                                                    17 October 1986

Source: Reproduced from Performance Indicators package.

**Health Advisory Service.** A relatively independent review of services is carried out by the NHS Health Advisory Service. It was founded in 1969 and is independent of the DHSS and Welsh Office. It 'exists to maintain and improve the standards of management and organisation of patient care services, mainly those for the elderly and mentally ill.'[3] Since 1985, its reports have become public documents In 1985-86, services for elderly people were reviewed in eleven districts and services for people with mental illnesses were reviewed in 22 districts. A two year follow-up report was made on a further 20 districts which had been visited previously. Members of the visiting teams are health service professionals, including administrators, nurses, remedial staff, clinical psychologists, psychiatrists, consultants in geriatric medicine and social service staff. Although this organisation probably makes a useful contribution to the improvement of services for elderly and mentally ill people, there are no lay members on the review teams to give a user viewpoint.

**Quality Assurance.** Many health authorities have now appointed officers responsible for 'quality assurance', one of the latest NHS buzzwords. This is an area of monitoring which, while focussing on process rather than outcome, may at least be amenable to local developments for district or unit needs. For example, health authority-run quality assurance activities such as quality circles, may provide valuable feedback not only to professional groups working in the service, but may also be more accessible to the general public and take more acount of their views.

# Monitoring outcome

As has already been described in earlier chapters most of the official health statistics collected relate to inputs and activity and there is little routinely collected information on outcome either in terms of effectiveness of health care or patient satisfaction. The Steering Group on Health Services Information missed the opportunity of making improvements in this area, concentrating instead on the information needed for NHS management:

'we have not tackled specifically the information needed by health professionals to evaluate the results of their care; nor that needed by individual professional bodies to review the resources available to and the professional work of their members.'[4]

It went on to say that it had made an exception for maternity services 'because of the interest and involvement of the relevant professional bodies'.

It also stated that:

'In our work we have not directly considered information about the occurence of disease or about the health needs of populations except in so far as these can be inferred from data about hospital episodes and certain community health programmes; nor have we made recommendations about data describing health status or the clinical and social outcomes of the use of health services. The former are outside the scope of our work; for the latter methods of measuring these important variables are not sufficiently developed to allow their introduction as a routine in health service information systems. When further research has identified those indicators which are not only sought by health service managers but are also capable of routine collection in all health districts, consideration will be given to their inclusion in the minimum data set.'[4]

Obviously it is much more difficult to measure outcome but these difficulties should not stop progress being made in developing these measures. The implementation of the new information system is consuming an enormous amount of financial and management resources, the result of which might well be a system which is not much better than the old data system. A joint working group of the Steering Group and the Faculty of Community Medicine has also expressed concern about the proposed 'minimum data sets'.[5] The report of this working group has identified serious deficiencies in the Steering Group recommendations and put forward proposals on how these deficiencies should be remedied. Also, relatively little is yet known about what statistics are likely to be emerge from the new system, or to what extent anyone outside the health authorities and DHSS will be able to use them.

It is not suggested that measuring outcome is a simple matter. There are currently few direct indicators of outcome of health care, these largely being confined to clinical trials of drugs and limited experimental comparisons of types of disease management or surgery. Many of the monitoring processes in the NHS are ones in which the medical profession monitors its own standards. A long standing example of this is the Confidential Inquiry into Maternal Deaths.[6] Some of these internal mechanisms for monitoring the quality of medical care are described by Robert Maxwell who suggests that the majority of British doctors take the view that self-audit is good and see external audit as a threat.[7]

Mortality data is widely used as a measure of outcome as there is still very little national data available on morbidity. This has obvious limitations, not least because mortality is not necessarily a good indicator of morbidity. Also it is extremely difficult to isolate the contribution of NHS care to peoples' health status from that of other factors including their home and work environment, informal sources of health care and heredity.

**Quality Adjusted Life Years (QALYs).** The interest of policy makers may lie in maximising or optimising 'health outcome' from the application of a given quantity of resources which is usually expressed in monetary terms. It has already been said that health resources will never be infinite, or adequate to meet all needs. In order to choose between competing priorities for resources, the people who make decisions on behalf of the wider public should be able to compare different treatments, or kinds of care, in terms of their likely effect on the future well-being of the patient, rather than concentrating solely on the number of inputs used or processes undertaken.

QALYs are one approach to measuring outcomes that can be compared across treatments. The application of this approach to making a choice between coronary artery bypass surgery and other treatments has been described by Alan Williams.[8] The idea is to relate resource inputs to health outcomes. In order to do this, some weighting needs to be developed to compare, for example, a year of good health to a year spent bed-ridden. The choice could then be made to put resources into treatments that offered the greatest gain in terms of QALYs for a given amount of expenditure. Obviously this is very complex and requires value-judgements to be made, particularly about the value of human life.

There have been quite a lot of doubts expressed about the use of QALYs. Some people think the use of QALYs will depoliticise decisions about what type of health care system we want. Another view is that every group of patients should be offered something and that to withdraw all spending on one type of treatment, such as kidney dialysis, in favour of another treatment, for example, hip replacements, would not be acceptable.

Measures of the 'economic' performance of health authorities which compare ratios of 'inputs' to 'outputs', such as QALYs need much further development before becoming universally practicable; and can never be completely 'value free'.

**Users' views.** There is no formal requirement for health districts to monitor users' satisfaction with the services they receive as this is seen as the responsibility of the Community Health Councils. Some health districts do however carry out ad-hoc studies of users' views sometimes jointly with the Community Health Council.

It has been argued that the 'outcomes of care' in terms of people's satisfaction or dissatisfaction with their local health service, are an essential element of the efficacy of that care. Users' views can at least be measured and acted upon, and this is increasingly being explored. Monitoring people's perceptions of care and its outcomes is an area which is ripe for more 'democratic' development, potentially involving Community Health Councils, District Health Authorities, NHS staff and community and user groups.

The National Association of Health Authorities have compiled a list of initiatives in the area of consumer relations.[9] One such initiative has taken place in Nottingham which has developed a public consultation process.[10] This has been organised by the city council and the voluntary sector as part of the preparation of the city's inner area programme and has involved the participation of the community unit in Nottingham Health Authority. The consultation process consists of meetings held twice a year in 17 different locations in the city. The health related questions asked or comments made at these public meetings have indicated that there is a need for more primary health services and that many people would like more information about health services. This exercise is a two-way process in which the public learns more about how health services are delivered and the health service learns about unmet need and consumer satisfaction.

**Public Opinion Polls.** One source of information about users' views on the NHS is from national opinion polls. The questions included in these polls usually concentrate on the amount of resources devoted to the NHS. For example, the National Association of Health Authorities (NAHA) and the Health and Social Services Journal commissioned a national poll from Marplan in both 1985 and 1986 to find out peoples views on the current level of NHS spending and their overall opinion of the NHS.[11,12] Some of the results from these two surveys are presented below.

The majority (72 per cent) of the 1986 sample thought the amount spent on the NHS was too low. Those respondents who thought the level of spending was too low were asked to state from which source the extra finance should be raised; 53 per cent wanted extra finance for the NHS to come from government expenditure.

The survey participants were asked to select the phrase which best described their overall opinion of the NHS in their area (Table 6.1). Three-quarters of the sample had an 'extremely good', 'very good' or 'fairly good' opinion of the NHS. The survey results suggest that people in London have a poorer opinion of the NHS; 16 per cent had a 'fairly bad' or 'very bad' opinion of the NHS compared with 9 per cent of the total sample. Questions on satisfaction with hospital services were asked if any member of the respondent's household had attended hospital within the last two years (Table 6.2). This applied to about 65 per cent of the sample and 59 per cent of those answering this question were very satisfied with the inpatient or outpatient treatment received. London appears to have the

**Table 6.1**
Which phrase best describes your overall opinion of the NHS in your area?

|  | Total % | London % | South % | Midlands % | North % | Scotland % |
|---|---|---|---|---|---|---|
| Extremely good | 8 (9) | 4 (8) | 10 (9) | 7 (8) | 8 (9) | 12(10) |
| Very good | 24(27) | 17(23) | 23(25) | 29(29) | 25(25) | 25(23) |
| Fairly good | 43(41) | 41(37) | 38(43) | 46(42) | 46(39) | 40(43) |
| Neither good nor bad | 10(12) | 12(12) | 12(11) | 7(12) | 11(14) | 7 (8) |
| Fairly bad | 7 (6) | 11 (9) | 7 (8) | 7 (4) | 5 (6) | 8 (5) |
| Very bad | 2 (2) | 5 (3) | 2 (2) | 1 (2) | 2 (2) | 4 (0) |
| Extremely bad | 2 (2) | 4 (6) | 3 (1) | 2 (1) | 1 (2) | 2 (1) |
| Don't know | 3 (1) | 5 (2) | 5 (4) | 1 (1) | 2 (1) | 1 (0) |

Source: Health Service Journal, May 15, 1986[12]
Figures in brackets are 1985 results

---

**Table 6.2**
Satisfaction with hospital inpatient or output treatment received by member of household in past two years

|  | | Class | | | Area | | | |
|---|---|---|---|---|---|---|---|---|
|  | Total | AB C1 | C2 DE | London | South | Mid-lands | North | Scotland |
|  | % | % | % | % | % | % | % | % |
| Very Satisfied | 59(62) | 60 | 57 | 49(56) | 56(59) | 61(67) | 58(62) | 71(60) |
| Fairly Satisfied | 28(25) | 28 | 28 | 34(27) | 32(25) | 25(25) | 29(24) | 15(28) |
| Neither satisfied nor dissatisfied | 3 (3) | 2 | 3 | 2 (4) | 2 (5) | 3 (2) | 3 (3) | 5 (4) |
| Fairly dissatisfied | 7 (6) | 6 | 8 | 10 (7) | 6 (7) | 7 (4) | 7 (7) | 5 (6) |
| Very dissatisfied | 3 (4) | 3 | 3 | 3 (7) | 4 (4) | 3 (2) | 3 (4) | 1 (3) |
| Don't know | 1(—) | 1 | 1 | 1(—) | 1(—) | 1(—) | —(—) | 2(—) |

Source: Health Service Journal, May 15, 1986[12]
Figures in brackets are 1985 results

---

highest proportion of people dissatisfied with hospital services. It also had the highest percentage of people dissatisfied with family doctor treatment received by members of their household in the past two years (Table 6.3).

Polls that ask very general questions may not always give very useful information. It is quite likely that people, whilst expressing general satisfaction with, for example, care received in hospital, might be quite dissatisfied with particular aspects of their care. A more useful approach may be to ask a lot of very specific questions.[13]

**Local Health Canvasses.** There is a growing need felt by independent bodies concerned with health and health services for information relating to the public's view of the NHS. The lack of information in this area has led many organisations particularly those involved in defending the health services such as trade unions and local health campaigns to carry out their own 'health canvasses'. Appendix 2 gives a few guidelines on how to conduct a local health canvass.

**Figure 6.3 Sampling methodology.**

## Sampling methodology

A quota sampling methodology was implemented in order to contact a sample of 1,500 adults aged 15 plus.

Interviewing was conducted in 100 nationally distributed constituencies, which were randomly selected from a sampling frame comprising all constituencies in Great Britain excluding those north of the Caledonian Canal. The frame was stratified by:

(i) Registrar General standard regions
(ii) Within (i) by area type
(iii) Within (ii) in descending order of Conservative/Labour vote ratio (from the 1983 general election).

A quota of men, housewives, and other women was issued together with controls on social class (AB, C1, C2, DE) and age (15-24, 25-44, 45-64, 65 plus); there is also a working control on working housewives.

The fieldwork was conducted between April 17 and April 21, 1986.

Source: Health Service Journal, May 15 1986.

**Table 6.3**
Satisfaction with family doctor treatment received by member of household in past two years

| | | Class | | | | Area | | |
| | Total | AB C1 | C2 DE | London | South | Mid-lands | North | Scotland |
|---|---|---|---|---|---|---|---|---|
| | % | % | % | % | % | % | % | % |
| Very Satisfied | 55 | 54 | 55 | 46 | 56 | 59 | 53 | 57 |
| Fairly Satisfied | 33 | 33 | 33 | 35 | 33 | 29 | 35 | 30 |
| Neither satisfied nor dissatisfied | 5 | 5 | 4 | 8 | 5 | 3 | 4 | 3 |
| Fairly dissatisfied | 5 | 5 | 5 | 8 | 3 | 5 | 6 | 7 |
| Very dissatisfied | 3 | 3 | 3 | 3 | 2 | 4 | 2 | 3 |
| Don't know | — | — | — | — | 1 | — | — | — |

Source: Health Service Journal, May 15, 1986[12]

One notable example of a successful canvass was the Watlington 'Who Cares' Campaign. All the 1,000 or so houses in the town were included in the survey and people were asked to give their opinion on various issues such as the principles of equal access to a free NHS.

The experience of groups such as Watlington that have conducted local health canvasses has often been that the survey has the equally, if not more important role, of obtaining publicity and informing people about local and national health issues.

Some examples of the types of issues that have been addressed by local health canvasses and some of the results obtained are given below .

**Table 6.4**
**The principles of the NHS**

1a) Equal access to the health service for everyone who needs health care, and health care free at the time of use?

| | | |
|---|---|---|
| Very important | 244 | (84%) |
| Quite important | 37 | (13%) |
| Not very important | 5 | ( 2%) |
| Other replies | 3 | ( 1%) |

1b) Health service paid for out of taxes rather than fees or private insurance schemes?

| | | |
|---|---|---|
| Very important | 177 | (61%) |
| Quite important | 82 | (28%) |
| Not very important | 25 | ( 9%) |
| Other replies | 5 | ( 2%) |

Sample: Wycombe and district Health Section interviewed 289 people in August 1984. The interviews were carried out in public spots in Wycombe, Princes Risborough and Booker.
Source: Wycombe and District Health Action Health canvass results, 1984

**Table 6.5**

A satisfaction with services

| | All | OAP | Non OAP | Female | Female OAP | Female non OAP | Male | Male OAP | Male non OAP |
|---|---|---|---|---|---|---|---|---|---|
| Do you think the service provided in recent years has:— | | | | | | | | | |
| Remained the same | 50·32 | 49·41 | 50·53 | 50·58 | 49·06 | 50·97 | 50·00 | 50·00 | 50·00 |
| Deteriorated | 41·90 | 42·35 | 41·80 | 43·24 | 41·51 | 43·69 | 40·20 | 43·75 | 39·53 |
| Improved | 7·78 | 8·24 | 7·67 | 6·18 | 9·43 | 5·34 | 9·80 | 6·25 | 10·47 |
| Are you generally satisfied with the service provided by local hospitals | | | | | | | | | |
| Yes | 50·94 | 55·56 | 49·87 | 54·34 | 55·56 | 54·03 | 46·70 | 55·56 | 44·89 |
| No | 36·27 | 34·44 | 36·69 | 33·21 | 35·19 | 32·70 | 40·09 | 33·33 | 41·48 |
| Don't know | 12·79 | 10·00 | 13·44 | 12·45 | 9·25 | 13·27 | 13·21 | 11·11 | 13·63 |
| Do you think support services for people who look after sick relatives are adequate? | | | | | | | | | |
| Yes | 12·10 | 14·44 | 11·53 | 13·04 | 18·52 | 11·56 | 10·95 | 8·33 | 11·49 |
| No | 64·58 | 55·56 | 66·76 | 65·22 | 53·70 | 68·34 | 63·81 | 58·33 | 64·94 |
| Don't know | 23·32 | 30·00 | 21·71 | 21·74 | 27·78 | 20·10 | 25·24 | 33·34 | 23·57 |

Sample: 1 in 10 sample of dwellings (474) taken during October 1984 in one ward (Picton) in Liverpool Mossley Hill Constituency.
Source: Health Service Survey, North West Region Labour Party

**Local Issues.** The future of the maternity unit at St. Albans City Hospital was in doubt because it was averaging only 1,000 deliveries a year. The Regional strategic plan maintained that units which delivered less than 2,000 babies each year were not viable. A question relating to maternity services was included in a survey which also asked people for their views on the NHS in general both nationally and locally.

**Table 6.6**

Availability of services

How important do you consider it that maternity services continue to be provided in St. Albans?

| | St. Albans | Harpenden | Total | Percent |
|---|---|---|---|---|
| Very important | 363 | 88 | 451 | 84 |
| Quite important | 38 | 13 | 51 | 10 |
| Not very important | 13 | 1 | 14 | 3 |
| Not at all important | 3 | 2 | 5 | 1 |
| No reply | 11 | 2 | 13 | 2 |

Sample: St. Albans and District 'Who Cares' campaign interviewed 534 people living in St. Albans Constituency. The interviews were done in the street on two Saturdays in September 1985
Source: 'Who Cares?' health service canvass in St. Albans and Harpenden

# Action

Given the range of monitoring activities currently being used or developed the question arises as to how often action to change a process or, more correctly, inputs to it, follow the discovery of a gap between targets and measured performance. Here the credibility of the monitoring processes may play an important part. This is especially so where monitoring is done by Community Health Councils or District Health Authority surveys, and not necessarily blessed by regions or the DHSS. In these, the results may challenge the performance of those with strong vested interests.

# Whose targets and whose priorities?

It is impossible to talk about how the health service should be monitored without raising the question of who controls it and in whose interests. In the 1980s, expensive and technically sophisticated new data collection systems are being introduced into the health service. Yet, as we have shown, these are severely limited in what they can tell us about the health service, because they were designed to monitor a narrow set of management objectives.

Thus there is a premium on maximising the level of activity in the health service without considering whether or not it benefits people receiving care. For example arbitrary national targets are set for a small subset of operations such as coronary bypasses. These specify the numbers to be done in the following year without any reference to the extent of unmet need for the operation or whether there are any alternatives. In competitive tendering, the word efficiency has become equated with downgrading the pay and conditions of the worst paid health service workers. There is not space here to discuss the many ideas[14,15] about how the health service could be run more democratically. We should say, however, that democratic control should not be equated simply with holding elections, as in local government. It means developing methods of consultation and organisation which are more sensitive both to the needs of the people who use the services and to the human potential of the people who work in it at all levels.

If these were our objectives, different data would need to be collected to monitor the extent to which they were being met. Although we should still need a common core of data collected all over the country, we should also need to know more about the extent to which local services are meeting local needs.

The data collection systems being introduced at present fall far short of what is required for this, and do not even fulfil the less ambitious aim of monitoring the outcome of care people receive from different parts of the health service. In particular, although shifting care to the community is seen as a major objective, there is no way of assessing the needs of the population or the extent to which they are being met. Perhaps this is because, as we have shown, one-off research projects show clearly that needs are not being met.

### References

1. Royal Commission of the NHS. Cmnd 7615. London : HMSO, 1979.
2. DHSS. Performance Indicators for the NHS — an introduction. Undated.
3. NHS Health Advisory Service. Annual Report (June 1985-June 1986).
4. Steering Group on Health Services Information. First report to the Secretary of State. London:HMSO, 1982.
5. Knox, EG. Ed. Health-care information. London: Nuffield Provincial Hospital's Trust, 1987.
6. Department of Health and Social Security. Report on Confidential Enquiries into Maternal Deaths in England and Wales, 1979-81. Report on Health and Social Subjects;29. London:HMSO, 1986
7. Maxwell,R.J. Quality Assessment in health. British Medical Journal 1984;288:1470-1472.
8. Williams,A. For debate: economics of coronary artery bypass grafting. British Medical Journal 1985;291:326-329.
9. National Association of Health Authorities. Index of consumer relations in the NHS. 1985.
10. Woodin, J. Facing up to public opinion of the NHS. Health and Social Service Journal, 1985:1364-1365.
11. Halpern, S. What the public thinks of the NHS. Health and Social Service Journal,1985:702-704.
12. Halpern,S. They want more money for the health service. Health Service Journal, 1986:654-5.
13. National Association of Health Authority News. Ask the right questions. p4, October 1985.
14. Progressive strategies for health. Reports, papers and information from the Progressive Strategies for Health Conference held on 17th September 1983. Sheffield: Sheffield Health Care Strategy Group, 1984.
15. Progressive strategies for health 2. Reports, papers and information from the second progressive strategies for health conference held on 13th October 1984. Sheffield: Sheffield Health Care Strategy Group, 1985.

# 7
# Has the health service achieved its original aims?

ALTHOUGH THERE is much we should like to see changed in the health service, this book has concentrated on what has happened through the 1980s and what is happening now. So we close, as we started, by looking at the current position in the light of the objectives set out in the 1944 White Paper[1] and in the National Health Service Acts which followed it. Are we moving nearer towards these objectives or further away from them?

Firstly, is there 'equal access to health services, irrespective of means, age, sex or occupation?'[1] We have shown that this is certainly not the case. In fact, racial differences in access should be added to the list. It is true that attempts have been made to iron out geographical inequalities in services through the process of NHS resource allocation. All too often, however, this has been done in ways which have widened other gaps, particularly at a subregional level. In addition, the rise of commercial medicine has shifted health care resources towards the most affluent and least unhealthy sectors of the population.

Next, is there a comprehensive service free at the time of use? Here again, there are negative trends. There has been a marked increase in the extent to which the family practitioner services are paid for by direct charges to users. Further increases in charges are planned for the financial years after the general election. Many people pay for the full costs of glasses, and dental and prescription charges have risen well ahead of inflation.

As we pointed out earlier, users of the services whose incomes are just above the exemption level pay the same charges as people who are much better off. Thus there is no sense in which people pay according to their means as would happen if the service were fully paid for out of taxation which is related to income. Furthermore, imposing means tests for services and benefits acts as a deterrent to people who are entitled to have them free of charge.

Lastly, has there been any shift towards the 'promotion of good health rather than the treatment of bad'?[1] As we have shown, there has been a lot of talk about this, but the promotional activities have largely taken the form of advice rather than measures aimed at tackling the social and economic causes of ill health.

While recent trends are depressing, it is important not to forget the achievements of our National Health Service. There are diminishing numbers of people left who can remind us, from their own experience, that setting up the NHS was a great step forward from an incomparably worse situation before the 1939-45 war. Similarly, as we have shown, our system compares very favourably with those in many other countries both in terms of accessibility and efficiency.

Having said this, it is disturbing to see that inequalities in health have persisted and, more recently, show signs of widening. This is perhaps not surprising, given the extent to which most of the causes of ill health and the measures which would need to be taken to reduce inequalities, lie beyond the scope not only of the health services, but also of the political agenda. This was predicted as long ago as 1946, when the NHS was being set up, in a book entitled 'Ill-health, poverty and the state'.[2] It concluded:

'it is possible on the basis of the above findings, to assess the value of the new National Health and other post-war reforms. Both the Beveridge Report and the Government's White Paper on Social Insurance presuppose the · continued existence of rich and poor. We can, therefore, say with conviction that they have not attempted to remove the root cause of ill health — poverty. These reforms will be as ineffective as those introduced since 1911.'

## References

1. Ministry of Health, Department of Health for Scotland. Department of Health for Scotland. *A national health service*. Cmd 6502. London: HMSO, 1944.

2. Hewetson, J. *Ill-health, Poverty and the State*. p.67. London: Freedom Press, 1946.

# Appendix 1
# Some questions to ask when looking at official health statistics.

IN THIS book, we have looked behind the statistics commonly quoted by the government and its supporters to see if the statistics justified the claims they make about health and the National Health Service. As we could not hope to cover them all, this appendix suggests ways in which readers can themselves question the interpretation of statistics. To lead into this, we say something about the nature of statistics and why they so often fail to answer the very questions we really want to ask.

**What do statistics mean?** 'Statistics' comes from the word 'state' and has a double meaning. Sometimes it means the numbers themselves and sometimes the science and art of interpreting them. The people who, just over 150 years ago, founded what is now the Royal Statistical Society saw their activities as a branch of political science to be pursued as an essential part of their wider interest in social reform.

Since then, statistical techniques have developed beyond recognition and are applied to a much wider range of topics. When it comes to the subjects of health and health care, however, statistics, in both senses of the word, are no less political in the 1980s than they were in the 1830s.

People tend to take two very opposite views of statistics. They are either seen as neutral, objective facts or dismissed as 'damned lies' plucked out of the blue to support whatever views are being put forward at the time. Often people veer from one view to another. As Bernard Shaw put it in his preface to 'The doctor's dilemma':

'the man in the street ... knows that "you can prove anything by figures", though he forgets this the moment figures are used to prove anything he wants to believe'.[1]

We do not think that either of these polarised views of statistics are helpful. Instead, we suggest that a better way of understanding statistics is to look at the way they come to be collected, processed and analysed.

**What do statistics measure?** Most of what are loosely described as 'health statistics' are collected by government departments and the National Health service as by-products of administrative or legal processes. The nature of these processes, which range from the registration of births, marriages and deaths to the administration of health services, inevitably affects the characteristics of the data which emerge from them.

Registration statistics date back to the mid nineteenth century. Birth and death registration started in 1837 in England and Wales, 1855 in Scotland and 1864 in Ireland. The collection of health service statistics grew up alongside the services themselves, such as school health services from 1907, maternal and child welfare clinics from 1915 and, during the second world war, the Emergency Medical Services.

Data collection expanded when the National Health Service came into being in 1948. As the Chief Medical Officer's Report for 1949 put it, 'The administration of the hospital and specialist services has made both possible and necessary the introduction of a uniform set of returns designed to keep the Minister and the hospital boards accurately informed of the amount and range of facilities at their disposal and the use being made of them.'[2]

Although the new data collection systems being introduced to replace the old 'returns' are much more sophisticated, the statistics they produce are not very different in character. They are administrative statistics, which tend to focus on the use made of facilities such as hospital beds, operating theatres and clinics and the work of staff in terms of numbers of hours worked, or visits made in the community.

Thus, for example, they tell us how many operations of a given type are done but little about the illnesses which preceded the operation, the people who were operated on, or the outcome of the treatment. Similarly, a death certificate can tell us what the doctor who completed it thought the person died from, but this may not relate very closely to their health problems when alive.

Thus, as we have shown in much more detail in our 'Unofficial guide to official health statistics'[3], these routinely collected statistics give a considerable amount of information about the activities of the health services and about the clinical causes of death. They tell us very much less about 'morbidity', which means the prevalence of ill health and disability in the population. Even when conscious efforts are made to collect data about particular conditions, as happens with cancer registration and the notification of infectious diseases, only people who have contacted the health services and had their conditions diagnosed can be included.

The only way to get round these difficulties is to do surveys which involve going out and asking people about their health problems, including those for which they have not consulted the health services. Of course, this can often be more expensive than analysing data from official records, which means that, at a time of public expenditure cuts, such surveys are becoming fewer in number and more limited in scope. It can also be difficult to frame the questions so that they can be answered in a comparable and valid way.

**Interpreting and using statistics.** Given the nature of official health statistics, it is not surprising if people find them at variance with their own experience. It is tempting, therfore, to dismiss them as error-ridden and irrelevant. Rather than do this, we hope that readers will try to confront the statistics and ask questions such as:

**How were the data collected?** The answers received depend on the form of question asked and this, in turn, can be affected by whether information is collected from case notes, input directly into a computer, derived from forms or collected by postal questionnaire or interview.

**How were the data coded and classified?** Sometimes data are slotted into a classification which is unsuitable or does not fit them well. For example, the International Classification of Diseases is designed to code the way illnesses and causes of death are diagnosed by doctors. This means it is unlikely to be the best way of classifying ordinary people's perceptions of their own health and ill health.

**How were the data tabulated and analysed?** Data may be tabulated in ways which ignore major geographical differences, such as those between the regions of a country or the four countries of the United Kingdom. Aggregated data can be tabulated for a whole year without taking account of seasonal variations. Age and gender differences can be masked when they are not tabulated separately.

**How were the statistics selected and interpreted?** It is hardly surprising if people involved in politics select and interpret data in a way which supports their case. Thus government statements are full of the new facilities which have been provided, but usually ignore those which have been closed. While watching out for simple tricks like this, it is also important to raise the much more relevant question of whether the sum total of facilities which remain are adequate to meet the needs of the population.

Similar considerations apply to the interpretation of data. For example, as successive hospital in-patient stays by the same person are not normally linked, ten in-patient discharges could mean that one person was admitted and discharged on ten separate occasions or that ten people have each had one stay in hospital. The government tries to imply the latter to support its claims of 'record numbers of patients treated'.

**What has been left out or ignored?** At each stage in the process of collecting or analysing statistics, decisions are made which may consciously or unconsciously ignore questions which are highly relevant. For example, irrespective of whether or not new hospital in-patient facilities have more beds than the old ones they replace, staff may be more concerned about whether they are well designed and convenient to work in and people who use the services will want to know whether the journeys they have to make to use them or visit relatives are long and inconvenient.

In this example, the relevant questions need to be asked at the outset. There are other examples, notably in government ministers' pronouncements and the annual reports of the Health Service in England, where the relevant statistics exist but are ignored. This is because, like the reduction between 1983 and 1984 in the numbers of nurses, they are politically inconvenient.

**'It can't be true — my experience was different.'** Even after closer scrutiny, people may still find that statistics are out of line with their individual experience. On some occasions, however, experience which is valid to them, may be very untypical.

For example, if one person reports an exceptionally long wait for an ambulance in an emergency, it would be unwise to assume, without making further enquiries, that everyone has an equally long wait these days. It could be that the person concerned was the victim of an unusually bad combination of circumstances. On the other hand, if the number of long waits really is increasing, the person's story can be useful in illustrating some of the consequences.

In general though, rather than relying solely on individual 'shock horror' stories, campaigning groups are on firmer ground if they go out and do a simple survey or canvass of the population. Doing this will enable them to collect their own statistics about the extent to which people are having problems in getting access to appropriate health care. The next appendix gives some notes on how to go about doing surveys of this sort.

Another reason why national statistics may not fit a local picture is that both the pattern of ill health and the provision of health services varies widely from place to place. As we have mentioned earlier this may not be apparent when statistics are aggregated and quoted for the whole country. Contacts with campaigns in other places is essential to compare experience. This is essential when the process of NHS resource allocation is used more to divide and rule than to ensure a more appropriate distribution and use of NHS resources.

## References

1. Shaw B. Preface to 'The doctor's dilemma'. London: Constable and Co.,1906.
2. Report of the Ministry of Health for the year ending 31 March 1949. Cmnd 7910. London: HMSO,1950.
3. Radical Statistics health Group. The unofficial guide to official health statistics. London: Radical Statistics,1980.

UNIVERSITY OF OXFORD
ECONOMICS LIBRARY, SOCIAL STUDIES
FACULTY CENTRE, MANOR ROAD, OXFORD

E-mail: library@economics.ox.ac.uk

or before the last date

302539945/